Quality of Service

MAKING IT REALLY WORK

QUALITY
—IN—
ACTION
●

SERIES EDITOR

BARRIE DALE
UMIST

Quality of Service

MAKING IT REALLY WORK

Bo Edvardsson, Bertil Thomasson
and John Øvretveit

McGRAW-HILL BOOK COMPANY
London · New York · St Louis · San Francisco · Auckland
Bogotá · Caracas · Lisbon · Madrid . Mexico · Milan
Montreal · New Delhi · Panama · Paris · San Juan
São Paulo · Singapore · Sydney · Tokyo · Toronto

Published by
McGRAW-HILL Book Company Europe
Shoppenhangers Road, Maidenhead, Berkshire SL6 2QL, England
Telephone 01628 23432
Fax 01628 770224

British Library Cataloguing in Publication Data
Edvardsson, Bo
  Quality of Service: Making it Really
  Work. – (McGraw-Hill Quality in Action
  Series)
  I. Title   II. Series
  658.562

  ISBN 0-07-707949-3

Library of Congress Cataloging-in-Publication Data
Edvardsson, Bo
    Quality of service: making it really work / Bo Edvardsson, Bertil
  Thomasson, and John Øvretveit.
       p.   cm. – (Quality in action)
    Includes bibliographical references and index.
    ISBN 0-07-707949-3
    1. Customer service–Management. 2. Total quality management.
  3. Service industries–Quality control. 4. Service industries–
  Management.   I. Thomasson, Bertil.   II. Øvretveit, John
  III. Title.   IV. Series: McGraw-Hill quality in action series.
  HF5415.5.E26   1994   94-15998
  658.8´12–dc20   CIP

2345 CUP 98765

Typeset by BookEns Ltd., Royston, Herts.
and printed and bound in Great Britain
at the University Press Cambridge

Printed on permanent paper in compliance with ISO Standard 9706

Contents

'Quality in Action' Series Preface

Quality is regarded by most producers, customers and consumers as more important than ever before in their manufacturing, service and purchasing strategies. If you doubt this just think of the unsatisfactory examples of quality you have personally experienced, the bad feelings it gave you, the resulting actions you took and the people you told about the experience and the outcome. The concept of Total Quality Management (TQM) is increasingly being adopted by organizations as the means of satisfying the needs and expectations of their customers.

Total quality management has been practised by the major Japanese manufacturing companies for the last 30 or so years. Their commitment to continuous and company-wide quality improvement has provided them with the foundation by which they have been able to capture markets the world over. In response to this competitive pressure Western manufacturing companies, first in America and then in Europe, started to embrace the TQM ethic, this was followed by commercial and service type organizations. The superior performing Western organizations now have some 15 or so years of operating experience of TQM.

Total quality management is a subject and management philosophy in which there appears to be an unquenchable thirst for knowledge, despite the considerable volume of published material. The objective of this major 'Quality in Action' book series is to help satisfy this need and fill what we believe are gaps in the existing range of current books. It is also obvious from the arguments advanced from some quarters that there is still a lack of understanding of TQM and what it is about. Hopefully the books in the series will help to improve the level of understanding.

McGraw-Hill has already published books by three of the best known and internationally respected quality management experts – Crosby, Feigenbaum and Juran. The 'Quality in Action' series will build upon the work of these three men; this in itself will be a challenge.

I was honoured when asked by McGraw-Hill to be the 'Quality in Action' book series editor. I have personally been involved in industrially-based TQM research for the last twelve or so years and from this experience believe I am well placed to identify the aspects of TQM which need to be addressed by new books on the subject.

The prime focus of the series is management and the texts have been prepared from this standpoint. However, undergraduate and postgraduate students will also find the books of considerable benefit in understanding the concept, principles, elements and practices of TQM, the associated quality management systems, tools and techniques, the means of introducing, developing and sustaining TQM and the associated difficulties.

One objective of the series is to provide some general TQM reading as guidance for management in introducing, developing and sustaining a process of continuous and company-wide quality improvement. It will focus on manufacturing, commercial and service situations. We are looking for recognized writers (academics, consultants and practitioners) who will be able to address the subject from a European perspective. The books appearing on this theme will not duplicate already published material, rather they will build upon, enhance and develop the TQM wisdom and address the subject from a new perspective. A second objective is to provide texts on aspects of TQM not adequately covered by current books. For example, TQM and human resources, sustaining TQM, TQM: corporate culture and organizational change, partnership sourcing, TQM and business strategy. It is likely that the authors of these books will be from disciplines (e.g. accounting, economics, psychology, human resources) not traditionally associated with quality management. A third objective is to provide texts that deal with quality management systems, tools and techniques in a practical 'how-to' manner.

My commitment to this series is that I am prepared to allocate time from my considerable research, teaching and advisory activities in order to ensure that it meets and hopefully exceeds the needs and expectations of our readers.

B. G. Dale, Series Editor

About the 'Quality in Action' Series Editor

Dr Barrie Dale is Reader and Director of the UMIST Quality Management Centre. The Centre is involved in three major activities: research into Total Quality Management (TQM), the Centre houses the Ford Motor Company's Northern Regional Centre for training suppliers in Statistical Process Control and the operation of a Total Quality Management Multi-Company Teaching Programme involving, at any one time, eight collaborators from a variety of industrial and business environments. He also coordinates the Bowater Corrugated Division Total Quality Performance Multi-Institute Teaching Programme. Dr Dale is also a Non-Executive Director of Manchester Circuits Ltd, a company specializing in the manufacture of high technology and complex printed circuit boards.

He is co-editor of the *International Journal of Quality and Reliability Management*, now in its eleventh volume. Dr Dale is co-author of *Managing Quality, Quality Costing, Quality Improvement Through Standards, Total Quality and Human Resources: An Executive Guide* and *The Road to Quality* and has published over 180 papers on the subject of quality management. Dr Dale has also led four missions to Japan of European executives to study the application of TQM in major Japanese manufacturing organizations.

Preface

The 1980s and early 1990s saw a dramatic increase in research into service management and service quality, and the growth of knowledge about service quality management as a distinct subject in its own right. Our own research and consultancy work at the Service Research Center in Karlstad, Sweden and the Brunel Programme for Service in West London, United Kingdom both contributed to this research, and also to practical developments in service companies which sought our help. Although most managers are aware of quality ideas, we have found in our research, teaching and consultancy that few are aware of the recent research and experience in service quality. We repeatedly find ourselves being asked to help rescue quality programmes which have failed because managers have force-fitted packaged solutions from the manufacturing sector into their service organizations. Introducing a quality approach is difficult enough, without starting-off with one which is entirely inappropriate for a particular type of organization and its customers. We have found this lack of awareness of the new service quality approaches to be greatest in the public sector, where the new ideas are most needed at present.

Our aim in this book is to make accessible to managers some of the new quality concepts and methods for services which have already proved their worth in the companies with which we have worked. We draw on our own and others research to show how managers can develop an approach suited to their business and apply this approach successfully. We introduce the concept of 'co-service' to describe how both providers and customers work together to create service, that the customer's needs must always be present in the minds of producers, and that services mostly are produced at the same time as they are consumed. We also argue that the new service thinking can help manufacturers to develop new approaches to quality by more clearly recognizing the integral nature of goods and services and the service dimension of their offering to customers.

Bo Edvardsson, Bertil Thomasson and John Øvretveit

Introduction

**To compete and win, we must redouble our efforts –
not only in the quality of our goods and services, but in
the quality of our thinking, in the quality of our
decision-making, in the quality of everything we do.**
(E. S. Woolard, President of DuPont)

More executives now have experience of quality programmes as the most
powerful means of improving customer satisfaction, customer loyalty,
competitiveness and, thus, profitability. Many previously-sceptical managers
now believe that quality gives them a competitive edge in both public and
private services. Quality was once something that concerned only specialist
production engineers, but now it is something that concerns everybody
working in successful organizations, as well as customers and suppliers.
The term 'Total Quality Management' (TQM), which we will define more
precisely, conveys this wider significance of quality.

In this book we describe new quality methods for services which are
different from those used in manufacturing, and present an approach to
Total Service Quality Management (TSQM). Taking a TQM perspective to
managing service quality, our approach is to show the link between service
quality and productivity, and to describe quality methods to improve both.
Our aim is to help others to improve the quality of their service by using
research and evidence about actions which do and do not work in different
types of service. We have drawn together our own and others' research into
a framework which people developing and managing services can use, in
both the private and public service sectors.

In this introduction we describe changes in markets and in society affecting service organizations, and introduce our ideas about how managers can respond by improving quality. Our approach is based on four premisses. First, that total quality management links actions to improve customer quality to actions to improve internal processes: it gives managers a framework to ensure that they relate their internal changes to customer requirements in the right way. Second, that producing a service is different from producing a physical product. Third, that because of this difference we need quality methods and philosophies which are suited to the nature of how services are produced and consumed and to staff values: ready-made quality methods from manufacturing applied to some services destroy the very quality which they seek to improve. The fourth premiss is that we need to recognize that many companies offer the customer a mix of service and physical goods, and that we should not seek to improve separately the quality of the product and of the service.

These premisses about the difference between producing services and physical products, and about the need to view and work on both together are not contradictory. First, we often think of physical products as performing a service for us, and, when they break down, we take them 'out of service': thinking of physical products as services and how to add value to them as packaged services to the customer can help improve their quality. Second, the quality of most organizations' offerings to customers depends on getting the right combination of service and product. It is only by recognizing the distinctive nature of service, and of ways to improve service quality, that we can also improve the quality of a service/product mix. This is not just a matter of designing and improving processes with service and product quality in mind. The approach we propose also involves using recent advances in service knowledge to redefine what the organization is offering the customer: its 'service concept'. Overcoming service/product thinking is the key to understanding and giving customers what they want and to process improvement. We use the term 'co-service' to highlight the unique nature of creating, rather than 'producing' service, in a co-service process with the service receiver as an active participant.

The subject of service quality is of importance beyond service organizations and their customers. Some claim that the low rate of growth in industrial productivity in many of the OECD countries in recent years is the result of the expansion of the service sector. Would a more service-intensive economy mean a less productive economy? The evidence suggests that the opposite is true – that developing new services and improving existing services supports and facilitates improvements in productivity in both manufacturing and public services.

In our view, both managers and researchers cannot understand and study productivity without taking quality into account. In public health and education services, increased productivity has to be accompanied with the better quality which customers now expect. In a quality framework designed for health services, Øvretveit (1992a) defines quality in a way that encompasses both customer satisfaction and productivity, and emphasizes productivity in the dimension of 'management quality'. We will show that, especially in services, it is possible and necessary to improve productivity and quality at the same time, and that methods which do not tackle both are costly in the longer term.

THE AIM AND STRUCTURE OF THE BOOK

The aim of the book is to review and synthesize, from a management perspective, what is known about quality in services and to offer guidelines based on our own and others' research. Considering service from a management perspective means the analysis, organization, control and development of service business activities. We use the term 'company' or 'business' for both public and private companies. We present an overview which includes the essential factors for successfully changing and developing business operations to improve service quality. We draw on management-orientated research about quality in services in Europe and the United States, and include the experiences of a number of private and public service companies. We note that the distinction between public and private service companies is already breaking down and, for improving service quality, the similarities are now more important than the differences.

The book aims for a 'scientifically-based overview', but one which illustrates principles with examples drawn from both the practical world and research. We show how to use concepts, models and research results in practical quality improvement. We draw a number of normative conclusions, where there is sufficient evidence to support them, but also recognize that managers and researchers will need to adapt the ideas for the particular circumstances of their service.

The book consists of nine chapters. In Chapter 1 we introduce our approach to total quality management in services. The chapter also describes how we are in the process of changing from an industrial society to a service society, and notes a number of clearly observable market trends. We believe it is important to place quality thinking in the emerging 'service society', part of which is the increasing interplay between the service and goods sectors. Goods and services are often closely related in various customer offerings and products. We consider a number of features of service production, which we think must be taken into account when analysing quality and planning quality improvement projects. Developments in quality thinking are leading many to view quality and productivity together, and we explain how we combine the two in the concept of 'co-service'. The chapter concludes with some examples of how companies use these ideas in their quality policies.

Chapter 2 surveys the quality field and deals with the relations between quality, productivity and profitability. We maintain that the link between the three concepts has not been sufficiently emphasized either in management literature or in research. Our thesis is that a quality approach is the main way in which modern organizations can improve productivity and thereby profitability.

Managing quality improvement projects is the subject of Chapter 3. Many people have ideas about what quality is, and how it can be achieved, and a few have tried to improve quality. Those who are successful have worked on quality improvement in a sustained and systematic way. They have carefully planned quality projects and gained support for them before starting to use internal marketing techniques. We present examples of quality improvement projects from different companies. The chapter also considers organizational culture, and how a quality culture can be created in a service organization.

Chapter 4 deals with quality analysis. Since the term quality is multifaceted and difficult to capture, we begin by discussing how to define quality. The rest of the chapter surveys various models for analysing quality. In our view of quality, the receiver of the service, the customer, plays the crucial role. Quality is realized with the customer. The customer is the person who ultimately decides whether a service has the right quality or not. In Chapter 5 we attempt to indicate what the term customer stands for, and how a business may be orientated towards the customer. We also discuss the importance of customer care and complaint handling.

Chapter 6 focuses on personnel and competence issues. In many service industries quality is very closely linked to the service provider as a person and his or her competence, commitment, willingness and ability to perform the service. Quality measurement is an important, not to say necessary, feature of quality improvement. In Chapter 7 we discuss approaches to and techniques for measuring the quality of co-service. We present a number of examples of how service companies measure their quality, internally and externally, and give guidelines to help managers to create measurement systems.

In Chapter 8 we consider the issues involved in service design and quality improvement. Many quality problems are the result of the wrong service concept or wrongly designed production processes and production systems. How can this be avoided or the current service altered to prevent inbuilt poor quality? We present a method for designing services and a number of tools for analysing problems arising from poor design. In Chapter 9, the final chapter, we draw together the main conclusions in ten theses about how to improve quality in services.

Quality and total service quality management

There is a lot of talk about quality, but quality is a dangerous word. Many customers are tired of broken promises about top quality. Promises are easy, especially for services, but customers increasingly want concrete evidence of service quality, a 'taste' before deciding.

WHAT IS QUALITY IN SERVICES?

The term is ambiguous and subjective: quality is like beauty, it is in the eye of the beholder. For many people, quality is fulfilling customers' expectations, both 'citizen' customers and company customers in the market. Customer-perceived quality is often defined as the relationship between the customer's expectations of the service and his or her perception of the service received. We argue for a definition of quality which is more than just customer satisfaction. The term quality is multi-faceted. We asked a group of consultants what they meant by quality. One of them replied that quality was when the customer was satisfied, when he was satisfied and when his boss was satisfied.

Talking of 'high quality' is not useful for managing quality, but we do need a general term and we propose the term 'right quality'. Right quality means that the service provider has met the specifications or requirements which were laid down for the service on the basis of the customers' demands and needs, and that the customers' expectations have been fulfilled.

In our view, quality is fulfilling expectations and needs: those of the customer, of the staff and of the owners. Right quality is when the customers, staff and owners are satisfied. Customers' expectations are based on their needs, their earlier experiences of the service in question and the reputation the service has in the market. We form and change our perceptions of service quality in a social process. We receive and interpret impressions in the present, we reinterpret previous perceptions, and we form future expectations of quality. In Chapters 2 and 4 we discuss in more detail the different concepts of quality and definitions of quality in services .

As we see it, total quality management stands for an holistic view of quality improvement, where the understanding, interest and commitment of top management is an absolute precondition for achieving success. Even more than in manufacturing, TQM for services depends on and creates a culture in an organization which involves everybody in quality improvement. Everybody can affect quality, but everyone must first realize this, and have the techniques and tools which are appropriate for improving service quality. Thus, TQM includes the marketing and dissemination of quality thinking and methods not only within the organization but also to customers, suppliers and other partners.

Our view of total service quality management for services is summarized in the following points, which we briefly comment on below:

● The importance of management
● The involvement, commitment and responsibility of everybody
● Quality in all processes

- Quality as strategy
- Focus on prevention rather than inspection
- Quality by design
- Continuous improvements
- Zero defects
- Meeting the needs of target customers
- Recovery
- Benchmarking.

Top management has the ultimate responsibility for quality improvement, but the commitment of managers at all levels is essential in the long term.

When we talk of everybody being involved, we mean the company's customers, suppliers and partners, all of whom can affect quality, as well as employees.

Service 'production' or creation consists of a number of processes, each of which affects the quality of service that the customer gets. The key process is the customer's 'pathway' through the service. Processes cut across departments and across organizations, and the right quality depends on the right relations between departments and organizations.

Quality as strategy means both that a company must have a strategy for improving quality, and that the quality strategy should be part of the company's business strategy in the market. Quality thinking is a driving force for both productivity and profitability.

Prevention rather than inspection indicates that service quality is not a matter of controlling quality afterwards. Instead, it is a matter of preventing poor quality at the earliest point.

Poor quality is often the result of wrongly-designed production processes. Old services need to be redesigned and new services designed with quality in the forefront. Service design is a way of avoiding inbuilt faults in the system from the start.

Continuous improvement means that one should take small steps, but progress on a continuous basis.

Zero defects is a strategy and a goal at one and the same time. Zero defects are in relation to the specifications laid down and grounded in the customer's needs. The concept originated in manufacturing, but is a key part of TQM for services.

Meeting the needs of target customers means adjusting the services to the requirements, needs and expectations of customers selected for the service, and avoiding dissatisfied customers. At the same time, we should make it easier for the customer to complain. An ongoing dialogue with the customer provides us with important information for making improvements. It also gives an opportunity to negotiate expectations before they become higher than those which the service can provide.

Recovery means acting quickly when the customer is not satisfied by, for example,

● recognizing the customer's perception and apologizing
● giving the customer a reasonable explanation for what had occurred.
● compensating the customer for the inconvenience
● ensuring that the problem does not occur again.

Benchmarking is comparing oneself with the standards of the best in a particular field, for example in handling complaints, stockholding, cash flow, etc. The comparison need not be with a competitor or even with a company in the same line of business. Better standards can often be found in other lines of business (see Chapter 7).

FROM AN INDUSTRIAL TO A SERVICE SOCIETY

In this section we consider the growing importance of service and service organizations to the economy and life of society. There are several factors that explain why services are becoming an increasingly significant feature of society. One of these is technical progress, which has resulted in changes in production methods so that more goods are produced by fewer people. The opportunities for rationalization and increased productivity have been greater in manufacturing than in parts of the service sector. Labour productivity growth in maufacturing in the United Kingdom was 5 per cent per annum, compared to 1.8 per cent in the 'service sector' between 1979 and 1987 (Boakes, 1988; Spencer, 1987). We later argue that this is in part

Index 1970 = 100

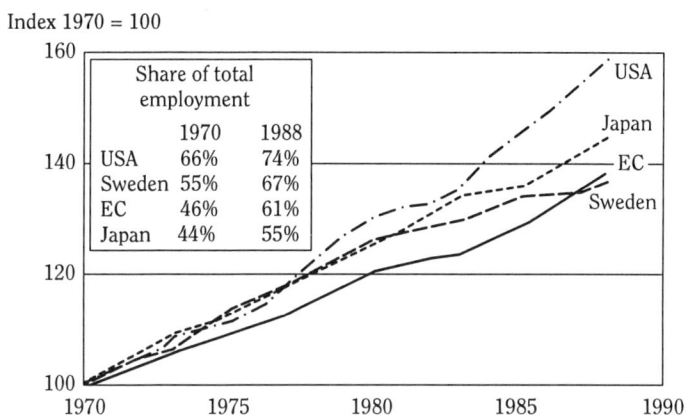

FIGURE 1.1   Growth in Employment in Services
Source: Swedish Coalition of Service Industries (Tjänsteförbundet)

due to service quality methods not being available or applied during this time. Generally, the rapid increase in productivity in manufacturing has led to a decrease in the price of goods relative to services, and hence a rise in the proportion of the economy accounted for by services in some statistics.

Services play an increasingly significant role in the global economy. It is in the service sector that employment and production will increase in the future. Services are extremely important for employment and the GDP of the economies of industrial nations. Even when it comes to investments, the service sector stands for a significant percentage. Figure 1.1 shows the increasing proportion of people employed in the service sector.

In the United States the number of people employed in the service sector has increased by nearly 60 per cent since 1970. The United States has the largest service sector and the fastest growth, primarily in business services, health care and financial services. The growth of the service sector in Japan is also considerable. Since 1970 the number of people employed in services has increased by 42 per cent. The proportion of employees in the service sector in Japan is 53 per cent of the total, a low figure compared with other industrialized nations.

Services account for the greater part of production and employment in all the EC countries with the exception of Portugal and Greece. The

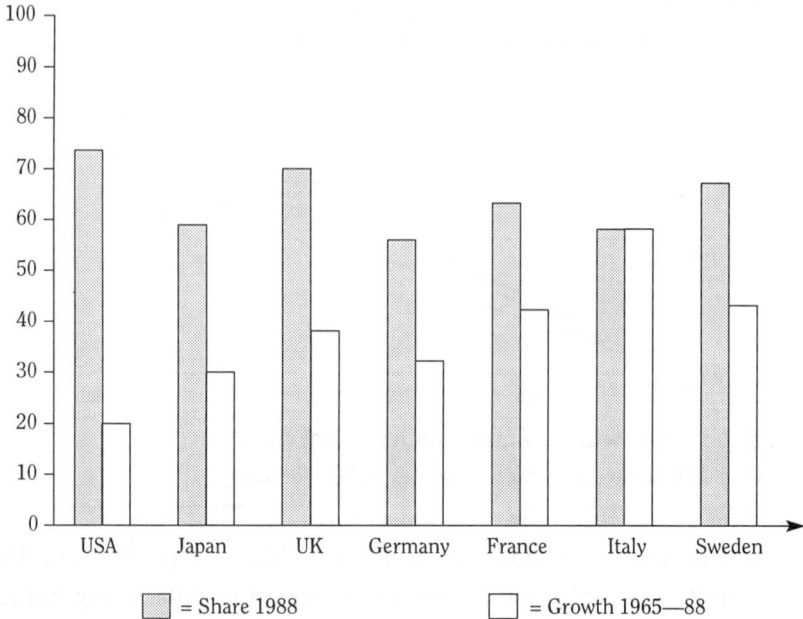

FIGURE 1.2 Share and Growth of Service Jobs

expansion of the service sector in the EC is fastest in those countries which have the lowest proportion of employees in services. The total number of people employed in the service sector in the EC has increased by 40 per cent since 1970. Figure 1.2 shows growth in the proportion employed in the service sector in a number of OECD countries.

To illustrate further the increasing importance of services, we will describe changes in Sweden, where there has been an enormous increase in the percentage employed in the service sector. In 1989 about 67 per cent of all those gainfully employed worked in the service sector, 30 per cent in industry including mining and only 3 per cent in agriculture. The proportion employed in services is continuing to grow, although not at the same rate as previously. The growth services are those based on information technology and services in the interface with industry.

During the years 1963–87 the proportion employed in manufacturing in Sweden decreased from just over one-half to scarcely one-third. During the same period, the number of salaried staff in industry increased from one-quarter to nearly one-third of those employed. From 1963 to 1987 private services' share of production increased from just over 35 per cent to just over 41 per cent in current prices. The same is true of consumption of services as a share of the total value of consumption. Private services' share of total domestic consumption increased from under 14 per cent to over 17 per cent.

A further factor which reinforces the impression of increasing service intensity is that household services, which were previously not registered, are now priced and included in the nation's balance. These include child care, care of the elderly, social welfare, etc. In Sweden the expansion of services has primarily occurred in the public sector. Sweden and Denmark are the two nations with the largest public sector in Europe.

Shortcomings in service statistics

In traditional statistical methods all economic activities are divided into goods or services. However, this distinction is rather arbitrary, and is increasingly inappropriate. The service content of manufacturing is increasing as is the use of technology in the production of services.

A significant part, perhaps half, of the growth in the private service sector in Sweden during the last 30 years is due to reclassification of the statistics. Manufacturing companies have, for instance, turned their computing divisions into separate companies. Statistically this means that the activities are classified as services whereas previously they were classified as manufacturing. Other examples of services which are now often purchased instead of being produced by the company itself are transport and property management. The production of these services has in most cases not grown at all while statistics show considerable growth.

Furthermore, several internal service functions in manufacturing companies, not least in engineering, have expanded. Examples are research and development, and services connected with products. This growing share of services in industrial companies and their offerings to customers is not taken into account in official statistics. According to compilations made by the Swedish Coalition of Service Industries, the internal service sector in industry now has 40 per cent of the total employed. About half of these are working on design and R&D, one-third in administration and the rest in marketing and distribution.

The forces behind these developments

The most significant force behind the development of the private service sector is to be found in the growth in manufacturing and business of knowledge-intensive methods of production. Within manufacturing the percentage of salaried staff has grown and there has been a shift towards a more qualified and more highly trained workforce. The new production methods increasingly require information- and knowledge-based services, more of which are being purchased externally. There are three reasons why more firms are 'buying-in' these services. One is that specialization enables service companies to perform services more cheaply. Another is that companies need a variety of types of specific external competences. A third factor is employment legislation, which has led companies in certain cases to avoid employing people in the short term. It is likely that the need for knowledge-intensive services and the purchase of external services will both continue to grow.

Technological developments have also played a key role in the structural changes in the service sector. Large service companies in banking and insurance have transformed their businesses over the last 10 years with information technology (IT). Perhaps more significant is how IT has changed relations between companies, leading to new structures and distribution patterns and complex inter-organizational networks.

> boundaries between transportation, communications, and travel-service indus-
> tries are disappearing as airlines begin to provide direct reservations, tours,
> conferences, auto and hotel arrangements, in-flight telephone service, electronic
> retailing, and package delivery services in competition – and coalition – with
> thousands of other service units. Accounting, software, and professional service
> firms are also breaking all traditional industry boundaries as they openly
> compete and cooperate to develop and supply new and better products and
> services to each other and to a wide variety of common customers.
>
> (Quinn *et al.*, 1990, p.67)

Services and goods are often interrelated

An important trend is the breakdown of the traditional distinction between services and physical products and between manufacturing and service industries. We would argue that there always was a close link, and that the distinction was more in theory than in practice. Part of the rapid postwar economic growth is due to innovations in the service sector which are closely connected to physical goods. Increased travel has meant that more cars, aircraft, hotels, etc., are needed. Many products are systems in which services such as installation, consultation, service and maintenance, financing, customer-staff training and guarantees all play a major role.

The emergence of a service society does not mean that manufacturing is no longer important. On the contrary, the role of industry is and will remain crucial. In the same way as the increased efficiency of agriculture in the nineteenth century was a precondition for the rapid growth of industry, increased productivity in industry has meant that fewer people are needed to produce the goods we demand. The new jobs will come in service industries and in knowledge-intensive service type work to design and run new manufacturing processes.

SOME TRENDS IN THE MARKET

Looking to the future, we describe below trends in the market which we believe are important for improving quality in both commercial and public organizations. The first is the increasing importance of integrating new high-technology products with service to make a usable 'package':

- We have moved from an industrial society to a service- and knowledge-based one. Manufacturing companies are becoming service companies. ABB Robotics, for instance, is no longer concerned only with industrial robots, but provides systems for developing productivity and rationalizing production, i.e. the robots have become parts of a service concept. The same is true of many other companies, e.g. ATLET, a Swedish company which now provides systems for handling stock, and not just trucks: trucks are now part of a service concept. Further, with advanced production processes, manufacturing companies are now facing new and different problems of quality control. They are finding that experience from manufacturing has to be complemented with knowledge of quality control in service production.

- We have seen a movement of strategic resources from capital to information, knowledge and creativity, and to 'human capital'. In many cases, the primary asset of a company is knowledge held by a few key employees. Further, knowledge is becoming obsolete at an increasing rate, which means that greater efforts must be made to develop the competence of the staff. The 'best' people are attracted to the companies which support personal development and self-fulfilment. Company growth now comes as much from employee development as from expansion with more employees, and this applies as much to front-line service-providing staff as to other professional staff.

- Most markets are complex and rapidly changing with new and more complex customer demands, products and services. Internationalization is increasing and international competition is intensifying in many markets. Deregulation alters market conditions. This is especially true of financial markets, but these changes also affect what are viewed as relatively stable public sector organizations. Health care reforms and public sector reform are sweeping through Europe creating new and more complex markets and inter-organizational relationships. Despite all these changes and complexities in markets, most companies are designed for a fairly stable environment with stable market conditions.

  To ensure the right quality, companies must be better at under- standing their environment and building-up the competence and ability to change before or at the same time as the outside world changes. This will involve organizing activities in smaller, independent, and flexible profit centres and in managing the links between them.

- Environmental issues will be central. The demand for quality in the outer environment will place greater demands on how companies conduct their business, which sources of energy they use, and how they design their products. Environmental taxes on emissions of sulphur and carbon dioxide will increase. Energy taxation is becoming more environmentally orientated.

● The boundary between the company and its environment as well as that between different lines of business is becoming less and less distinct. Companies are cooperating more and more with other companies and with strategic customers. Through co-ownership, alliances and joint ventures, constellations of companies are formed into networks which compete with other networks. Several companies, including pure service companies, cooperate to build power stations, bridges, tunnels and other major projects. Railway companies and airlines cooperate with travel agents, car hire firms and hotel chains. Large computer manufacturers conclude agreements with or purchase shares in computer consultants. Other consultancies cooperate with finance companies, advertising agencies and other services. More than ever, customers are demanding total solutions and one company is managing a network of specialists to provide the solution.

In recent years there has been a major change in the services offered by banks. A range of new services has been developed, which forms a complement to traditional banking services. Banks have expanded their activities and devote more and more time to providing a financial and legal advisory service to both private customers and companies. They have adapted their activities to the demands of various groups of customers. This move towards customer-adapted advisory services will probably continue. Manufacturing companies are adding services such as advice, service, maintenance, training and financing, to their goods.

One way of summarizing these trends is in terms of increasing specialization and the need for coordination. The increase in specialization and in knowledge services means that customers find it more difficult to know the services and combinations that they need. Customers, individuals as well as companies, are increasingly demanding that the service fulfils a complete function: that the service manages and coordinates a set of specialists to provide a 'package solution' to the customers' problems.

Leonard Berry, one of the leading academics in the field of service quality in the United States, expressed his view of quality in services in the 1990s in the following terms:

> In my view, the most significant service challenge for the 1990s is to raise our service aspirations – to raise our service quality ambitions in this country. It's time for American executives to declare war on service mediocrity. It's time for American executives to become indignant over shoddy service and to become intolerant in the face of so-so service.
>
> (Berry, 1989, p.25)

We believe that this challenge applies with greater force to European managers, who often do not even notice the poor quality of their own and others' services, and, if they do notice, do not believe that they can do anything about it. Because services cannot be exported as easily as products, European managers have become complacent. However, times are changing, with new technologies and service design and operations systems, and rising customers' expectations of public and commercial services. We predict that more overseas companies will offer services of a higher quality, and will be able to take over local companies and introduce new service provision systems. This will happen in all sectors from professional and knowledge-based services to consumer services such as fast-food and hotel services.

CO-SERVICE

In this section we turn towards how service companies are to respond to these changes by improving quality. At the beginning of this chapter we summarized our approach: first, that TSQM is a framework for linking internal changes to customer needs. Second, that producing a service is different from producing a physical product. Third, that because of these differences we need quality methods and philosophies that are suited to the nature of how services are produced and consumed. Fourth, we need to consider and improve service quality and product quality together to create the service and product mix which many customers want. Here we develop further the last three points.

How does producing a service differ from producing a product? In the 1970s, and before, service and marketing researchers noted the difference between goods and services, but mostly in terms of an end-product. With an increasing awareness of process improvement and research into customers' experience of services as processes, service researchers recognized the significance of the process of production of service. From research and development work in health and social services, one of us noted the difficulty of breaking from the manufacturing concepts, a difficulty which service providers experienced even though they were the first to criticize the damage done by manufacturing analogies:

> Delivering a service package is an entirely appropriate way to describe how some services are provided. The 'package' is left on the doorstep for the client to unravel. The clients' involvement is to place an order, sometimes to sign for it, if they are available when it is delivered – the 'producers' do the rest, 'assembling' the 'package' from the items 'in stock'. The product and production metaphors are now limiting our ability to think about better ways of giving service, helping other people, and of cooperating with others to do so.
>
> (Øvretveit, 1993b)

Taking a TQM perspective, our approach is to show the link between service quality and productivity, and to describe quality methods to improve both. The term 'servuction' was used by Eiglier and Langeard (1987) to draw attention to questions of productivity in services. In services, production, delivery and consumption are overlapping processes and the customer participates as an active co-producer. We use the term 'co-service' to highlight the unique nature of creating, rather than 'producing' service, in a process with the service receiver as an active participant. The term 'co-service;' recognizes that giving and receiving service is not like consuming or using a product, either for an individual or for an organization. Often persons in need of service work with others to meet their own needs – they take the fullest part they can in co-producing the service by co-assessing, co-planning and co-providing.

Quality in services must be based on insight into the special nature of co-service. Knowledge in this field has been built up over the last 15 years, and service management is now an established discipline with theories that do not regard services as merely an appendage to goods. This has opened the eyes of researchers and practitioners to the fact that services and service activities should be treated in different terms to goods and manufacturing processes. The deeper understanding of the central features of services has had an effect on how successful service companies organize their business, how they market their services and control quality.

Services is not a uniform concept. There are major differences between, for instance, professional consultancy services and cleaning services. Despite these differences, there are certain general characteristics in services:

- The customer often participates directly and actively in the production process as co-producer. Therefore it is important to make sure that service staff and customers can have effective dialogue, and that relationship is kept to the forefront of everything that is done.
- Do-it-yourself production systems and customer education play an important part in most services. The customer's role, involvement in and responsibility for co-service must be clarified in order to achieve the right quality.
- Services are often abstract and therefore difficult for the supplier to explain and for the customer to assess. Marketing must do more to avoid creating wrong and often excessive expectations in customers. It is the responsibility of the service provider to ensure that the customer does not have unrealistic demands on and expectations of the service. Control of customer expectations is often neglected in quality improvement.
- Many non-standardized services are very closely linked with the service provider as a person. 'For some services, the people involved in delivering the service is in essence the service', say Crane and Clarke (1988). Major quality factors from the customer's perspective are the knowledge, commitment and attitude of the staff.
- Services are often made up of a set of services/products. The customer assesses the whole. The value, quality and attractiveness of services depend on the customer's perception of the whole.

In all co-service it is important to define exactly the service concept, and communicate it within the organization so that it is accepted by the employees. Unless employees know what the object of the business is, what they are meant to do, which customers they are to serve, which needs, demands and expectations customers have, then they cannot give a quality service. This is true not only of the services offered to external customers on the market but also of internal services and in relations between internal customers.

In manufacturing, one can control quality by purchasing components which ensure the right quality, by using and adjusting machines to assemble the components into products with a quality that is specified in advance. At every part of the process of design and production there are detailed controls. Through inspection (physical control) possible faults and defects are discovered, which can be dealt with before the customer receives the good.

Conditions are often very different for co-service. The customer is present and participates in the production process. Each customer has personal ideas, suggestions and feelings and will behave differently from another customer, but also may behave differently on different occasions. The customer sees and experiences what is happening during the co-service. He or she notices any chaos in the 'service factory', and can hear the staff speaking ill of the customers, or sense lack of motivation in the staff. Customers also interact with each other – a further uncontrollable factor in co-service. All these give tangible clues by which the customer assesses a service provider and the quality of the service. A good experience of the competence, motivation and attitude of the staff, of order and modern equipment, and positive impressions from other customers are powerful signals to the customer that the quality is good.

The basic problem with services compared to goods is that there is less opportunity to control how the service is provided and experienced. Just one example is fluctuations in demand: although services can do much to influence demand to match their capacity, there are always sudden unpredictable peaks or staff absences which lead to uneven quality.

The presence of the customer in the 'service factory' and his role as co-producer has implications for quality improvement. It is not possible, as in the manufacture of goods, to apply inspection, and thereby avoid exposing the customer to incorrect or defective services. The right quality must be built into the production system and all parts of the service process from the start.

The service company's employees play a central role. In many cases, it is the service provider's knowledge, skills and attitude that is most important for the customer's perception of quality. How can one steer employees towards the right quality? How can one mentally prepare employees for the right quality? Perhaps Picasso's description has lessons for us: 'Painting is something that takes place in your mind.'

The service company does not have the same opportunity as the manufacturing company to control the details in production. The demand for flexibility is therefore both greater and different. Robots are used to an increasing extent in manufacturing. The service provider's employees cannot be 'adjusted' in the same way as robots to achieve the desired behaviour. Indeed, to seek to do so shows a lack of understanding of the nature of service: quality controls which undermine the human core of giving service destroy quality in service, rather than enhancing it.

This is not to say that customers do not want consistency or that service quality must not be controlled: rather that the approach to control and the methods of control must be appropriate. In this context a clearly defined service concept is crucial because it provides staff with guidance but allows flexibility: we will see in later chapters how important this balance is to service quality. Before looking at how to improve service quality in more detail, we need to consider the arguments for improving quality in the emerging service society.

WHY QUALITY IMPROVEMENT?

The top managers of the 500 biggest companies in Europe viewed quality to be the most important field for strategic development during the 1990s. The

American Society for Quality Control (ASQC) conduct an extensive biannual survey of how American executives see quality and work with quality issues. The most recent study, by Gallup in 1989, found that the most frequently mentioned means of improving customer satisfaction were through improvements in service quality (QUALITY: Executives' Perceptions on Quality in a Competitive World).

Quality in services was given the highest priority among a number of critical issues facing American companies in the coming three years (50 per cent means that half the respondents judged the factor to be crucial).

Service quality	54 %
Product quality	51 %
Productivity	32 %
Government response in bringing products/services to market	26 %
Cost of material and labour	22 %
Product liability	18 %
Capital availability	15 %
Labour relations	14 %

In a later chapter we consider the costs for a company of the estimated 30 per cent of the staff engaged in putting right what others have done wrong. Doing things right from the start raises productivity since it lowers costs and also increases income. What costs is not quality, but the lack of quality.

High quality also makes it possible to charge a higher price, which increases income and profitability. High quality produces satisfied customers who are loyal and help to spread a positive image of the company in the market. This leads to a reduction in marketing costs. Further, the staff get positive feedback from the customers, which makes them feel appreciated, staff turnover decreases and it is easier to recruit competent employees. The company is in a virtuous circle.

That quality is profitable is abundantly clear from the major international 'PIMS' study (Luchs, 1986). PIMS stands for Profit Impact of Market Strategies. About 3000 business units were analysed and divided into three groups on the basis of the customer-perceived quality of their goods and services. The group with high customer-perceived quality was six times as profitable as the group with low quality.

Quality improvement is primarily a matter of adapting to the customer and developing long-term, trustful customer relations. The customer becomes a partner. The successful organizations in the 1990s will have the customer's development and quality as the cornerstones of their strategic development.

The right quality presupposes competent and motivated staff. In tomorrow's company the competence and commitment of the staff will, even more than today, be the critical resource. Many people talk about the importance of developing human capital but few companies have accepted the consequences of this. Most companies invest twice the amount of resources in maintaining and developing their computer systems as in developing their staff. Japanese companies spend more than twice as much as Swedish companies on staff training and, in the United Kingdom (e.g. Nissan), as much as 20 times more than comparable British companies.

In tomorrow's companies and organizations an increasing number of people will come into contact with the customer. The marketing function will be spread throughout the company and most people will be part-time marketers and must be aware of their role and tasks in the company's marketing. This is true of switchboard operators, technicians, service staff, etc. All are ambassadors who affect the customer's perception of quality.

THE DEVELOPMENT OF QUALITY THINKING IN SERVICES

It is only in the last 10 to 15 years that the subject of service quality has become an established discipline. According to Gummesson (1991a), it is to all intents and purposes a phenomenon of the 1980s. Modern quality thinking has its roots in manufacturing, mainly in the United States (Shewhart, 1931), and was primarily concerned with increasing productivity in production. Methods were developed to control systematically quality in manufacturing processes and thereby reduce the costs for faults and wastage. Requirements and internal standards were laid down.

Gradually the focus has shifted from production and internal conditions to the customers, their needs, requirements and expectations. It is these that form the point of departure for quality analysis and quality improvement in the new quality thinking. This does not mean that the demand for internal quality in production – fewer faults and defects – has been set aside but rather that the term quality has been given wider significance. In the new quality thinking – total quality management – quality improvement is a strategic issue for management and company boards rather than a concern of only production engineers (Gummesson, 1991a).

The development of quality thinking can be viewed in four phases (see, e.g. Godfrey, 1986). The first phase is inspection, and is many thousands of years old. Inspection means checking that the product does not have any faults when it comes out on to the market. The faulty products are sorted out before they reach the customer.

The second phase is represented by 'quality control'. This approach can be traced back to the 1920s and Walter A. Shewhart's introduction of the control chart and statistical methods. A range of techniques for quality control were later devised, but they are mainly limited to producing physical goods (Gummesson, 1988).

The third phase comprises Company-Wide Quality Control (CWQC). This entails working continuously to improve quality with the aid of systematic feedback from customers. Various types of quality analysis, quality measurement, quality circles, etc., are of great value here. It was primarily the Japanese who introduced this approach and devised methods for implementing quality improvements. The methods of policy deployment and quality function deployment are described later in the book.

We term phase four as 'quality by design' meaning that quality is built-in early at the development and design stage, and that services and product quality are viewed together. Gummesson (1987) originally used the term 'design quality', and this is a rapidly developing field in service research.

The ability to design services systematically is much less developed than is the case with goods.

Gummesson proposes two quality strategies that must be adopted right from the design of the service: prevention and zero fault strategy. Prevention means ensuring that the design of the service avoids quality problems arising when the service is provided. Often staff cannot give good service because the design of the service not only prevents them from doing so, but causes them to make errors. If the design is right then quality service depends on staff doing things right and a zero fault strategy.

Quality thinking in services

Quality in services became a subject in its own right about 15 years ago, but it is only in recent years that services have used some of the findings from research, and that models and theories have been tested. In the chapters to follow we will develop our argument that quality improvement in service organizations must be based on the special conditions and nature of co-service.

This is not to mean, however, that service researchers and managers cannot learn from the long tradition and the extensive experience of quality improvement in the manufacturing industry. Quality thinking started with inspection and ensuring that faulty products did not come on to the market. We noted above that this approach does not work for services. More recent quality approaches emphasize prevention, and this philosophy is more suited to services, even though many methods for quality improvement in services are different. Prevention means that the right and even quality is built into all parts of the production system and all links in the service chain from the start – hence our emphasis on design quality.

However, improving quality in services depends on getting the right balance between techniques and methods for improving processes and systems, and staff attitudes, behaviour and the service culture. This balance is particularly important in health services and other services with a professional ethic: to put the emphasis on both people and processes, motivation and methods, and the service spirit as well as systems (Øvretveit, 1992a).

In services, quality appears in behaviour, and has to do with fundamental values, corporate culture and attitudes: relationships between staff and between them and customers are critical. People's attitudes, their undertaking and commitment to continuous learning and development are as important as their understanding and use of quality methods and systems. It starts in the mind and heart and finds expression in decisions and actions.

Quality techniques and control systems do not work on their own: quality is created by people in an organization and this is especially so in service companies. It is people aided by techniques, methods and systems, who can achieve the right service quality, but they must want to do so and gain satisfaction from giving and improving service quality.

Modern quality philosophies view quality not as a goal but a journey, where the destination is not given but is continually changing. New opportunities for improvements are continually arising. New demands from customers mean that what used to be the right quality no longer is so. Customer demands come in part from competitors providing higher quality. To really be better, one must be better than one's competitors at being better.

Modern quality thinking emphasizes the importance of having the right quality throughout the service chain, in all parts of the service company. The concept of total quality management has gained general acceptance but not general application. Since co-service is largely a set of processes that can be described as a chain of internal customer relations, the chain must be so designed as to ensure the right quality. David Bowen, an American researcher on quality, uses the phrase 'the seamless service' to convey this idea. The quality chain is as strong as its weakest link.

The links in the chain are not merely service providers within the service company but also external suppliers, partners and customers. The same view of quality and the same quality requirements must permeate all the links in the chain. The challenge is to get quality thinking and responsibility for quality to permeate the whole company, and external suppliers' organizations.

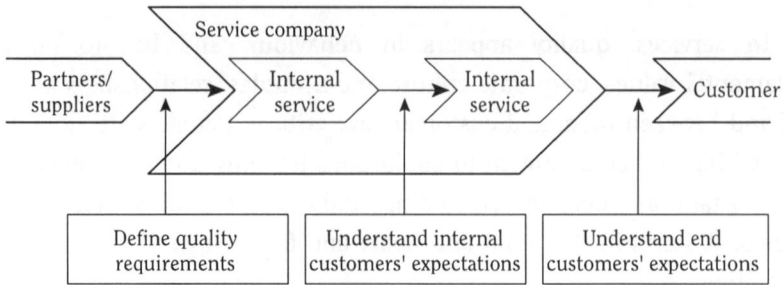

FIGURE 1.3   The Service Chain
Source: Based on Edvardsson, 1991.

For people to take responsibility for making quality improvement and feel committed to the changes, they need to understand their part in business operations. All those involved in the links in the service chain – partners and suppliers, departments and functions in the company and customers – should know what is expected of them, and what 'right quality' means (see Fig. 1.3).

The one thing that all quality consultants agree on and research has shown consistently is that the commitment of top management is essential for successful quality improvement. In services we believe that this is because top management has a critical role in creating the necessary culture and values that we emphasized above. If managers set an example for their employees and practise what they preach, then the talk about the importance of investing in quality becomes credible.

These ideas are illustrated in Lilja and Schröder's (1990) report of their experience of quality improvement in Saab Aircraft Division:

> Our experience at Saab Aircraft division has shown that to build a quality environment one must:
> - Create clear goals and objectives, easy to understand and communicate.
> - Stress the necessity of the top management commitment.
> - Stress the necessity of the full middle management commitment.
> - Create well-defined and well-known standards and requirements on all levels.

We consider below two examples of how service organizations have drawn on quality ideas in their quality policies.

Examples of quality policy

> For us in Swedish Telecom our new quality thinking means that we are sowing seeds that will grow into a new kind of spirit and a new way of working, both with colleagues and with the world outside. When everybody in Swedish Telecom has accepted the right quality, we can also fulfil the demands and wishes on which we are agreed with our customers. Then our customers will be satisfied and we can also feel satisfied with our work. It is always the customer who ultimately decides whether the quality is right.
>
> (Swedish Telecom's Quality Policy)

In the introduction to Swedish Telecom's Quality Policy, Tony Hagström, the director-general, writes:

> The RIGHT QUALITY is necessary for our business today and in the future. The RIGHT QUALITY is very profitable and provides security for all of us in Swedish Telecom. It creates a feeling of confidence in our customers, suppliers, owners and the community in general. We create the RIGHT QUALITY ourselves. Our profitability is dependent on our ability to produce services and products that our customers are satisfied with. Our customers demand – and have the right to demand – the RIGHT QUALITY.

Our quality policy means that we provide faultless and competitive products and services which fully satisfy the customer's needs and demands.

> Our quality policy means for each one of us that:
> We focus on the customer.
> We set up requirements that yield the right quality.
> We have achieved the right quality when the requirements are fulfilled.
> We create expectations which we can meet.
> We strive at all levels to produce faultless work.
> We give priority to preventive quality measures.
> We know that the right quality is a personal undertaking and a task for us all.

The result is the greatest possible value both for our external customers and for all those working for Swedish Telecom.

The American information technology company Bell & Howell has the following quality policy:

> We will be number one in customer satisfaction in each of our markets. Every Bell & Howell employee is responsible for always delivering to our customers, both external and internal, products and services that conform 100% to mutually agreed upon requirements. In implementing this policy, Bell & Howell will observe the following supporting principles:
>
> 1. Require that all employees participate fully in the process and lead by example.
> 2. Build a spirit of working together toward common goals.
> 3. Promote a climate of open communication and feedback.
> 4. Encourage and recognize innovation and teamwork.
> 5. Provide honest, fair and equitable treatment of all and develop an atmosphere of trust and mutual respect.
> 6. Recognize the right of every employee to understand the requirements of his or her assignment and to be heard when offering suggestions for improvement.
> 7. Take prompt action on opportunities, problems and conflict.
> 8. Encourage every person to strive continually for understanding of and mutual agreement on all requirements of customers and suppliers.
> 9. Require that products will not be shipped nor services performed if they do not meet customer requirements.
> 10. Actively and continually evaluate competitors' performance.

These examples show the importance these companies attach to a systematic approach to quality improvement, that quality control requires both detailed instructions and flexibility, and that a common quality definition and clear quality goals are formulated and generally accepted. In later chapters we consider how to make these ideas part of everyday working life.

Quality: the driving force for productivity and profitability

Quality, productivity, and profits are triplets; separating one from the other creates an unhappy family.
(Gummesson, 1990b, p.6)

In a TQM perspective, quality, productivity and profitability are intimately related. This is not just a theoretical proposition, but an accepted fact in companies that have successfully implemented TQM. The link is well recognized in manufacturing companies such as the Japanese automobile industry, but now also in service companies like Federal Express and Florida Power and Light (FPL), the latter being one of the largest power companies in America with over 15 000 employees.

FPL was the first non-Japanese company to receive the prestigious Japanese quality award – the Deming Award for 1989. Since 1983, FPL has systematically applied its 'Quality Improvement Program'. Among the results are a reduction of the average length of power cuts by half, a reduction by a third of the number of complaints, and a stability in the price of electricity. FPL's quality programme consists of four main sections: customer satisfaction, continuous improvement in all processes with the aid of the Deming circle of 'plan–do–study–learn', management by fact and the commitment and involvement of the whole staff. In 1989 over 25 000 suggestions were submitted by various improvement teams and problem-solving groups.

FPL's quality programme has proved a very profitable investment. In the years 1985–89 the company invested US$2 million per annum to improve quality. The result – apart from better customer-perceived quality – was an annual saving of US$10 million.

In this chapter we consider productivity, quality and profitability in services, mainly in the form of 10 statements based on research and experience in service management. We conclude by drawing on this research to give guidelines about how to improve productivity in service businesses.

PRODUCTIVITY, QUALITY AND PROFITABILITY BELONG TOGETHER

This first statement forms the point of departure for our view of service businesses, and we demonstrate our point below in considering quality costs. Productivity should always be seen in relation to quality and profitability. Even though productivity and quality are both concerned with income as well as expenditure and tied-up capital, there is a different emphasis:

- Productivity: the emphasis is on the utilization of resources, which often entails cost reduction and capital rationalization. The focus is on production.
- Quality: the emphasis is on customer satisfaction and revenue. The focus is on customer utility.
- Profitability: the result of the relation between income, costs and tied-up capital.

A noticeable shortcoming in many studies of productivity is that they do not take quality and income into account. In the modern world productivity without quality is commercial suicide: the Japanese discovered this when they overemphasized production and put the customer in second place, and Eastern European and Asian companies already recognize this. One problem is that quality is more difficult to measure, especially in services. However, measures of both productivity and profitability are based on assumptions and value-judgements.

Quality and costs

The commonest objection to improvements in quality is the cost: 'It will be too expensive.' Crosby (1988) claims that the opposite is true, and we can see from his early work the links between quality, productivity and profitability. For Crosby, quality is free, and it is non-quality that costs, that is everything that was not done right from the beginning. On the basis of his work Crosby concludes that:

- In manufacturing companies 20 per cent of the company's costs are caused by faults and their correction.
- In service companies 35 per cent of the company's costs are caused by faults and their correction.
- If you concentrate on quality, you can increase profits by 5–10 per cent of the sales.

Another way of looking at the cost of quality is to divide it into the cost of conformance and the cost of non-conformance. The first is the cost of maintaining and improving quality while the latter is the cost caused by quality defects. According to Musgrove and Fox (1991) the latter generally outweighs the former in most businesses.

Quality costs are usually divided as follows:

- *Preventive costs*: the cost of avoiding faults, e.g. staff training, the planned and 'robust' design of the service.
- *Control costs*: the cost of monitoring and ensuring that the service provided fulfils specifications, e.g. the costs for controllers and surveys among customers.

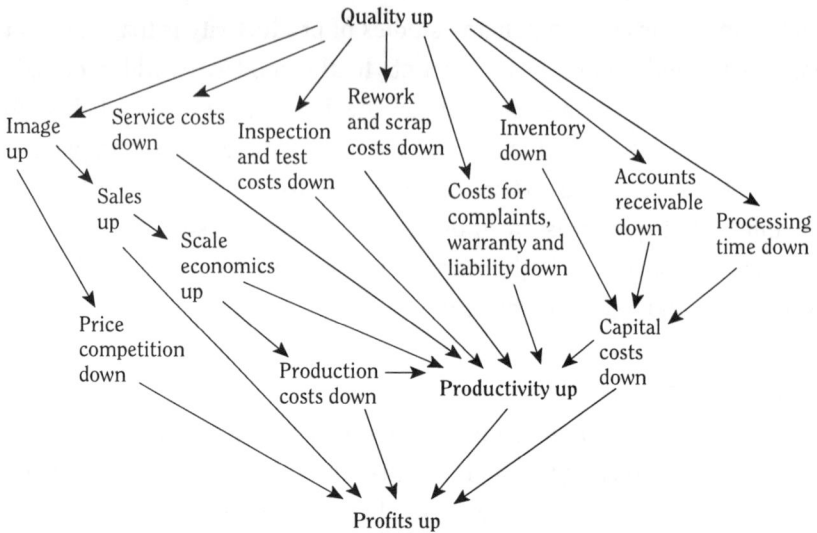

FIGURE 2.1   The Link Between Productivity, Quality and Profitability
Source: Gummesson, 1992b.

- *Fault costs*: the costs caused by faults, e.g. extra work and the loss of an irritated customer.

Crosby proposes that quality costs are usually apportioned as follows: 2–3 per cent are preventive costs, 20–25 are control costs, and 70–80 per cent fault costs. He believes that fault costs account for a larger proportion of the total quality costs in service businesses than in manufacturing industry.

In short, making a mistake is expensive, results in poor quality, and reduces productivity and profitability. These connections are shown in Fig. 2.1.

Improvements in quality also affect capital costs: fewer goods need to be kept in stock, less storage space is needed, smaller stocks of forms are required, fewer invoices remain unpaid while the customer is waiting for things to be put right, etc. Techniques such as just-in-time (JIT) manufacturing, one of the TQM methodologies, also help to reduce stocks, and these techniques are also being used in service industries. This has a direct effect on profitability.

With improved quality the costs of dealing with complaints and refund claims are also reduced. The unknown but higher costs are the effects on staff morale and the costs of the customer's dissatisfaction. The risk of losing customers is considerable. An American study of service companies (Krauss, 1987) shows that consumers do not usually complain: 96 per cent of those who were dissatisfied do not complain and 65–90 per cent choose a new supplier. Of those who complain, 54–70 per cent can be recovered if the problem is solved, up to 95 per cent if it is done rapidly. If complaints are handled efficiently, customers may have a more positive perception of the service provider than before (Edvardsson, 1988b).

Improvements in quality reduce the costs of re-doing work, which may take up considerable staff and customer time and also disrupt the flow of work. Inspection costs are also reduced: if you know that something works, you do not need to check it continuously, thus reducing costs for inspectors, and instruments, and minimizing the erosion of a sense of responsibility which comes from being inspected. All these costs – complaints, reparation, inspection – directly affect productivity.

Improving quality also increases income. When the service functions better and is more reliable, it is better adapted to the customer's needs. When the customer can rely on it being well performed, the company has an opportunity to improve its image. This in turn affects sales volume and price competition if the company takes advantage of the improvement. Increased sales often allow economies of scale, which can raise productivity. Greater freedom to determine prices – either raising them and retaining the same volume or lowering them to increase the volume – directly affects profitability.

Note, however, that costs for prevention may rise with design, internal marketing costs, bonuses, etc. However, these should be seen as investments. They are costs on which there will be returns over the longer term. The key question is thus not whether to invest in quality improvements, but by how much, and which are the most important improvements in which to invest, given the market conditions. Øvretveit (1992a, 1993a) argues that quality programmes must be linked to business strategy and the market, and that over-investment in quality can be as disastrous as under-investment when a particular market will not bear higher prices, whatever the quality.

BUSINESS CONCEPT, STAFF CONCEPT AND CORPORATE CULTURE

The business concept forms the framework for the company's activities. It is within this framework that productivity, quality and profitability are to be achieved. The idea or concept must be translated into action through goals and strategies (Townsend and Gebhardt, 1986).

An illustration of the business concept comes from a project by the Swedish Property Owners' Association and the Swedish Association of Municipal Housing Companies. The project was to change the business concept from 'quality of dwellings' to 'housing quality'. The Housing Board's old modular strategy was that there is a single best way of building a dwelling. In this business concept of the 'quality of the dwellings', productivity and quality are the same. If everybody has identical dwellings, productivity will rise. The quality of the physical dwelling will probably also increase as doors, windows, etc., will be constructed to more carefully tested standards. If the standards are wrong, e.g. for sound insulation, the quality will be low.

The business concept of 'housing quality', on the other hand, also includes the opportunity for customers to influence the plan of the dwelling, to choose materials and colours, and to have some control over their situation by choosing the site. It also includes having neighbours they like, having stairs cleaned, getting service for the elderly, and so on.

The business concept of a service organization indicates in simple terms what the company is in business for and what it wants to achieve. Other examples are:

- Linjeflyg, the Swedish domestic airline: 'To minimize travel times for the Swedish nation from door to door across the whole country.'
- Scandinavian Airline System, SAS: 'We shall be the frequent business traveller's preferred airline.'

- For Xerox, quality is integral to the business concept: 'Quality means providing our external and internal customers with innovative products and services that fully satisfy their requirements. Quality improvement is the job of every Xerox employee.'

The 'staff concept'

A problem in many service businesses is that it is difficult to motivate and retain staff. Cleaning and washing-up staff are a case in point. These jobs are often seen as temporary and many of those employed in them are immigrants, often with poor language skills. The jobs are characterized by low pay, very repetitive tasks, a narrow work content, lack of appreciation from the customer, poor working environment and shift work. Given this, it is difficult to expect the employees to have a sense of commitment and responsibility for quality and productivity. If staff turnover is not controlled, both productivity and quality will fall. In this situation the staff concept is extremely important.

But the staff concept is also essential for personnel in knowledge companies, such as consultancies or education. Here specialists who are employed and who often have a long education, expect a great deal in the form of development, motivation and independence. The business concept needs to be complemented with a staff concept for service. The staff concept should include guidelines for employee recruitment, development and outplacement. It should describe needs for knowledge and competence and measures for motivating staff to give good service. Both the business concept and the staff concept have to be part of the corporate service culture and reflected in the attitudes which staff hold. As an illustration of this we show below different attitudes which are linked to quality and productivity – which are more likely in a service you know?

- The customer shall leave here satisfied. I must find a way of solving her problem.
- The customer will do as we say. I am just obeying the rules.
- The customer will like it better if I smile and am good-humoured.

- The customer should be pleased that he does not have to wait more than 15 minutes.
- I admit that our information is not clear. I shall see to it that it is improved. Can I help you with your problem?
- The problem is the result of the customer misunderstanding our information and getting it wrong.

The business and staff concepts are discussed further in Chapter 6, and culture in Chapter 4.

UNDERSTANDING CO-SERVICE

The production, delivery, marketing and consumption of services is often a simultaneous process, so the term service production is less than satisfactory. We proposed the term 'co-service' to emphasize the nature of services and to indicate the difference between the production of goods and the production of services (Øvretveit, 1993a). Relationships are a key feature of co-service as represented in Fig. 2.2.

The individual customer is in the centre, and his or her perception of quality is affected by four types of interaction:

1 The customer interacts with different contact staff (also called front-office staff or the front-line) such as cashiers, receptionists, workmen, and doctors during the production of the service. In this interaction the

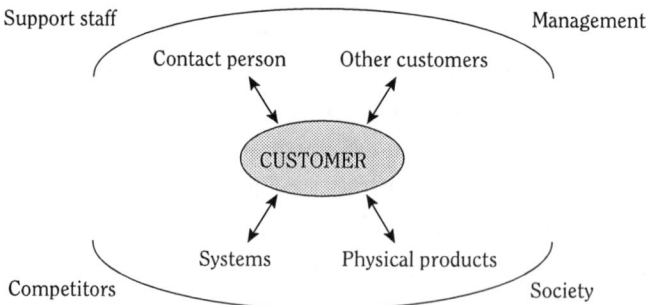

FIGURE 2.2   Co-service with the Customer in the Centre
Source: Gummesson, 1993.

customer partially consumes the service and is involved in the co-service process. Much of the work of improving service quality has concentrated on the customer–contact person interaction. This was the case with the famous charm courses organized by SAS and British Airways.

2 The customer is also affected by other customers. The service provider may be able to influence the interaction between customers and affect their perception of the quality of the service. An example is in how the service provider or service design organizes queues. Customers often wait for other customers, and queue discipline and the way people behave play a large part in people's perception of service quality. An example of this was Linjeflyg's campaign to get passengers entering the aircraft first to sit at the back. The object is to save time in embarkation but also to avoid irritation in the queue. Other ways of reducing the time for embarkation and disembarkation are technical, i.e. having doors both at the front and the back of the aircraft and making it easier for people to stow their cabin luggage and overcoats.

3 The third customer interaction is with the physical environment, e.g. with a hotel room and its equipment. Services are also delivered by telephone, e.g. information about ticket prices. Some services are performed in the customer's environment, e.g. cleaning services. A cleaning company strives to adjust its services to the customer's need for cleanliness, to his or her requirement that the cleaning be carried out at certain special times and to what the customer is prepared to pay. If the cleaning company can have a say in the layout of an office before it is built, it can then provide a better quality cleaning service and maintain higher productivity. If the building is difficult to clean, a certain amount can be achieved by choosing the appropriate methods and aids, but this is less satisfactory than designing the building from the start to make cleaning easy. Anyone who has spent time in a badly designed kitchen knows about the importance of this aspect of service.

4 Fourthly, the co-service system must be understood and accepted by the customer and be attractive to him or her – it should be 'user friendly'. An example is cash dispenser systems at banks. The banks' primary aim has

been to reduce costs by replacing staff with machines. However, it is not clear whether costs have really been reduced. Quality has improved in that cash dispensers and telephones are available 24 hours a day, but has diminished in other respects. It may, for instance, be difficult for older people to handle the system. Other recurrent quality failings are the lack of banknotes in the dispenser and technical faults in the link with the main computer. The system also includes the support functions, often termed back-office, which include all the work that is done behind the scenes to make the co-service process work. In this description we considered co-service from the viewpoint of the customer. For a fuller description we would have to take the perspectives of service providers and others into account – we consider their part in co-service later.

THE UNIQUE FEATURES OF SERVICE QUALITY

Two approaches to quality which are important to service quality are:

1 Customer-perceived quality and the needs of the market. This approach is characteristic of service research. It is market- and income-oriented, externally oriented with the focus on the customer.
2 The other approach is directed towards quality control: how we control the processes in our organization to achieve quality. It is primarily internally oriented. Service research has so far shown less interest in this approach.

Figure 2.3 presents a model of quality in services.

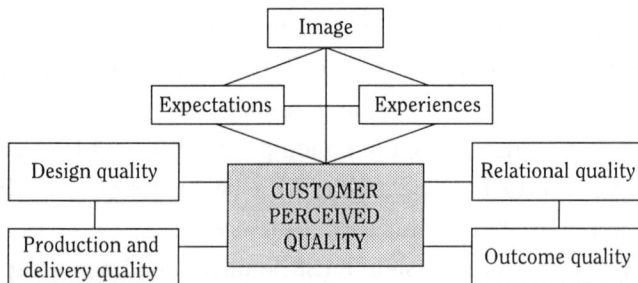

FIGURE 2.3   Customer-perceived Quality
Source: Gummesson, 1993.

The centre of the model is the customer's perception of quality. This is affected by the customer's expectations, which are related to his or her experiences. Perceived quality is further affected by the image of the business, i.e. the reputation of the supplier and the service in the market. An image can be better or worse than the real thing, but it acts as a filter for perceived quality. Perceived quality as a concept is difficult to grasp because it contains both subjective and objective factors and is dependent on the characteristic features of the customer: education, income, life style, values, state of mind, etc. Consequently market segmentation, which we consider later, is important. To improve quality, it is necessary to influence expectations, experience and image – this is the task of a marketing department and others who have contacts with customers including front-line staff. Quality improvement need not always be directly linked with the service offered.

For a customer's perception of quality to be satisfactory there are four qualities for a service to meet – '4Qs'. The first, design quality, relates to how a product or service has been developed and put together. When building a house, drawings and specifications are an essential aid for the design of the house. Similarly, services must be designed, but in a different way which we describe in Chapter 8. The second Q, co-service quality (production and delivery quality), relates to the ability to follow the design of the service exactly. Poor co-service leads to disruptions, the correction of faults and missed sales. The third Q concerns the consumer's immediate perception of quality during the co-service process, relational quality: how pleasant the staff are, if they give the impression of being competent, if other customers are troublesome, etc. The fourth Q is the future utility or end-quality of the service, e.g. that the renovation of an apartment has been done well and will last or that an operation will not cause the patient trouble in the future. These four quality factors are different in nature but all are important.

Like other quality concepts, some aspects of the four Qs are more easily measured than others. However, in co-service, closeness to the event is essential – interviews and statistics are generally late and not particularly useful. If one is close to the event and understands the processes, it is easier to act and achieve continual improvements. It is to measuring productivity that we now turn to pursue our thesis of the links between quality, productivity and profit.

PRODUCTIVITY MEASUREMENTS IN SERVICES

The term productivity in services describes how resources are utilized. A simple and common measure is work productivity which indicates the number of units produced per hour of work. The shortcomings of this measure are that the effects of other resources such as capital, information and material are not taken into account. To include all the various resources, resource consumption can be expressed in monetary terms: total productivity thus being equal to the number of units produced in relation to the actual cost. Sometimes the term 'capital productivity' is used. This refers to the relationship between the units produced and the market value of the resources needed to produce them. Another term of relevance is 'process value productivity'; this refers to the quotient between process value and the number of hours worked or the number of employees. Process value is the market value of what is produced, minus the cost of the resources purchased, divided by the number of hours worked. Process value productivity is often used to compare different business units to provide a basis for strategic decisions.

Productivity measures in services often have major failings. In health care, for instance, it is common to use the relationship between the number of patients and the cost of the treatment; in schools the number of pupil hours per week in relation to the cost of education. This type of operationalization of the concept of productivity produces misleading information and makes productivity and quality appear to be in conflict. There is much discussion about whether productivity should be measured in monetary or physical units. Jones (1988, p.317) maintains:

> There is little doubt that as far as the business is concerned performance should
> be measured in monetary terms since it is actual performance that is important

here. But for measuring productivity, and capacity management too for that matter, it may be better to use physical rather than financial measures. For instance, seat occupancy in a restaurant or customers served per hour in a supermarket are physical measures of capacity management.

We have argued that the production of services and of goods is interlinked in several respects. The one is dependent on and affects the other. High productivity in goods production often depends on the availability of services and on services which are essential for using the good in question. We noted in the last chapter that this service aspect may have been transferred to a separate company and, in the statistics, will thus be classified as services. Often it is such services that are difficult to standardize and mechanize, thus there is little or no potential for improving productivity. This results in productivity, when measured in the traditional way, falling, or at least not rising. Service businesses have thus taken over parts of what used to be an integrated part of goods production. The effects of these structural changes are that there is a rise in the productivity of goods production, while the things which are difficult to standardize are considered services. This 'burdens' developing productivity in service, or more exactly in the services that cannot be standardized.

There has been considerable discussion about how to evaluate fairly the 'output' of service-producing organizations. A major French study (De Bandt, 1988) points out that the development of productivity in the service sector has been the driving force behind the development of the industrial sector. When the traditional way of measuring productivity in industry is applied to the service sector, co-service is undervalued. Some aspects of the improvements in productivity are not credited to the service sector but appear in the industrial sector as a factor favouring its productivity development. Allen *et al.* (1989) maintain that the models used to measure the development of productivity systematically undervalue the 'output' of co-service.

If we consider changes in stock market prices in the United States from 1963 to 1987, we find the trends in share prices for companies which can be assigned to the service sector are much better than those for manufacturing companies (Baumol *et al.*, 1986b). How is this possible, given that they have shown a weaker productivity trend? If the development of productivity really is lower in service companies than in manufacturing companies, should this not have a negative effect on share prices over such a long period? Part of the explanation is to be found in the problem of measuring productivity at aggregated levels and over time:

> Measuring productivity at aggregated levels is only meaningful as a comparison over time with the units of analysis/sector grouping that satisfactorily reflect the organization of industry and commerce. Partly as a result of the development of the quality concept in the private service sector, the usefulness of traditional sector grouping is being lost.
>
> (Hjern, 1990)

Maccoby (1989) uses the term 'technoservice'. His view is that technoservice is characterized by customer-adapted products and services for customers and clients both within and outside the organization. A technoservice organization is characterized by networks and teams, a flat hierarchy and freedom for the front-line staff to make decisions to satisfy customers and adapt to changing conditions; productivity measures that are based on customer satisfaction and profitability; management as strategic planning and leadership which develops a motivated corporate culture that supports teamwork. This view echoes Forsman's (1989) view that: 'There are researchers who maintain that the most important gain in quality and productivity, primarily in the social services, comes from a change of attitude, approach and motivation in the staff in relation to pupils, patients, those in need of care, clients, etc.'

We now turn to the part that service design plays in improving both productivity and quality in services, and to designs for co-service.

THE IMPORTANCE OF SERVICE DESIGN

Before manufacture, products are carefully designed and tested. Manufacturers test ideas both technically and in the market, prepare drawings and specifications of the components, manufacture prototypes and make a pilot series. They also plan and redesign the production process. This design work is to ensure that the item can be easily produced, in the amounts required, at the lowest cost and corresponds to the needs of the customer. Designers increasingly use computerized design and production control (CAD/CAM programs). Large industrial companies like Ericsson have several thousand designers. In many sectors, manufacturers are moving to producing single items or batches, designed for individual customers, using more flexible production processes which can be quickly retooled.

Design in most services, where it exists, is more like nineteenth-century design in manufacturing. Service design is a very neglected field, but is perhaps more important than in manufacturing for quality and productivity. In many services, design is complex as it involves considering the process of service and the whole package offered to the customer: the quality in physical goods, in the service and the interplay between them.

In public services, design is mainly concerned with buildings or management structure. Readers can judge the success of these designs if they think of their last visit to a hospital or other public service: from driving or arriving by public transport to leaving. The simplest of customer needs, knowing where to go, often in an anxious state, is frequently not met even at the basic level of signposting. While public services may involve a rationing element, the lack of attention to the customer's experience and needs in design is the cause of much dissatisfaction, and cannot be appeased for by the most customer-friendly staff. Public policies governing the design of such services rarely have a coherent 'service concept'.

Poor service design builds-in quality problems before one brick of the building is laid, before staff are selected and trained in customer relations to overcome the deficiencies in design. Customer and staff frustration are guaranteed before the first customer arrives. Problems that can only be satisfactorily solved at source are left to the front-line and the customer to deal with. Both customer and staff may try to resolve the situation by circumventing the system in a bold and flexible manner. Usually the building, equipment and service systems have not been designed to work together to facilitate service: the co-service process has not been designed as a whole.

Prevention through design is the most important quality strategy: 'Get it right from the start.' The first opportunity to get it right is at the design stage. Once a fault is built into the system, it is continually repeated. W. Edwards Deming maintains that 94 per cent of all failings are caused by built-in system faults: the design of the service, the organization of the company, leadership style, what he terms 'general causes'. These create the conditions under which the service is performed. Only 6 per cent have 'specific causes' such as carelessness, ignorance, bad temper, etc., in the operative and front-line (Deming, 1986). Olsen (1992) shows that about 60 per cent of the critical incidents in banking services can be assigned to shortcomings in service design.

This is not to suggest that front-line staff are not important. Firstly, the ratio between 'general' and 'specific' cause varies between different services. Secondly, some of the built-in system faults can be corrected in contacts with the customer, even though the cost is unnecessarily high. Thirdly, through their continuous contact with customers, the front-line staff discover recurrent problems, and can be helped to report them or suggest or carry out changes. Better service design, or redesign call for contributions from different skills and departments in a company. Neither productivity, quality nor profitability can be delegated to a specialist department or team.

New and tested methods of service design are already being used with success. The most well known, is Shostack's 'blueprinting' (1977, 1987). This is a combination of flow chart, programming, network planning and methods engineering which provides an overview of the co-service process, taking into account the unique features of services. The service blueprint or drawing gives an overview of the service, and helps to choose whether to include or exclude certain steps, combine manual and mechanical aspects and calculate the cost of individual steps. Another method is the 'quality tree' (Dale and Wooler, 1990) which uses decision-analytic techniques to clarify the quality dimensions of a service, their relative importance for the quality of the service and the company's current competence to meet the requirements.

Service design involves making it possible to give a more individual service to each customer. The trend is towards individualized service, just as the trend in manufacturing is towards customized products. Some services have always aimed to design and provide a service for each person: architecture, consultancy, some financial services. Health services call for individual patient plans which then have to be well coordinated. Designing the conditions under which a service provider can then easily 'design' an individual service is a new field of service design. The overall design of a service must be such that the person or team designing a service for an individual is able to draw together the different elements that they need. This often means that they have a database of the service they may need, and can arrange and coordinate these services for the customer. Øvretveit (1993b) describes designs for health and social service teams which then make it possible for the team to design services for each patient or client.

Good service design sets the right conditions for the co-service relationship between customers and providers: we now consider their roles in service quality, productivity and profitability.

THE ROLES OF THE CUSTOMER AND THE SERVICE SUPPLIER

In co-service the customer interacts with the provider and with other customers. Productivity, quality and profitability in the service are affected by how each acts and understands his or her role: what should customers do and what should the supplier do for co-service?

A simple example is where the customer has 'free time', that is, time where he or she is not doing anything and would rather be doing something. The most common example is the 'service queue', a subject in its own right, but other situations are during travel. In these situations the customer could possibly perform some part of the co-service process. A customer can do certain things better and more quickly than the staff, e.g. filling in a form with background details. Perhaps the customer wants to be active and feel that he or she has control over the situation. In health services, especially mental health services, an active role for the 'patient' is often essential for a good outcome.

A good example is the supermarket, because it shows how important it is to get the balance right. The customer can carefully select the goods she wants without having to stand in a queue except when she pays. This may be good from a quality angle, but it can be bad because it is often hard to find anybody to ask. Goods must be easy to find, the message must be clear, it must be easy to move between the shelves. When it comes to perishable goods, this approach has proved difficult. Staffed meat, fish and cheese counters have been introduced. The staff of the shop provide two basic services: making the goods available and receiving payment. Productivity is increased by customers doing work which they prefer to do. The example also shows where the balance of co-service is wrong: where, at the checkout, customers are worked like robots on a production line, placing goods on the counter or belt and trying to pack them at the same time.

SEGMENTATION

Each customer's needs are different. Ideally a service should be designed for each person rather than as a mass service, but the costs of doing so are too high for many people. The alternative is to design service for people with similar needs – to do so may also be better if people want to be with others who are similar to them, for example some holiday services. Segmentation is a marketing term for identifying customer groupings, and doing so is one way to improve service productivity, quality and profitability.

> A service cannot be all things to all people ... Groups or 'segments' of customers must be singled out for a particular service, the needs determined, and a service concept developed that provides a competitive advantage for the server in the eyes of those to be served ... Segmentation is the process of identifying groups of customers with enough characteristics in common to make

possible the design and presentation of a product or service each group needs.

(Heskett, 1986, pp. 8–9)

Øvretveit (1992a) argues that:

> The lesson from research into services is that, unlike manufacturers who can make a great variety of products, few services are able effectively to provide more than one type or level of service. The secret is to decide which type of customers to serve with a particular type of service. In health services this translates into defining different health needs and designing different types of services to meet these needs. Segmentation methods are useful for identifying customers with homogeneous health needs which can be met more cost-effectively by designing a service specifically for them.

Segmentation methods have developed from mass marketing, to division into rough segments according to socio-demographic variables, taste, etc. More recently segmentation is on the basis of life style, and has led to tailor-made mass production where each individual or purchasing organization is its own segment.

These should be seen as alternative ways to examine customer needs. Standardization is essential for keeping costs down and keeping productivity up. Examples of this are casualty insurance for households, which are collective solutions which keep costs down. When it comes to pension insurances, a collective basic insurance can be complemented with an individual solution. Another example is Shouldice Hospital near Toronto, cited by Davidow and Uttal (1989) as an example of a successful service based on segmentation and designing the right service package for the targeted clients.

> By segmenting the market of sick people according to their complaint, then concentrating on a single segment, Shouldice has gained the ability to optimise its operations far more than general hospitals can. Its doctors have become highly proficient after doing hundreds of hernia repairs a year using Shouldice's special technique.

(Davidow and Uttal, 1989, p.49)

Note, however, that segmentation has to be used in conjunction with service design to improve quality and productivity and profit: sometimes segmentation does not result in improved productivity even if it does increase profits for a period:

> But which customers are the best targets? Those who are the most valuable compared with the likely costs of serving them.
>
> (Davidow and Uttal, 1989, p.38)

'Modularization' is one way to individualize services for different customer segments. A single module means one variant; several modules can be assembled in several different ways to produce a limited number of variants; a large number of modules gradually leads to individualized products. In the service sector, travelling is an example of a combination of modules. The travel agent tailors the journey from these modules and the customer complements it with individual services such as taxi journeys or car hire. Increasingly, education services are provided to students and employers on a modular basis.

THE IMPORTANCE OF INFORMATION TECHNOLOGY AND SOFTWARE IN SERVICES

Computerized and automated production was the key to increased productivity quality and profits in manufacturing. The key in services is information technology (IT). IT in data processing and telecommunications is at the centre of many service companies' activities, for example airline and hotel booking systems and for handling 'money' in banks and insurance companies. According to Quinn and Gagnon (1986) the service sector in the United States and the United Kingdom accounts for 70–80 per cent of all investments in information technology.

For data processing and telecommunications to be effective, the elements of computer, telephone, telefax, etc. – the hardware – and the computer program – the software – must work together. Both can be problematic with low productivity and low quality as the result. However, it is often the software that causes most problems, e.g. access to the system, program flexibility and the availability of terminals. The program must provide the right information and do the right things. Examples of the opposite are insurance companies' demand routines, where computers keep on producing demand notes for payment of premiums on insurances that have long been cancelled. This has a very bad effect on customer-perceived quality.

Quality assurance is especially important in software, and this has to include how the software forms a service system with hardware and people. Frequently software is only designed by computer programmers and without considering service design.

THE CUSTOMER CAN TAKE OVER SERVICE FUNCTIONS

Finally, to improve quality productivity and profitablity we would like to suggest the most radical measure: get rid of services! A radical way to raise productivity and quality is to make service superfluous. This is the case with machines and equipment that are designed to enable the customer to carry out service by cleaning or where parts are assembled in units and whole units can be easily changed by the customer.

Small copiers work on this principle. These used to need a service contract, and small companies were a lower priority for service compared to large customers. The greatest problem for the customer is breakdowns, not being able to use the copier and not knowing when it is going to be repaired. The customer sees self-service as higher quality. Another example is cars. Usually motorists have to wait before the garage has time to repair their cars, and they are also unsure of the quality of service that has been provided (Thomasson, 1989). If the need for servicing can be reduced through the conscious efforts of the designer, the customer will feel that the car has better quality.

TQM-BASED IMPROVEMENTS IN PRODUCTIVITY

This chapter argued for considering quality, productivity and profit together, and proposed the concept of 'co-service' to emphasize this link in services. We illustrated the connections in different areas and gave examples of how services could raise quality and productivity at the same time. The following summarizes these ideas in five suggestions for managers.

1 Work on productivity and quality simultaneously and devise measures for both. There is a risk that companies will carry out cost reduction and capital rationalization which will have negative consequences for the customer's perception of quality and thus for income.

2 Use the business and service concept as an aid. The business concept sets the limits for the company's business but creates opportunities at the same time. It defines the scope within which the employees can act and indicates the main purpose of the activities. In service businesses, the staff concept is a particularly important complement to the business concept since so many of the employees have contacts with customers and since productivity and quality depend on the personal efforts of so many individual employees. These concepts should be the core of the corporate culture.

3 Make sure you know how your company's services are produced and received by the customer in the co-service process. Services are different from mechanical components and engineering approaches may be irrelevant or damaging in some services. Above all, the interaction between customers and the service provider's staff is central to service activities. It is essential to clarify what you as the supplier are to do and what the customer is to do.

   Services are also highly dependent on equipment and systems. Computers and telecommunications are particularly important and the heart of these is software. If the company provides service for machines and equipment, the best strategy may be to design the product so that the need for service is eliminated or at least minimized.

4 Clarify how quality is created and destroyed in your business and how it

affects productivity and profitability. The point of departure must be customer-perceived quality. Different customer segments perceive quality differently, thus the choice of segment is of major importance. Make sure that the sources of quality – design quality and co-service quality – are right for the segment and measure whether the outcome satisfies the customer's various needs.

5 Go beyond the symptoms to the built-in system faults in your business. Symptoms arise as problems in contacts with the customer and in recurrent unnecessary tasks which reduce productivity. These faults may also lead to missed sales opportunities and reduce quality. Each task by itself may be of minor importance, but because it is repeated, it becomes significant. System faults are often due to defects in service design: consider service redesign in terms of the cost of poor quality.

Organizing and managing quality improvement

A few years ago, top management's interest in quality was typically an intellectual exercise; today, it is a strong personal commitment manifested through strategic leadership.

(John Condon, Managing Director, American Society for Quality Control)

Total quality management (TQM) is not just a 'programme' but a complete change in an organization's culture and way of working. While quality improvement initiatives can be undertaken without top management involvement, the evidence is that substantial and sustained change does not happen without top management commitment. This is true for the success of any substantial change in organizations, but especially for TQM. With TQM the aim is to establish a culture and systems which also survive changes of managers.

It is not sufficient for management merely to say that quality is important and request employees to pay greater attention to quality issues. To be successful, quality improvement must be organized and managed:

there must be a quality strategy and quality systems. Quality improvement depends on teamwork in a network, involving everybody, and to which everybody has to be committed. Any change with these ingredients is likely to be successful, but few changes in organizations have these ingredients. The power of quality methods and philosophies is that they can secure and sustain this degree of commitment – but only if their introduction is properly manged. The power also lies in the mutually-reinforcing effects of the changes, but for this to happen managers have to oversee and integrate the different initiatives using TQM frameworks.

The first two sections describe the managers' role and contribution to quality improvement, and their part in leading a quality strategy. The next section shows how to get the message across to everybody in the organization – and to suppliers and other partners – through 'internal marketing'.

The fourth section shows how managers can translate the business concept into clearly stated goals for the departments and teams. It is this link, together with measurement and accountability, which makes quality improvement a reality for staff rather than an abstract idea. In the fifth section we describe how quality improvement should be organized and illustrate this with an example of successful quality improvement carried out by Telia (Swedish Telecom).

If they are used as part of a TQM strategy, quality circles are a powerful way for getting staff to use quality methods and to take responsibility for quality improvement. They help to establish and sustain a quality culture, which extends beyond the circle, especially as many quality circles involve staff from different departments and professions. The next section considers corporate culture for quality improvement in more detail. Culture is difficult to define, especially for insiders, but a quality culture is perhaps even more important in services than in manufacturing. Managers need to stand back and understand the possible cultural obstacles to quality improvement before making changes. We draw these considerations together in the final section to describe a TQM approach for service managers.

THE ROLE OF MANAGEMENT

> The responsibility for and commitment to a quality policy for the service organization belongs to the highest level of management.
> (International Standard, ISO 9004-2, *Quality management and quality system elements: Guidelines for services*)

Quality improvement is often started by an enthusiast, who then has to arouse the interest of the management team to get them to believe in the idea and to gain their wholehearted support. Both research and practical work repeatedly show that quality improvement cannot be successfully carried out without top management commitment. Too often managers pay lip-service to quality and delegate quality issues. Staff judge managers by their actions and know, often better than managers do themselves, what is important to their manager. Quality policies alone are not sufficient: managers have to be wholeheartedly involved in the work.

Quality improvement cannot be achieved by order or administration. It is changes in managers' attitudes and behaviour that count: they have to take an active part in meetings, and other work on quality improvement, and reward staff for improvements that they make. Management at all levels must be encouraged to give priority to quality improvement. According to Kahn (1989) you cannot start 'a little on the quiet' and gain acceptance from management later. Kahn says, 'Quality starts at the top and is total'. The initiative can be taken by anyone in the organization but management must be involved. According to Kahn, experience from industry shows that investments in quality where management is not involved, only have an impact on 20 per cent of the employees. With full commitment on the part of management, the figure will instead be 80 per cent. A finding of a recent three-year evaluation of the British National Health Service's TQM programme was that the lack of change in many hospitals was due to poor top management commitment.

The American, W. Edwards Deming has worked longer than anyone on quality issues, primarily in the manufacturing industry but also with service companies. Deming emphasizes the importance of a long-term approach to quality improvement, and of creating a work climate where the employees feel secure. With security comes the courage to point out what is wrong, something which managers need to find out from all of their staff. Deming's (1986) 14 points for leadership in quality improvement are a good guide for service managers:

- Create constancy of purpose towards improvement of product and service.
- Adopt the new philosophy. We are in a new economic age.
- Cease dependence on inspection to achieve quality.
- End the practice of awarding business on the basis of price alone. Instead, minimize total cost by working with a single supplier.
- Improve constantly and forever every process for planning, production and service.
- Institute training on the job.
- Adopt and institute leadership.
- Drive out fear, so that everyone may work effectively for the company.
- Break down barriers between staff areas.
- Eliminate slogans, exhortations, and targets for the workforce.
- Eliminate numerical quotas for the workforce and numerical goals for management.
- Remove barriers that rob people of pride of workmanship. Eliminate the annual rating or merit system.
- Institute a vigorous programme of education and self-improvement for everyone.
- Put everybody in the company to work to accomplish the transformation.

Deming's points are well formulated and, we believe, with him, that they are applicable to services businesses. However, we would add one which Deming himself stresses: measurement, which we further consider in Chapter 7.

QUALITY STRATEGIES

Managers have to stop thinking about quality merely as a narrow effort to gain control of the production process, and start thinking more rigorously about consumers' needs and preferences. Quality is not simply a problem to be solved: it is a competitive opportunity (Garvin, 1987).

Many managers we have worked with find TQM confusing and are overwhelmed by the magnitude of the changes that they will have to make. It seems that they have to change everything at once, at the same time as ensuring that routine services do not suffer. Their understanding of TQM has disabled them rather than empowered them.

The starting point for managers at every level is diagnosis of the current state of quality in their area. We later describe simple as well as more sophisticated quality diagnostic methods, for example frameworks based on ISO 9000, BS 5750, the Malcolm Baldrige National Quality Award, or the Wel-Qual framework. From diagnosis, managers can then develop a strategy for quality improvement. One of us warns of the 'perils of quality over-saturation' (Øvretveit, 1992a) and proposes 'phasing-in' quality methods and changes in four stages at a pace with which staff can cope.

Quality improvement often calls for reorganization at various levels, new routines and changes in work teams. However, there is a danger in drawing up too detailed plans. Mintzberg (1989) describes two strategic approaches. The first is familiar to many managers: a systematic analysis of the market and the company's own resources, giving the basis for detailed planning. Afterwards, checks are made to see whether the plans have been realized. Mintzberg explains the second approach by means of a metaphor. Management develops its strategy as a craftsman does. A potter, for instance, sits with his material, clay, thinking about how to use it. He sits between his previous experience and his coming products. He has learnt from experience and he can use the material in different ways. He looks forward and combines the past with the future. In the same way, says Mintzberg, management should work with its material – organization and its resources. Visions of what the result may be are good but it is important not to fasten in a specific attitude.

Managers need to recognize which approach is best for quality strategy and use a mixture. For some changes they need detailed planning with critical paths, milestones and reviews. For others it is better to shape direction and to go with the flow.

Strategic planning also entails mapping the obstacles to change that exist within the organization. Lawrence (1969) maintains that there are three reasons why opposition to change is so common: uncertainty about the consequences of change; unwillingness to give up one's own privileges; and awareness of the problems and difficulties in the imminent changes. Strategy formulation involves identifying barriers to change and devising ways through or around them. It is important to analyse opinions about weaknesses in the proposals. They may concern planning oversights about the effects on the organization of the planned changes. Involving the staff concerned at an early stage means that valuable insights can be included right at the start of the planning stage, and also helps to implement the changes.

In our work with managers introducing TQM we have found it useful to draw on managers' past experience of different changes in the organization – what helped and hindered these changes – and the lessons for TQM change. In any change there are two opposing forces – 'driving and restraining forces' – forces that support and drive changes forward and ones which counteract changes. To formulate a strategy it is helpful to list the different forces for change. In principle, there are three ways of dealing with these forces. One is to reinforce those that support changes and the second to weaken those that oppose changes. The third way is a combination of the other two. Reinforcing the supportive forces often results in the strengthening of the counteractive forces as well. In TQM strategies the combined approach is more likely to be successful.

INTERNAL MARKETING

Internal marketing was originally devised to 'sell' a product to staff so that the staff would better be able to sell it to customers. Internal marketing has gradually gained greater importance as an organizational development method. It is no longer a matter of simply selling a product, but primarily of selling the company's business concept.

We proposed in Chapter 2 that a company should have a clear and viable business concept as a guideline for all work. This is as true of the public sector as of private industry. The business idea should be simple and easy to understand and indicate:

- for whom the company exists
- what the company should produce
- how the customer should be served.

But for the business concept to give direction for all work, not just in customer contacts, managers have to market it internally so that everybody in the company understands it and is committed to realizing it. Properly conducted, internal marketing results in the staff being better informed and more motivated. The business concept and internal marketing increases the will and ability to cooperate and all pull in the same direction. Managers have a key role in internal marketing in that they provide an example for everybody else in the company. Even the company's external marketing has repercussions. What the company communicates externally also has an effect internally. It is often the staff, not the customers, who pay most attention to the company's advertising.

Internal marketing as part of TQM has several aims:

- To make clear what is being done.
- To influence attitudes to work.
- To alter behaviour towards both external and internal customers.
- To increase commitment.
- To improve communication with external customers.
- To improve communication between internal customers.

According to Grönroos (1990), internal marketing is a management strategy for producing customer-conscious employees. Skilful internal marketing is needed at an early stage of quality improvement. There is no contradiction between quality improvement with the customers in mind and quality for the company's employees. The introduction of the concept of internal customer is an aspect of internal marketing. Suddenly being seen as a customer in your work situation may make each task easier and the work more enjoyable. Virtuous circles emerge that have synergy effects throughout the organization.

The task of management is to encourage and stimulate the internal marketing process. The company's information system often has channels for spreading the quality message, so it need not cost much to market the new quality thinking internally. Quality goals, which we discuss in the next section, must also be marketed internally.

QUALITY GOALS

When we embark on a journey, we generally have a goal or destination. The same is true of quality improvement. For people to be enthusiastic about and committed to quality improvement, they must have attainable goals to aim for, which are clearly defined, and measures of their progress towards the goal. Managers' task is to formulate goals that meet these criteria and that are oriented towards external customers. A goal can be set to satisfy an internal customer, but there must be a demonstrable link between this goal and value for external customers. Sometimes people use the term 'standard' rather than goal, and although we are not going to distinguish the two here, it is worth noting that 'standard' is often a more static idea.

In formulating quality goals, managers translate the business concept and customer demands into actions for themselves and their staff. Goals exist at two levels: the overarching ones must be broken down to the right level and operationalized. Below we list a number of guidelines for formulating these goals, which also serve as criteria against which a manager's quality goals can be judged:

1 The goals must be based on the expectations, requirements and needs of the customers. If the customers are not satisfied, the goals have failed.
2 The goals must be related to the company's business concept and must not contradict it. If there are contradictions between goals and business concept, one of them must be changed.
3 The goals must be realistic, but also sufficiently ambitious.
4 The goals must be so clearly defined that there is no doubt when they have been attained. They should be measurable in some way.
5 The goals must be clear and unambiguous so that they are not

interpreted differently by different people. They must not be contradictory.

6 The attainment of the goals must be someone's specific responsibility.

7 The goals must have a time limit. The latest date for attaining them must be indicated.

8 The goals must be subject to change, reflecting changes in the environment.

Regular monitoring and feedback to those concerned are essential in a development process. Goals are not given once and for all. The environment is continually changing and improvements in one's own organization may necessitate changes in the goals and the level at which they are pitched.

Part of the manager's task is to break down goals into sub-goals for staff working in different sub-processes. The Japanese method for doing this is *hoshin kanri*, which we describe later in Quality Policy Deployment (QPD). Florida Power and Light is one company which uses Quality Function Deployment (QFD) to break down the overarching goals and make them measurable at all levels in the organization.

Each company must determine its own goals, but this does not mean that a company cannot compare itself with other companies. The term benchmarking is used for this type of comparison – we select a company, which we know to be exceptional in a particular field, and measure ourselves against it. It need not be a competitor or even a company in the same line of business. If, for instance, we know of a company that is especially good at handling complaints rapidly and smoothly, we can learn from its approach and use its results in complaint handling as our own goal (see Chapter 7).

CARRYING OUT A QUALITY STRATEGY

The RIGHT QUALITY is not achieved by chance but is the product of planned cooperation between various people and it results in competitive goods and services.

(From Telia's [Swedish Telecom] Quality Policy)

For a quality strategy to be effective, it has to be carefully prepared and planned. But it is not sufficient for managers to formulate and initiate a strategy, they must guide it, adjust it and take part in it. A major factor is the interest and commitment of the staff (cf. Chapter 6). Everybody must be involved if the strategy is to have a chance of success. Service managers can learn from the four-stage programme of American Express, who have successfully pursued quality improvement since 1978.

The first stage is to form 'quality improvement groups', made up of people from different departments. Apart from focusing on quality issues, the group members learn a great deal about each other's work and also receive training in working in groups.

The second stage is to spread the 'quality message' throughout the organization by means of internal marketing. Staff are constantly reminded of the quality programme through posters, badges, etc. There is constant education and training in quality.

The third stage is to establish goals for service quality. Every employee should know what is required of him or her and they should all understand the goals and the reason for them.

In the fourth stage the task is to ensure that everybody knows the cost of quality errors. Quantifying quality errors in cash terms helps to convince those who are otherwise opposed to quality improvement.

This programme gives one example of how to carry out a strategy, but we would argue that it is not sufficient to form groups with just internal participants. In most cases companies depend on subcontractors and partners, who also need to take part in the quality development process in order to ensure the right quality in their contributions to the business. One example is in air travel. Customers have to rely on taxis or buses to reach their final destination, and airlines cooperate with different transport companies and sell tickets for ground transport. Health care is another case in point; the operation may well be successful but the patient may suffer because of low quality post-operative care. Links with subcontractors and partners are often more important to service quality than internal processes: there is no point recognizing these links in design and ignoring them in carrying out quality strategies.

With quality training, employees' ideas and suggestions can make a big contribution to quality improvement. Acting on these ideas is the best way for managers to show that they are serious about quality and for progressing a quality strategy. Ignoring these ideas or not giving convincing explanations for why the ideas cannot be pursued is a quick way for managers to signal both that staff involvement is not wanted or valued and that quality is not important.

Our experience is that many companies are bad at handling suggestions from employees, and are not able to follow through when they do set up such schemes. In practice, a few basic rules are sufficient if they are followed and it is surprising that European and American service managers have not adopted them to any great extent. These rules are:

1 Give rapid feedback to the person making the suggestion.
2 Reward suggestions that can be implemented.
3 If a suggestion cannot be realized, explain why not in detail.
4 Ensure that as many suggestions as possible are accepted, even if they involve only small improvements.

Many of the principles are similar to those about dealing with customer complaints or suggestions. Set a limit for how long people making suggestions have to wait for an answer. Even if the answer is negative, it is better to receive it in a few days than to wait for weeks in uncertainty. While waiting they will probably not make any new suggestions. Deal with suggestions rapidly, seriously and in a positive spirit. Set up a reward system so that nobody feels exploited by the company. If the suggestion is profitable in economic terms to the company, the person or team that made the suggestion should receive part of the 'profit'.

In the long term, the fourth point is probably the most important. Implementing a large number of the suggestions for improvements has a powerful psychological effect. The employees feel that not only can they influence their own situation but also they can contribute to the development of the company.

Although there are cultural differences, many Japanese companies with suggestion schemes find that 90 per cent of the employees come with suggestions for improvements. In many cases, over 95 per cent of these suggestions are accepted and implemented. Every employee makes on average between 30 and 50 suggestions per annum. Many of these are small and seemingly insignificant, but together they are of great importance for involvement in, and a sense of ownership of, a quality strategy.

A suggestion scheme is part of the philosophy quality as a journey without end, a never-ending process of seeking improvement (cf. Deming's fifth point). This idea is well summed up in the Japanese word: *kaizen* – that everything can be improved, whether it be a product or a service, a process or a single activity in a larger process.

Telia (Swedish Telecom) – An example of one approach to quality improvement

Companies that are successful in quality improvement see it as an organized process, but how to organize this process depends on the type of company, its market and its history. Telia provides one example of how quality processes can be organized and used on a long-term basis. It also shows how one company uses a quality award as the basis for a company-wide framework for a comprehensive approach to quality, something which we consider in Chapter 7. The following summarizes the company's approach, starting with the general quality statement, developed after much discussion:

> Quality is a way of working and an attitude to work. In more philosophical terms one could say it is a way of living ... Companies who want to be successful in quality must go about it in a methodical manner. Isolated efforts in a company seldom produce lasting effects ... To be successful and achieve measurable results, quality improvement must be organized and structured.

Telia has a quality support division, 'MQ', which assists the various companies in the group to formulate a unified approach and an awareness of quality improvement. The division provides an education and training service to managers, and aids and methods which help them to produce measurable improvements in quality. To ensure a common approach to quality, MQ uses a framework which extends from overarching strategies to concrete operations. The following summarizes part of the framework document.

From strategy to action – Telia's quality policy

The planning cycle

Working consciously with quality improvement strengthens competitiveness, raises internal efficiency and improves profitability and gives both greater customer satisfaction and greater job satisfaction to all employees. Management handles resource allocation for quality improvement, but the result is produced through an interplay of resources and operational quality improvement activities that create the successful company.

To achieve this, senior management carries out strategic quality planning (SQP), planning which has its point of departure in the improvement areas and in the criteria for the Telia Quality/Swedish Quality Award. The result of this SQP is the input for a continuous improvement process in four steps: (1) plan; (2) execute; (3) measure; (4) evaluate (the management's planning cycle). This process then goes on continuously and is based each year on an overall assessment of the company's quality situation in relation to the criteria in the above award.

Strategic quality planning

To achieve a common understanding of the criteria in the Telia Quality/ Swedish Quality Award, the management group as a whole works through a SQP process.

1 *Business concept and vision.* All business operations should be based on a clear business concept, firmly implanted throughout the entire company. If this is not the case, you have to begin the first step by creating and implanting the business concept in the entire organization. You then have to define the company's vision. This is strategically very important in that it determines the direction the company will take in the future.

Many units within our company today have the vision of 'the successful service company'. Success is measured primarily by the satisfaction of our external customers, but the overall result is also dependent on a healthy economy and a committed staff.

2 *The path/strategy.* The path leading to the successful company is described in the Telia Quality/Swedish Quality Award in the form of criteria divided into seven improvement areas, which have been allotted different weightings depending on how important they are from the total quality viewpoint. The main areas are then divided into 30 sub-areas. The most important area is customer satisfaction, which has been allotted 300 of a total of 1000 points.

3 *Assessment.* Each of the seven improvement areas and the 30 sub-areas are assessed and described. The answers should describe the dimensions: approach, application and result. The description should be brief and factual and statements supported by data if possible. If the account is based on information from another unit in the group, this should be indicated.

4 *The current situation.* Based on these descriptions and on an evaluation model with the three above-mentioned dimensions, an assessment is made of the current situation. A total assessment is then made for each sub-area/criterion. After analysing and describing all the improvement areas/criteria and evaluating them with the aid of the model, senior management now has a total view of the current quality situation in the whole company and its relation to the outside world.

5 *Rate of improvement.* The process has now reached the stage where it is time to establish the short-term and long-term goals for quality improvement in the whole company. When the goals have been defined and established, management must also decide on the rate of improvement for each area, that is, at what level on the scale, non-existent (0%) to first class (100%), the company will find itself for example, in one or three years' time.

6 *Plans.* The rate of improvement is then described in short-term and long-term action plans. These plans are broken down into activity plans and

concrete activities. The plans clearly spell out who does what, and the various related deadlines.

7 *Measurement.* The planning process has now arrived at the point where a measurement model has to be found to measure and follow up the improvement results. This measurement model must contain both subjective and objective performance indicators. The overall measurement is carried out in the annual self-assessment against the criteria in the Telia Quality/Swedish Quality Award. The description of the current situation which emerges from this assessment forms the point of departure for a new quality improvement plan. Improvement area 6 in the Telia Quality/Swedish Quality Award includes the important results criteria.

Telia works with a quality index called TQIX, Telia Quality Index (see Chapter 7). In a trial run in four Telia regions, the index contains 36 core performance indicators which provide information about developments within the areas of service, economy and job satisfaction. By this means we can measure the achievement of our goals; in other words, the degree of satisfaction among our owners, customers and employees.

8 *Evaluation.* These measurement results are evaluated and fed back to the internal improvement activities. At the same time, they also provide the basis for new plans for the continuous process of improvement. The performance indicators are integrated into a tree structure that enables the results to be read at several index levels. Each indicator and index level carries a weight reflecting its importance to the total quality concept. This enables the index to be used to manage and set the priorities for the continuous and daily improvement work.

9 *Improvements.* To achieve and maintain the highest level of competitiveness, the continual improvement of our products/services and processes is essential. This attitude must permeate the whole business, its management and staff. Evaluation forms the point of departure for a new planning process that results in continuous improvements in a never-ending process.

Strategic quality planning – conclusion

This strategic quality planning model – the 'SQP' model – gives a framework for the company's quality improvement work. The planning ensures active participation by senior management in the quality improvement process. There is a structure for managing the process, setting priorities and following up the results of this work. Other companies, such as IBM, are increasingly using broader frameworks for organizing quality than quality systems like ISO 9000, or BS 5750, and we discuss the Malcolm Baldrige National Quality Award for these purposes in Chapter 7. Øvretveit (1993d) provides more details of other approaches, and describes a computer process for self-assessment against award criteria – the 'Maps-Qual' process (Øvretveit, 1992c).

QUALITY CIRCLES

Turning to more specific aspects of an organized approach to quality, we now consider a simple and effective part of a quality strategy – quality circles. These small groups of staff are often the backbone of a quality strategy and one of the main ways of introducing quality thinking and methods into an organization. They were originally started in Japan in the 1950s. In the beginning they were often a failure because they were not an integral part of an overall quality strategy, and because basic rules for setting them up were not followed. Some organizations may have to reintroduce them in a new way to overcome their poor reputation, but used in the right way they are a key part of a TQM approach.

The basic idea of quality circles is that they should involve staff in planning and implementing quality improvements using proven quality methods. People should be given the opportunity to improve their own work situation, which will also give them the feeling of belonging to and identifying with the company. The success of quality circles presupposes a people-oriented management style which respects, believes in and trusts staff, and proves this by carrying out changes proposed and properly resourcing quality circles.

One approach to forming a quality circle is to create a group of four to ten volunteers who have more or less the same type of job. The circle meets regularly to identify the causes of and to devise solutions to problems at the workplace. The circle is a working group that uses quality methods, makes decisions and assumes responsibility for transforming the decisions into action. It is different from a simple problem-solving group in that the group uses systematic methods and quality tools – for example the 'seven QC' tools described by Ishikawa (1985) and Imai (1986), and discussed by Bergman and Klefsjö (1991).

It is the employees, not management, who run the circles and managers who take part can find difficulties if they adopt a traditional management role in the group. Allowing the staff to run the circles does not mean that management has no responsibility for the results. According to Barra (1989) a condition for the success of quality circles is that management fully supports the work and accepts the following responsibilities:

- Management must actively encourage the view that staff can and should exert greater influence.
- Management must ensure that the work in the circles receives the necessary support.
- Management must find a system for rewarding the results achieved by the circles.

Barra claims that about one-third of the quality circles are successful, one-third achieve some success and one-third fail. Failures, he maintains, are due to the lack of maturity in management regarding improvements through quality circles. Barra draws a slightly patronizing but evocative parallel with sowing and cultivating: it is not enough merely to spread the seed and hope for a harvest – the sowing must be carefully prepared and the plants tended as they grow.

Quality circles have been primarily used in industry, but in recent years they are increasingly used in pure service companies, both private and public. Westinghouse started using quality circles in 1978. Today there are quality circles at over 200 Westinghouse establishments in North and

South America and in Europe. Westinghouse has become a 'quality circle' model not only for industry but also for service companies, with hospitals, banks and public authorities successfully using the Westinghouse approach (Barra, 1989).

QUALITY IMPROVEMENT TEAMS

A second practical step towards an organized approach to quality is the quality improvement team, which is similar to the quality circle. The principle is that many people, in time everybody, in the organization can be involved in and contribute to continuous quality improvement. To make this possible and to deal with and implement suggestions and ideas for improving quality in all the activities, the work has to be done in an organized and systematic manner. The task and responsibility of quality improvement teams (QITs) is to identify and analyse the potential for improvement and ensure that various improvements are initiated and implemented. The following gives some principles for organizing QITs, their working methods and how they can get started.

- The QIT must not be a separate organization but should be in the mainstream of the company's activities. Each team consists of seven–nine people. The team leader (TL) may, for instance, be a divisional manager.
- It is important that the team is headed by the manager to underline the significance of quality improvement. To lighten the load on the manager, there should also be a deputy team leader (DTL). External consultants should also be on hand when needed.
- The DTL has a key role in quality improvement. Much of the practical work will rest on his or her shoulders and he or she must be very committed and prepared to spend more time on quality improvement than the others.
- At least one QIT should be started in each profit centre. It is important that the members of the team are motivated, believe in and are fully committed to quality improvement. If there is any doubt, the QIT should not be started.

- To stimulate and follow up quality improvement, a quality improvement board should be set up, with the managing director or equivalent, an internal quality specialist and an external consultant. The internal specialist should be trained in using various tools for measuring, analysing and improving quality and thus act as a resource for the QIT.
- The QIT should meet once or twice a month during the first six months. After this the frequency of the meetings can be evaluated. Each meeting should last two–three hours. The quality improvement board should meet four times a year.

QIT working methods

- The QIT should work on their own terms and take up issues which they consider important. The team will be offered various tools for customer attitude surveys, etc., and models for describing processes. They should follow these common principles to increase their effectiveness:
  - All quality improvement should be based on facts.
  - Everybody should work in accordance with the four phases of the 'quality improvement wheel':
    (i) Identifying problems and development potential.
    (ii) Describing and analysing the current situation. Describing the goals or desired situation.
    (iii) Developing a plan for achieving the goals, desired situation.
    What should be done? Description of activities.
    Who is responsible for implementation?
    What resources are needed?
    When is the work to be completed? Timetable.
    How should the work be followed up?
    (iv) Implementation and follow-up/evaluation. Documentation and possible further activities.

Getting started

- To start the process, a first meeting should be held with representatives of all the units in the company, the aim being to motivate them for quality improvement, train them in certain basic tools and discuss and gain support for the QITs and the wheel.

- This meeting should be planned by the managing director together with the consultant. Further, the divisional managers involved should also be consulted. A follow-up meeting should be held after six months.
- The consultant should be available to provide the QIT with advice and to train them to use the necessary tools.

ORGANIZATIONAL CULTURE

The concept of culture was developed in anthropology and sociology and was used by organizational theorists to conceptualize a general mode of thinking and acting within an organization. Culture is based on learned habits and traditions and evolves slowly over time like a language. Like a language, culture cannot be changed easily by those in authority, but managers can and do need to create a quality culture for successful quality improvement – we consider in this section how they may do this.

Organizational culture consists of fundamental values shared by all the members of the organization. It is a form of ideology within the organization. Successful companies often have a strong culture which is shared and accepted by everybody in the company. Schein (1987, p.6) puts it in the following terms:

> The term 'culture' should be reserved for the deeper level of basic assumptions and beliefs that are shared by members of an organization, that operate unconsciously, and that define in a basic 'taken-for-granted' fashion an organization's view of itself and its environment. These assumptions and beliefs are learned responses to a group's problems of survival in its external environment and its problems of internal integration. They come to be taken for granted because they solve those problems repeatedly and reliably.

Schein sees culture as a tool for the management of an organization to influence its members to act in a certain direction. He believes that one of management's most important tasks is to create an organizational culture and to manage the development of that culture, integrated with the development of the business. When management attempts to change the existing culture, its task is to formulate visions and coin terms which reflect the new way of thinking which it wishes to introduce. This does not mean that all old assumptions and values should be thrown out, but some may need to be renewed and complemented with new insights into how the everyday work of the company is to be carried out.

Øvretveit (1992a, p.133) argues that many quality programmes have failed because those introducing them have not understood the organizational culture, or have assumed that they can change it quickly to a culture which values customer satisfaction above all. His aim has been to develop an approach to quality suited to the values, ethics and culture of different services, health services being one example,

> 'Off-the-shelf' quality programmes can be force-fitted into a service – some developed for manufacturing are used in commercial and now public services. The argument is: change behaviour and changes to attitudes and culture will follow. Some of these programmes are successful for a short time. But unless the programme directly addresses health service culture or happens to be suited to the culture, it dwindles rather than gathering momentum and producing the continual quality improvements that are the aim. 'Culture' tends to be a catch-all term used to explain something which people find difficult to explain ('history' is another). Structural changes, such as changing and defining roles and relationships and developing teamwork help to change culture. Leadership by example is also important to changing culture. The approach described here focuses on changing attitudes by showing staff that there are tangible benefits for them in improving quality, and that quality is a way of upholding professional and caring values.

Quality culture

> A strong internal service culture is likely to lead to higher quality in service delivery, which in turn will lead to higher perceived service quality from the customer's point of view.
>
> (Bitner, 1991, p.23)

A part of the company's culture is attitudes towards quality and customers and knowledge and use of quality methods and concepts. It is this culture which sustains the use of quality methods, and also helps to create a common approach across the company. An investment in quality improvement can be an instrument for influencing the whole organization. If the company concentrates on developing the quality of all its functions, this will have synergy effects throughout the system. There will be a better understanding of what constitutes quality, of what quality is, at the same time there will be a better chance of offering the customers the right quality. This is what is meant by cultivating a quality culture.

The point at which we should start cultivating a quality culture does not lie in the interaction with customers. Front-line staff depend on support services, the quality of the physical equipment and the internal, interactive quality in the company. Before a company uses quality as a competitive measure and increases customers' expectations, the whole organization must be prepared to meet these expectations. There must be an effective back-up system. On the other hand, customers' demands and expectations must, of course, underlie quality improvement.

A story is told of an American car manufacturer who annually exported a small number of cars to Japan. On one occasion some of the American company's management visited their Japanese agent. The first thing the American guests saw was a large workshop. Somewhat surprised, they asked the Japanese why they had set up such a large service workshop near the port for such a small number of imported cars. They received the answer when they entered the workshop. The American cars were completely dismantled and then immediately reassembled. The Japanese did not rely on the Americans' assembly work but wanted it done with more precision. The story – true or not – shows that quality is something very tangible, which can be affected by a conscious effort to make improvements. It is a matter of introducing a quality thinking which permeates the whole organization and of developing and strengthening a quality culture.

Many companies try to develop common quality thinking. Ericsson has concentrated on developing a quality culture in the company to ensure that employees understand that they are contributing to the total quality of the company's offering. It is not just the quality of the physical products that is decisive. The customers' quality assessment is based on a total impression of the company's products, services and staff. Ericsson underlines that 'the customer is the final judge of Ericsson quality' (Gummesson, 1987, p.28).

We have mentioned a number of companies in the private sector who are working on quality. Quality is not of course the preserve of private companies, and many professions have long been concerned with improving quality, although they have been slow to adapt the new techniques. It is in the public sector where the challenge to introduce a quality culture is greatest, even though there is a long history of a service ethic. Intensive quality improvement is being carried out in the public sector, for instance, in health care, child care, elderly care, regional social insurance offices, etc. An example of what the Swedish government is doing to improve the quality of public service and create a quality culture is the Administrative Procedures Act, whose objective is to adapt public services better to the demands and wishes of the users. Inscribed in this Act are the obligations of the government, the county and municipal councils to the citizens. Tens of thousands of civil servants are going through a special training programme to ensure that the law is properly applied by the various authorities. The Swedish government's bill (1990/91:90) on research, states: 'The public sector's services are generally not finished products. Greater influence on the part of those requiring the services will enable the services to be better adapted to the demand. This is largely what is meant by quality in services.' The British government has also introduced a number of customer-care initiatives. Our own view of public sector approach to quality in the United Kingdom and Sweden is of a failure to address both culture and quality systems, and a tendency to take a relatively superficial approach to quality.

Changes in culture

A quality culture is the context within which staff use the tools and systems of quality – it is the culture which sustains the motivation and interest to use the

new techniques and which sets the norms for how staff interact with external
and internal customers. It is the air that people breathe or the water they swim in.
Øvretveit (1992a)

Cultivating a quality culture entails organizing for quality and implanting a quality thinking which reaches everybody in the company. Managers will become more familiar with phrases like the preceding one – changing an existing, familiar culture which has been established for many years is easier said than done. Frequently quality programmes fail because new or 'old' managers have not understood the existing culture, or seriously attempted cultural changes as well as the technical changes. They need to lead a mental revolution in the organization, with new values, new insights and a changed attitude to customers and colleagues.

One danger when attempting to change an existing culture is over-optimism. It is wrong to believe that changing the culture will of itself lead to changes in behaviour in the organization. But changes in managers' behaviour do lead to changes in culture. If managers show by their actions that they give quality improvement high priority, and not just talk about it, then a quality culture may be developed. Questioning old, accustomed patterns contributes to changing the culture. In a company that you know, as a customer, visitor or employee, where do you park your car? In one large company the managers had their parking spaces near the entrance to the main building. Other staff and customers had to park their cars further away. The company appointed a new managing director and he immediately changed the parking system so that customers and other visitors could park as close to the entrance as possible. Then came the parking spaces for the staff, so arranged that the higher a person's position, the further he had to walk. The managing director parked his car furthest away. The idea was to underline the fact that the customers were the most important people and that the managers were not more important than their staff. At the same time, as they walked from their cars, the managers would have a perfect opportunity to exchange a few words with their staff. Of course, a small change cannot alone alter an existing organizational culture, but changing habits and patterns of behaviour and getting people to think along new lines may contribute to the development of a new culture.

Even if it is difficult to change an existing culture, the latter must not be neglected. Successful quality improvement requires an understanding of culture. We think it is of great value to analyse one's own company's culture to gain a greater understanding of the obstacles to improving quality. Culture has many elements, some are easy to register, others more difficult to grasp and interpret. One aspect of culture is the managerial style that may be observed in an organization. It is easy to see whether it is formal or informal, dictatorial or democratic. Øvretveit (1992a) suggests that culture is also revealed as follows:

- in formal and informal status hierarchies
- by looking at the actions and the people that are formally and informally valued in the service (e.g. a respected secretary, manager, or practitioner)
- in the language (e.g. the non-professional words commonly used to categorize clients, or to describe 'difficult' or 'good' clients, or a successful worker)
- in images and myths – the often retold stories about the last manager, or what one of the staff once did
- to understand culture and values and their power, managers should imagine actions that would cause trouble, or create uproar.

Managers need to understand the fundamental norms and values that exist in the company. Their norms and values are often not shared by others. In the following we describe how sub-cultures can act as anti-cultures, among other things, because specific professional standards control behaviour.

Sub-cultures – anti-cultures

One obstacle to changes in culture lies in the fact that there are sub-cultures of various kinds, which in many cases go against the general culture if there is one. Many social groups in organizations, especially professions, have their own alternative culture that isolates them from the overall culture. There may be considerable opposition to altering the existing culture.

Vocational or professional sub-cultures exist in many organizations. These have both negative and positive features from a management and quality improvement perspective. A professional culture may to some extent be an anti-culture to the current organizational culture. Professional cultures are often marked by a monopolization of a certain type of job, while, at the same time, members are 'forbidden' to perform tasks that lie outside their ordinary range of duties. Professional competence may be so special that it makes it difficult for the person in question to see beyond his or her own sphere and understand that it may sometimes be necessary to change behaviour so that other groups can offer customers the right quality in the services. One positive feature of professional cultures is that they often include quality thinking. Professional pride forbids the practitioner to let the quality sink below a certain level. In extreme cases this level may be too high to achieve the 'right' quality.

BASIC APPROACHES TO QUALITY IMPROVEMENT

> To promote the right value system which is sensitive to Total Quality managers have to learn to do one thing. They must learn to love their people as they do their own family and themselves. Learning to love people, looking at them as people, not staff, or hourly paid or blue collar workers, but people, is a major step. Looking at your people from the neck up, not from the neck down, is a good starting point.
>
> (Atkinson, 1990, p.13)

This quote is a bit extreme for some, but the general point is valid – that managers' attitudes and behaviour towards their staff form a key part of a quality approach. Some managers will not be successful with quality improvement if they just focus on the technical aspects of quality without an inner change of values towards people. Total quality management (TQM) means that management formulates strategies and plans and implements them with the aid of internal marketing. Management is also responsible for organizing quality improvement but management's responsibility extends even further. Managers must ensure that the goals are operationalized and that the activities are followed up and evaluated in relation to the goals at various levels. TQM also means that quality improvement concerns everybody in the company and managers at all levels have a quality responsibility. TQM stresses the importance of common basic values, i.e. what is right or wrong, good or bad, correct or incorrect.

A similar approach to TQM is total quality control (TQC), which has so far mainly been used by manufacturing companies. 'Total' means that it is not a special department that is responsible for quality improvement; all staff at all levels are involved and it is all these people in cooperation who can develop the quality of production. The Japanese sometimes prefer the term 'company-wide quality control' (CWQC) in order to underline the fact that all the staff are involved.

We wish to underline the fact that quality improvement takes place in continuous interaction between planning and action. Improvements are preceded by planning. Each implemented improvement gives experience for further planning in an ongoing upward spiral. Each step gives staff a greater understanding of how quality can be improved, greater confidence in the approach and their own abilities, and makes quality more a part of the organizational culture.

The analysis of quality – definitions, concepts and models

Words and concepts are the tools that unite divided thoughts in agreement and action.
(Anon.)

M any of us have experience of services that do not work as we expected: postal delays, a return visit to the dentist because of incorrect treatment, a train that does not keep to the timetable. People have complained about bad service, but in the past they did not always think of the faults in terms of quality. Things have changed: people talk about good and bad quality in products, and they are beginning to use the same terms for services. Usually, by a poor or low quality service they mean one that does not come up to their expectations and requirements.

Management in some companies does not see developing quality in services as a high priority – in other companies management sees the need but does not know how to go about it. In our experience the starting point for both is analysis and measurement. Without careful analysis it is difficult to plan and implement developments with good results, not least when it comes to quality, however committed the senior management.

In this chapter we set out to answer four questions. First: what is quality in our business? To anwer this question, managers need to look at existing descriptions and definitions of quality to see whether they can use these as a starting point for defining and understanding quality in their business. Quality definitions should be clear and distinct so that different people perceive them in the same way. Further, the definitions must serve to create acceptance and to act as guidelines for quality in day-to-day work.

The next question is: What languages and what concepts should we use in our development work, in our service, at this time in our quality journey? We need a relevant set of concepts and a language to describe the current situation, the development process we are about to start, and the goals we wish to attain. The concepts are tools for describing the quality of our co-service and, therefore, they must be both distinct and easy to use. They must be defined in a way that all can understand and accept.

The third question is: What are the most important quality factors in our development work? Quality is a multi-faceted concept and we need to know which factors to concentrate on. We need a number of factors, both general and specific and, because not all quality factors are of equal importance, we need to draw up a list of priorities.

The fourth question is: Are there suitable models which people in the business can use for analysing quality? We are concerned with models for increasing our understanding of co-service and with analytical models to help find the causes of quality problems.

In service quality improvement, we feel three things are fundamental to success. These are:
- the service concept
- the co-service processes which create the service – the customer pathway process, and the internal support processes
- the co-service system, as it is designed to resource the creation of the service.

We will return to these three aspects below in the section on quality analysis and relate them to models for analysing service quality, and in Chapter 8 on design.

Definitions of Quality

The word 'quality' is not neutral. When we use it alone without an adjective such as poor or good, we generally give the term value. When person A says, 'Bicycles had quality in the old days', she means the quality was good. To indicate the opposite, person B would have to add a negative qualifier: 'the quality of bicycles was worse in the old days'. Quality without a qualifier means good or first-rate quality.

What do A and B understand by the word 'quality'? What person A means is that cycles were more robust, stood more rough treatment and lasted longer than modern cycles – their quality was better. B means that cycles used to be heavy and clumsy to handle, they had no gears and were harder to pedal, that is they were, in her eyes, of a poorer quality than modern cycles. A is referring to the quality of the physical product, B is making a user assessment of the function. This illustrates how important it is to make clear the factors included in the term quality, and also to indicate the degree or level of the quality, so that a listener, or reader, customer or supplier may understand it in the way that was intended.

The prevailing wisdom is that a business should be steered by the customer's perception of quality, the customer being the external customer. As regards service quality, it is, we believe, the individual's experience of a service that forms the basis for her assessment of its quality. It is of great value to listen to customers and study their reactions. Townsend and Gebhardt (1988) speak of 'Quality in Fact' and 'Quality in Perception'. Quality in fact means conforming to specifications. Quality in perception means that the customer thinks she has received the quality she expected. It is no use achieving factual quality if the perceived quality is not right.

Nor must we forget internal quality. To achieve the right quality for the customer, not only is an internal awareness of the importance of quality for the customer essential, but also a perception by the staff of the quality of their own and others' work. Internal quality, which creates commitment and willingness in all the company's employees, is a prerequisite for achieving quality for the customer. Quality concerns everybody in the organization. Quality systems and techniques are tools for achieving the right quality, but it depends on people whether the tools are used in the best way. We shall consider this in more detail in Chapter 7.

It is not easy to define 'quality'. If we asked a number of individuals what they mean by quality, we would probably get as many answers as respondents. Pirsig's (1975) discussion starts by defining (or not defining) quality in a circular argument: quality is a feature of life and thought which is identified by a process beyond thinking. Since definitions are always products of strict, formal thinking, the concept cannot be defined. Pirsig also maintains that even if the concept of quality is difficult to define, we know what it means anyway. Pirsig's argument illustrates a dilemma involved in defining quality. We all have an idea what it means, but nobody can define it in a clear and unambiguous manner. Pirsig goes on to say that our ideas about quality are based on the images we have in our memory. We base our assessment of quality on analogies with what we have experienced in the past. This explains why a group of people with similar backgrounds and more or less the same knowledge make approximately the same quality assessments. He uses the assessment of essays as an example, where it is often the case that a fairly homogeneous group of students can easily agree on the ranking of essays from a quality viewpoint.

The difficulty in defining quality often leads to general definitions of quality being vague and meaningless, and thus difficult to operationalize and concretize. The danger is that service providers use their own definitions of quality – of what they think that the customer wants. We need both a general definition indicating the 'quality spirit' of the whole company, and more concrete and specific definitions expressed by means of rules for the level of quality to be attained and for how this is to be achieved. It does not save time to copy the quality definitions of other companies: they are often irrelevant when set in a new context with other conditions. The work of creating definitions of quality is itself an important developmental process for a company. However, companies can build on and learn from the way others describe quality. Clarifying what quality stands for in one's own business and finding relevant definitions is an important first phase in all quality improvement.

Many have tried to find general definitions of quality, for instance 'conformance to specifications' (Crosby, 1980) and 'fitness for use' (Juran, 1982). The question is whose specifications and who decides suitability for use? These definitions do go beyond the simple concept of quality being the same as customer satisfaction, which is a concept of quality which has led many health services to reject early manufacturing approaches to quality. In the health field, more multidimensional general definitions of quality take into account customer satisfaction as one element of quality, but recognize that customers do not always know what they need. In defining quality in health services, Øvretveit (1992a) distinguishes between customer quality (whether a service gives patients what they want), professional quality (whether a service meets patients' needs as diagnosed by professionals), and management quality (whether a service is provided with no waste and errors, at a low cost and within legal and other regulations). This wider definition is used in some services with a high professional component. A general-purpose broad definition of quality is given in the 1990 international standard for service quality: 'The totality of features and characteristics of a product or service that bear on its ability to satisfy stated or implied needs.' (ISO 9004:2, *Quality management and quality system elements – Guidelines for services.*)

General definitions of quality give everyone an idea of the end result they are working together to achieve: they unify departments towards the same objectives. Quality policies give more specific guidelines about how work should be done. Many companies formulate a quality policy as the basis for all work in the company and as a guideline for how customers are to be treated. An example is the quality policy of a well-known ferry company: 'Everything we do is to be performed in such a way that our guests and customers will speak well of us and will be pleased to come back to us.'

General definitions of quality used by some service companies

American Express:
'Quality is our only form of patent protection'

Federal Express:
'The presence of value defined by customers'

AT&T:
'Meeting or exceeding competitors' quality'

Florida Power and Light:
'Meeting the desires and expectations of customers'

Marriot (American Hotel Chain):
'Quality is Conformance to Requirements. Requirements are determined and modified through continuous communication between customers, frontline associates and management.'

An insurance company expresses it thus: 'Our overarching goal is to do everything right from the start and attain our established goals.'

Most definitions and policies are linked to the customer's perceptions of quality and to customer relations. Edvardsson (1988a, p.91) argues that:

> Quality is a matter of finding out what creates value for the customer and achieving it. For this it is necessary to really understand the customer and the current situation. Of fundamental importance is to define the customer's demands in the right way. If this is not done, good quality cannot be achieved. Knowledge and understanding of what the customer needs must then be translated into a demand specification for the services. In the next step the demand specification must be transformed into concrete services.

A general definition of service quality is that 'the service must correspond to the customers' expectations and satisfy their needs and demands'. The definition is customer-oriented but it should not be interpreted as suggesting that the service provider must always comply with the customer and her wishes. That the customer decides what is good or bad quality does not mean that she is always right. Placing the customer in the centre does not mean always complying with her wishes. On the other hand, it is important first to listen to the customer and then help her to formulate her requirements. In many cases the customer needs help to clarify her needs and quality demands and it is here that the competence and professionalism of the service provider is important. Simply doing what the customer says is the same as devaluing one's own competence. The customer comes to the service provider – the professional and the specialist – to get help, whether it be for heart problems, toothache, taxation matters or a troublesome car.

Involving the customer in defining the level of quality

It is not only the quality of service offering that the service organization must define – it is just as important to determine the level of quality. It is not enough to say, 'the quality of our services shall be at the highest level'. In a management perspective it is more relevant to talk about the 'right' quality rather than high quality. What then is the right quality? The answer is not simple, but even here the customer must be involved. For us, customer is an overall term for users, consumers, patients, clients, etc., or, in other words, the person to whom the service is directed, the receiver of the service. (See further our discussion on customer orientation in Chapter 5.) The level of quality can be defined as the relation between expected and perceived service from the perspective of the customer. Expectations can be influenced and it is crucial not to create greater expectations that cannot be fulfilled. Further, it is important to make it easier for the customer to assess quality. One way of achieving this is to make visible parts of the co-service process which have previously been hidden from the customer, for instance allowing the customer to see how the food is prepared in a restaurant or letting a garage customer accompany the mechanic into the workshop and watch or even assist him in his work. Involving customers further in the co-service process may even increase their understanding of the difficulty of maintaining the right level of quality.

Other interested parties should also be involved in defining quality. As we see it, there are three groups whose expectations should be met, whose needs should be satisfied and whose demands should be fulfilled. Apart from the customers, these are the staff or employees and the owners. Naturally, other groups are also involved but we see these three groups as the main ones as regards quality issues. This does not lessen the importance of the customers as regards quality because to be able to offer customers the right quality, the other two groups must also be satisfied.

In summary, we define 'the right quality' in the following terms:

> The right quality is achieved when expectations are fulfilled, needs satisfied and demands met: those of the customers, staff and owners.

It is not easy to achieve quality with so many interested parties involved. However, the expectations, needs and demands of these groups need not be incongruent and they often coincide. It is better to examine and work-through conflicting views and demands where they arise at this early stage. Satisfied customers are a prerequisite for the survival and development of an organization. When the customers are satisfied, this satisfaction spreads like circles on water and the staff are satisfied and eventually the owners: quality improvement is a game where everybody wins.

LANGUAGE AND CONCEPTS

To communicate the quality message within the organization and to build a quality culture we need a language that everybody understands. Language consists of concepts, and concepts have meanings which are interpreted differently by different people. It is therefore of the greatest importance in quality improvement to develop a language that is understood internally. This does not mean that we need to create an entirely new language, but it is essential to ensure that everybody has the same interpretation and understanding of the concepts used to explain what we want to achieve as regards quality in the organization. The following considers a number of quality concepts that have helped to form a common language in top service industries in recent years. They are general in nature and can be used in all types of services.

Two useful service concepts are 'technical' and 'functional' quality (Grönroos, 1983). Technical quality is what the customer gets, and functional quality refers to how he or she receives the service. The company's profile or image is a 'filter' in the customer's assessment of the quality of a service. If a company has a positive image, it is easier to accept minor faults in the service delivery, the customer sees them as a temporary aberration. Grönroos's quality model, with the three concepts of technical and functional quality and image, is discussed in more detail below. In a similar vein, Lehtinen and Lehtinen (1983) use the terms physical quality, interactive quality and corporative quality. Physical quality includes both physical products and physical support in the total service delivery. Interactive quality arises in the interaction between the customer and the staff (or machines) of the service company. Corporative quality is the quality of the service company's image and profile.

These concepts inform Gummesson's model, developed on the basis of work carried out in manufacturing industry. Gummesson (1987) proposed the terms design quality, i.e. the quality that is built into the design of a service; production quality, which indicates how a service is produced; delivery quality, i.e. the way in which a service is delivered; and finally relational quality, which refers to the quality in the interaction with the customer. Gummesson points out that relational quality concerns not only the relations between customer and service provider, but every company is part of a network where the relations with the other participants are important, such as suppliers, competitors and higher authorities.

Relational quality is process-linked, that is, it is coupled to how the service is produced and provided, but it can even be affected by the result – by what the customer gets. A result which is much worse than the customer expects can drastically change the relationship. A customer who is dissatisfied with the result can break off all relations with the company, irrespective of how good the design, production and delivery quality is. The company's relationships must be constantly maintained and strengthened. Good relations are based on trust between two or more parties, a trust which can take a long time to build up, but which can be destroyed very quickly. Good customer relations can be established, developed and sometimes retrieved by means of customer care and complaint handling, as discussed in Chapter 5.

These quality concepts are general in character and applicable to all types of service company. On the other hand, the concepts must be specified and given a content which is adapted to the specific activities of the company. For instance, technical quality is not the same in health care as in education, and relational quality has a different meaning in consultancy than in entertainment.

QUALITY FACTORS

Clarifying the 'quality factors' in a service and judging the importance of each helps to decide priorities for quality improvement. 'Factors' is an overall term for what some researchers call determinants, others dimensions or categories. It is quality factors that produce the customer's perception of the quality of the service. Understanding these factors for a service is part of the work of creating more specific definitions of quality for a particular service. We can start with the results from several studies which have charted the factors that are of particular importance for the customer's perception of the quality of service. Although each service has to find out the quality factors that apply to it, there are some common factors for all services.

A customer's perception of the staff of the service company involves a number of factors: their experience, knowledge and competence, combined with their commitment and willingness to serve the customer. It is a matter of both the ability and willingness to serve, and the latter is not the least important factor. Reliability and trust are also central to quality from the customer's perspective. The customer wants to feel that he or she can rely on the service being provided as agreed, and on getting what was promised, i.e. that his or her expectations are fulfilled. The staff must inspire confidence, give the customer the feeling that they are trustworthy and reliable as suppliers, that they have the competence and capacity to deliver the desired service. A third factor, which is usually termed empathy, refers to interest in the customer. Empathy means personal attention and consideration, which is a major quality factor for most customers.

A fourth factor is the handling of critical incidents and customer complaints. This entails having the ability to see that the customer has suffered and is dissatisfied, that it is possible to do something about the situation and set things to rights. It is when the customer does not receive what is expected that he or she becomes aware of what is actually received. In these deviant situations the service provider has a golden opportunity to communicate and demonstrate competence. The professional handling of critical incidents and customer complaints has proved to be a means of strengthening customer relations and improving the customer's perception of quality. An unprofessional handling of these situations can, on the other hand, lead to great dissatisfaction or the end of the relationship. Furthermore, it may result in poor reputation in the market. The effects of this may be significant and very costly. (Chapter 5 gives more details on how to handle critical incidents and customer complaints.)

There are several studies which concentrate on the description of the factors that affect customer-perceived quality in services. Berry *et al.* (1988) have identified five quality determinants in services: tangibles, reliability, responsiveness, assurance and empathy. An example of a study of one type of service is Lindqvist (1988), who in a customer study on a cruise ship found 21 quality dimensions in the consumer phase, from the behaviour of the staff, price level, opening hours, accommodation comfort to willingness to provide information and conference facilities. Another customer study in the travel sector was one conducted by British Airways, which found the following four quality factors are most important for the customer's perception of quality, all are related to the behaviour of the staff:

1 *Care and concern*
The customer feels that the organization, its employees, and its technical systems are devoted to solving his or her problems.
2 *Problem solving capability*
The contact employees are skilled in taking care of their duties and performing according to standard. The rest of the employees in the organization are also trained and trained to give good service.
3 *Spontaneity and flexibility*
The customer feels that the employees are willing to take care of the customers' problems and solve them in a proper manner.
4 *Recovery*
If anything goes wrong, or something unexpected happens to the customer, the employees should be able to make a special effort to handle the situation.

(Albrecht and Zemke, 1985)

British Airways were aware of care and concern and problem solving. What they did not know were that spontaneity and recovery were of great significance to the customers: they had simply not thought of them as a part of good service. This would also probably be the case for other service providers. In a study of garage customers, Thomasson (1989) shows that their perception of quality can be described in a number of categories, with confidence as an overarching category and honesty/reliability/responsibility, personal contact, accessibility/willingness/attitude and competence as sub-categories. The study is presented in more detail in Chapter 7. A range of studies of customer-perceived quality from various countries show similar findings. Grönroos (1990) integrated the findings of these studies as a guide for service activities and for improving quality and produced a list of six criteria of good perceived service quality:

1 *Professionalism and Skills*
The customers realize that the service provider, his employees, operational systems, and physical resources, have the knowledge and skills required to solve their problems in a professional way (outcome-related criteria).

2 *Attitudes and Behavior*
   The customers feel that the service employees (contact staff) are concerned about them and interested in solving their problems in a friendly and spontaneous way (process-related criteria).

3 *Accessibility and Flexibility*
   The customers feel that the service provider, his location, operating hours, employees, and operational systems, are designed and operate so that it is easy to get access to the service and so that they are prepared to adjust to the demands and wishes of the customer in a flexible way (process-related criteria).

4 *Reliability and Trustworthiness*
   The customers know that, whatever takes place or has been agreed upon, they can rely on the service provider, his employees and systems, to keep promises and perform with the best interest of the customers at heart (process-related criteria).

5 *Recovery*
   The customers realize that, whenever something goes wrong or something unpredictable happens, the service provider will immediately and actively take action to keep them in control of the situation and find a new, acceptable solution (process-related criteria).

6 *Reputation and Credibility*
   The customers believe that the operations of the service provider can be trusted and give adequate value for money, and that he stands for good performance and values which can be shared by customers and the service provider (image-related criteria).

(Grönroos, 1990, p.47)

We would add a further criterion of good quality, namely personal contact. Both practical experience and our research suggest that in many service businesses quality is highly dependent on the customer's personal contacts with the staff. In many cases personal contacts are more important than the company's image on the market: a customer's trust is often more related to persons than to companies. In health care trust is central to good relational quality (Øvretveit, 1993b). The customer's confidence in the company and its staff is also coupled to the latter's ability to solve problems and handle critical incidents.

A common feature of the studies we have described is that they concentrate on the factors which in the first place affect customer-perceived quality. These studies reveal that it is primarily factors that affect the process of how services are provided which result in customer perceived quality. We now turn to the fourth of our questions for this chapter: which models help to analyse the sources of quality problems?

MODELS FOR ANALYSING QUALITY

There are many models for analysing service quality, but the choice of model depends on the purpose of the analysis, the type of company and the market situation. A prerequisite for successful quality improvement is first to understand how quality is perceived and valued by the customers. There are a number of useful models which help managers and front-line staff to learn what is important to customers and to make sense of customer survey data. These models may be divided into three groups, according to the focus on:

- customer-perceived quality, or
- the processes in the creation of the service, or
- the whole service ('systems models').

Model of customer-perceived quality

We noted above the concepts of technical and functional quality described by Grönroos (1983) in a model of the customer's assessment of service quality. Technical quality is result-related and dependent on what the customer receives. Functional quality is process-related and dependent on how the customer receives the service. Both technical and functional quality are 'filtered' through the customer's image of the company. In forming a full assessment of service quality, the customer contrasts perceived quality with expected quality, which in its turn is affected by a number of factors. If the perceived quality corresponds to the expected quality, the customer is satisfied. If customer expectations are too great in relation to the perceived quality, the quality will not be satisfactory in the customer's eyes, even if it is classified as good by the service provider. Figure 4.1 shows how the total

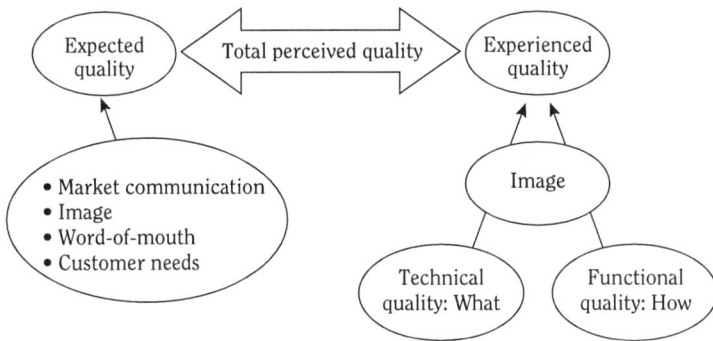

FIGURE 4.1 Customer-perceived Quality
Source: Grönroos, 1990.

perceived quality is revealed on a spectrum between expected and perceived quality.

Technical quality concerns the products included in the service package: technical solutions, machines, computer systems, expertise of the staff, etc. Technical quality may relate to the food served to a guest in a restaurant, the operation performed by a surgeon, the transport of goods from one place to another, the loan a bank grants a person, etc.

Functional quality is based on the attitudes and behaviour of the staff, on accessibility, on the physical environment, on internal relations, etc. Functional quality may consist of, for instance, the restaurant's opening hours or the doctor's surgery hours. The behaviour of a waiter, bus driver or consultant as the representative of a service company and how it affects relations with the customer is another aspect of functional quality. If the technical quality of the same service offered by different companies is perceived as identical by the customer, then functional quality becomes a major competitive factor.

The model shows that the customer's perception of quality, both technical and functional, is affected by the company's image. A positive image may lead the customer to overlook certain quality faults, since he or she feels the shortcomings are temporary. The company's image may be affected by various PR and marketing measures. In large well-known companies, the company needs the assistance of the media in creating and forming the image. Expected quality is affected by the company's market communication in the form of advertising, PR, sales campaigns, etc., i.e. activities that are controlled by the company itself. Image and 'word-of-mouth' factors can only be indirectly controlled by the company. Note also that the customers' needs influence their expectations of the quality of the service.

The model places the customer in the centre. It is the customer's quality assessments and perceptions that are the touchstone for the company's quality efforts. Our experience is that managers and service staff find this model helpful to understand how different factors, which they can influence, affect the customer's perceptions of the quality of the company's service.

The 4 Q model

A model, which helps service providers take an holistic approach to quality, is one developed by Gummesson (1987) from extensive empirical material from a large company manufacturing many different high-technology products. To be viewed as high quality, these products depend on sophisticated services for installation, training and after-service. The 4 Qs stand for four different qualities: *design quality, production quality, delivery quality* and *relational quality.*

Design quality means that the product is designed from the start to meet the demands of the customer. In this the customer may need help in formulating personal requirements and this may form part of the service included in the 'package' that the customer buys. However, design quality is not usually determined by the external customer alone. In most services there are many internal customers who make demands on the design and contribute to achieving the right quality with regard to production, storage and distribution.

Production quality relates to manufacturing. Contributions to production quality come not only from the manufacturing department but also from the design, purchasing and marketing departments, etc. The third Q, 'delivery quality', concerns the promises made to the customer, such as level of quality and consistency when giving the service to the customer. In manufacturing, the dispatching department has a key role in ensuring 'delivery quality', and it in turn depends upon other departments 'downstream' such as design, manufacturing and marketing, etc., taking their share of the responsibility.

Relational quality refers to relations between people. It covers professional and social relations between representatives of the company and customer, suppliers, agents and authorities, as well as between people within the company. Delivery companies and customer companies cooperate to an increasing extent to develop products, equipment or systems. In many cases, several suppliers work together in order to manage large complicated deliveries. Networks are formed, joint projects started and finished. All this makes relational quality increasingly important. Good relational quality can in many cases counteract minor shortcomings in the other three qualities.

This model is both customer-oriented and process-oriented. It stresses the importance of maintaining the right quality in the service right from the design stage until the service is delivered and accepted by the customer.

An integrated model

Gummesson and Grönroos (1989) combined the two above models, and this integrated model may be more appropriate for some services at a particular stage in their quality evolution (Fig. 4.2). Both models have a holistic perspective, and stress that customer-perceived quality is crucial. The difference between them is that the 4 Q model indicates the sources of quality, while the first model (Grönroos, 1983) is based on what the customer receives and how he or she receives it. A reason for combining the models is that the 4 Q model originated in a manufacturing company, while the other was derived from service research, but many companies sell or use both goods and services in their business and are recognizing that an integrated approach to quality is required.

A framework encompassing service and product quality is increasingly called for as new forms of cooperation, networks, and project organization

```
┌─────────────────────┐          ┌─────────────────────┐
│ Design quality      │          │                     │
│ Production quality* ├──────────┤ Technical quality   │
│ Delivery quality**  │          │ Functional quality  │
│ Relational quality  │          │                     │
└──────────┬──────────┘          └──────────┬──────────┘
           └──────────┐        ┌────────────┘
                ┌─────┴────────┴─────┐
                │ Image              │
                │ Experiences        │
                │ Expectations       │
                └──────────┬─────────┘
                           │
              ┌────────────┴────────────┐
              │ CUSTOMER–PERCEIVED      │
              │ QUALITY                 │
              │ =                       │
              │ CUSTOMER SATISFACTION   │
              └─────────────────────────┘
```

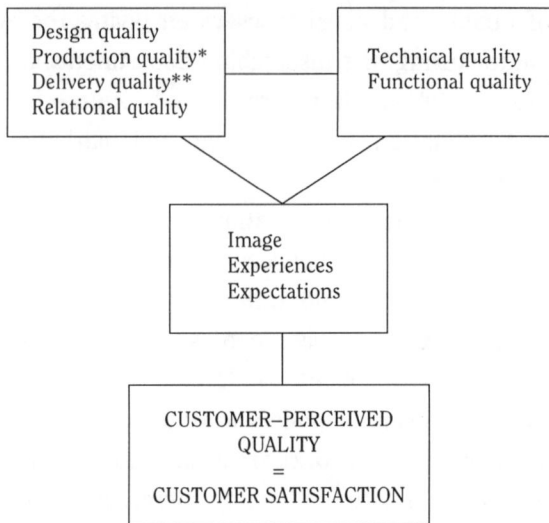

 * Visible/Invisible
    Interactive/Non-interactive
 ** Own/Subcontractor's

FIGURE 4.2   Grönroos–Gummesson Quality Model
Source: Gummesson and Grönroos, 1987.

---

are continually emerging. Intermediate organizations emerge at the interface between goods and service production and a common framework is essential for two or more organizations to cooperate around quality issues.

Vicious and virtuous circles

A further model is particularly useful to service organizations finding themselves in a downward spiral of poor quality, with fewer and fewer resources to invest in quality, or even to service organizations finding difficulty in making significant improvements. Normann (1991) describes how quality in a service company can change depending on whether the company gets into a vicious or a virtuous circle. According to Normann, service companies are seldom average, they are either good or bad. Our view is that there are many service companies, especially public services, that remain in existence for decades without having excellent quality in their services, but neither is their quality extremely poor. However, the model is helpful to both average and poor quality services trying to understand how to break out of their situation (Fig. 4.3).

A vicious circle tends to arise if a service company tries to reduce its costs by reducing its service, often the peripheral (secondary) service (the left-hand side of Fig. 4.3). The reduction in costs is marginal but customers quickly observe a tangible deterioration in service, which leads them to feel that the quality of the service as a whole has deteriorated, although they are paying the same price as before and thus they are less satisfied. Their dissatisfaction affects their relationship with the staff and soon some of the customers turn to other suppliers. The company's profitability decreases

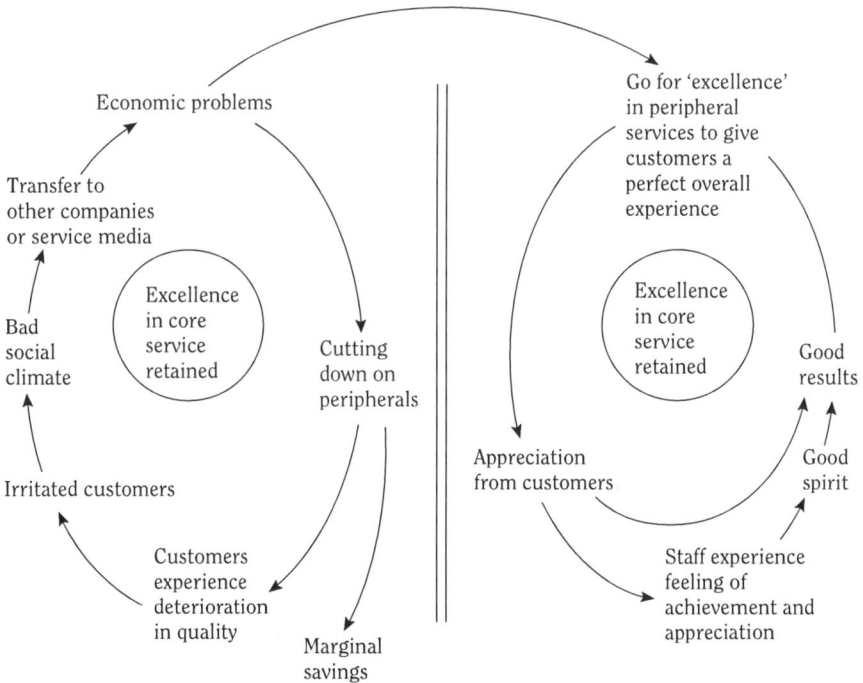

FIGURE 4.3   Vicious and Virtuous Circles
Source: Normann, 1991.

and it makes further cuts to reduce costs, which leads to further deterioration in the service. More customers are dissatisfied and leave the company. The company is in a vicious circle and may soon become bankrupt unless it finds a way out of the vicious circle into a positive one. Øvretveit (1992a) describes a similar spiral, drawing on his research into quality in the British National Health Service (Fig. 4.4).

Just as a vicious circle can start in the peripheral service so can a virtuous one (the right-hand side of Normann's model; Fig. 4.3). Customers notice a small improvement in the service which makes a positive impression on them. The relationship between customers and staff improves and a virtuous circle is started. It is easy to get into a vicious circle but it can be difficult to get out of it, unless one finds out where the

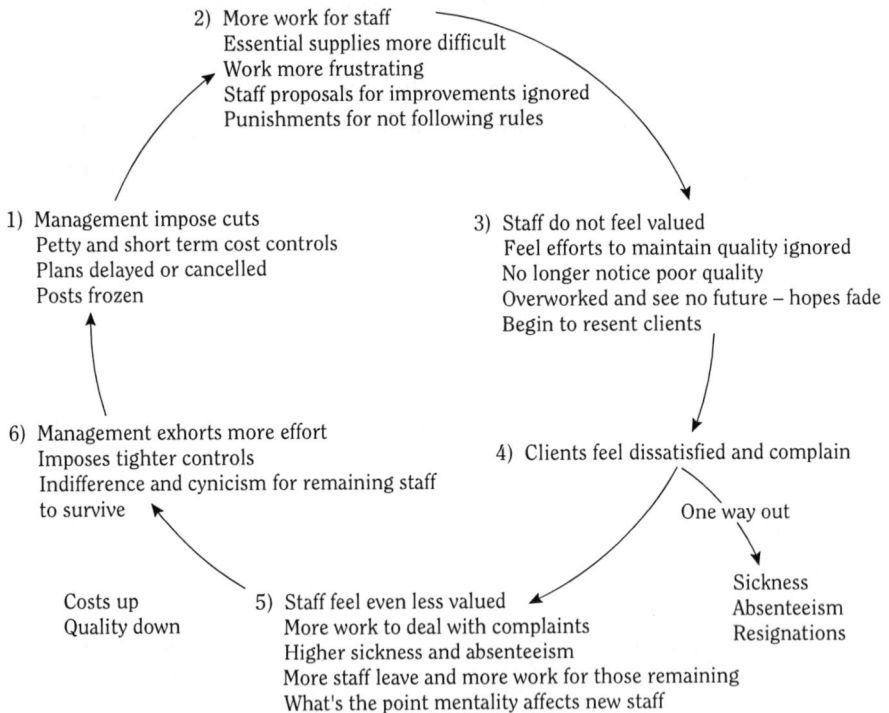

2) More work for staff
Essential supplies more difficult
Work more frustrating
Staff proposals for improvements ignored
Punishments for not following rules

1) Management impose cuts
Petty and short term cost controls
Plans delayed or cancelled
Posts frozen

3) Staff do not feel valued
Feel efforts to maintain quality ignored
No longer notice poor quality
Overworked and see no future – hopes fade
Begin to resent clients

6) Management exhorts more effort
Imposes tighter controls
Indifference and cynicism for remaining staff
to survive

4) Clients feel dissatisfied and complain

One way out

Costs up
Quality down

5) Staff feel even less valued
More work to deal with complaints
Higher sickness and absenteeism
More staff leave and more work for those remaining
What's the point mentality affects new staff

Sickness
Absenteeism
Resignations

FIGURE 4.4   The Effects of Poor Quality
Source: Øvretveit, 1992a.

shortcomings lie that caused it. The model shows a way out of a vicious circle into a positive one. In many businesses tough competition has resulted in many companies performing the core service in a similar manner. In this situation, raising the quality of the peripheral services may put the company in a positive circle. Note, however, that in most sectors simply standing still and not improving quality will lead the company into a vicious circle as competitors increase their quality and customers come to expect more.

The consistency model

A model, which helps to identify the causes of quality problems and errors in services, is described by Edvardsson and Gustavsson (1988b, 1990). The following describes this model because managers and quality specialists can use it to highlight the areas, factors, structures and processes which either can be changed or must be analysed further (e.g. by blueprinting). This helps to manage several service processes in order to prevent poor quality, both internally and externally. The assessment approach is based on the view that quality problems vary between service organizations and that the general models of quality determinants are only useful up to a point: quality problems must be identified and analysed in each service, and this framework helps to do this.

The service management system

The Edvardsson and Gustavsson assessment model draws on the management model proposed by Normann (1984) and starts by analysing a service organization in terms of the following components:
- Target group
- Service concept
- Organizational culture and image
- Co-service system.

Target group/market segment
Services need to distinguish between primary and secondary target groups,

and identify different customer segments: for example, to distinguish private persons or consumers from companies, and private companies from organizations in the public sector. The market analysis should cover previous, present and potential customers.

The service concept

The service concept refers to the core benefits or advantages offered to the target group. It usually consists of complex combinations of values some of which are more concrete, while others lie on a more psychological or emotional plane. Some are of greater importance than others and may be designated as the core service, while others are more supportive in character and may be termed 'peripheral services'.

It is important that the service concept be designed on the basis of the needs, requirements and expectations of the target group, and to distinguish between primary and secondary customer needs. For an airline, the flights from City A to City B constitute the core service, which should meet the customers' primary needs to get from A to B. But customers often have other needs as well, e.g. how to get to the airport or to contact their secretary while travelling. Peripheral services in this case would be taxis and telefax equipment. In health services the core service is to relieve symptoms and cure illness, and peripheral services are mostly hospital 'hotel' services. Quality often lies in being able to offer a system of services which together satisfy both primary and secondary customer needs, and this combination gives a significant competitive advantage.

A basic requirement for developing an appropriate service concept is to understand the customers for a particular service and their needs and preferences. Many companies say they are customer-oriented but lack this fundamental understanding of their customers' expectations and of ways of assisting them. This explains a number of quality problems which start from poor service design. The best way of understanding customer requirements is to seek out the most demanding and engage in a dialogue with them, and to involve them in designing the service.

Organizational culture and image

This element of the model refers to the general principles on which the service organization operates. These principles are often informal, but have a real impact on operations and their quality. The three most important aspects are: (1) basic norms and values, (2) management and decision-making styles, and (3) social codes, such as dress and behaviour. Image is the view that the customers and staff have of the service company and of its individual services. 'Profiling' is the term we use for the various measures and steps that the company takes to position itself in the market and to create a favourable image.

The co-service system

The most important difference between service and goods production from a quality management point of view is the fact that the customer is involved in the co-service process and that the service provider has less control over the environment and the behavior of the actors. It is in these, not easily controllable, conditions that the perception of service quality is created in the interaction between the customer and the service. The co-service system consists of four basic components. At the centre are employees and customers, and the other two components are the physical environment and organizational structure.

The employees are frequently looked upon as the key resource; however, recruitment, training and outplacement are often not managed in a systematic way from a service quality point of view. Other important factors in this context are the reward system and career opportunities. The customer is, of course, a key factor in the co-service system; without customers, there would be no business. The co-service system should be constructed in a way that makes it easy for the customer not only to participate but actively to contribute to the production of the service. Customer education/training may be of great value. Relations between customers may also be of great importance for service quality. Customers can help one another physically and psychologically and, as a result, improve perceived service quality.

The physical environment provides tangible clues to quality or the lack of quality. The co-service system should include, for instance, equipment, 'office dress', and a location which reflects overall quality ambitions and customer expectations. Given the critical role of service employees, it is not good policy to have different quality standards for the physical environment in the front and back offices, especially if service-giving staff work in both areas. The fourth co-service component is organizational structure, which refers to the distribution of responsibility and authority, the planning and information systems used, the cooperation between the different depart-ments or sections of the company, as well as administrative aids such as computing systems and information systems, and accessibility, which has to do with the ease with which customers can contact the company when necessary.

Fields of analysis

The assessment model adds two further ideas to the components described above. The first is the disparity that always exists between the formal statements in the organization and service providers' own views. The other dimension refers to the basic disparity in all social systems between the idea (goal) and action (outcome) (see Fig. 4.5).

The assessment model gives four 'fields' for analysing service quality:

- *Formal goals*. Data for this field come from the goals as stated by the top management level, obtained from content analysis of the company's business concept, goal descriptions, policy documents, strategic plans, and plans of action as well as from in-depth interviews with the chairman of the board and management representatives.
- *Subjective goals*. Here the analysis concentrates on how the various actors within the organization perceive the organization's goals. The factors, which have the greatest impact on decisions and actions, are not those related to the formal goals, but those resulting from the interpretations of the goals made by the various actors. It is the objectives that top managers see as most important that are, in fact, the most influential.

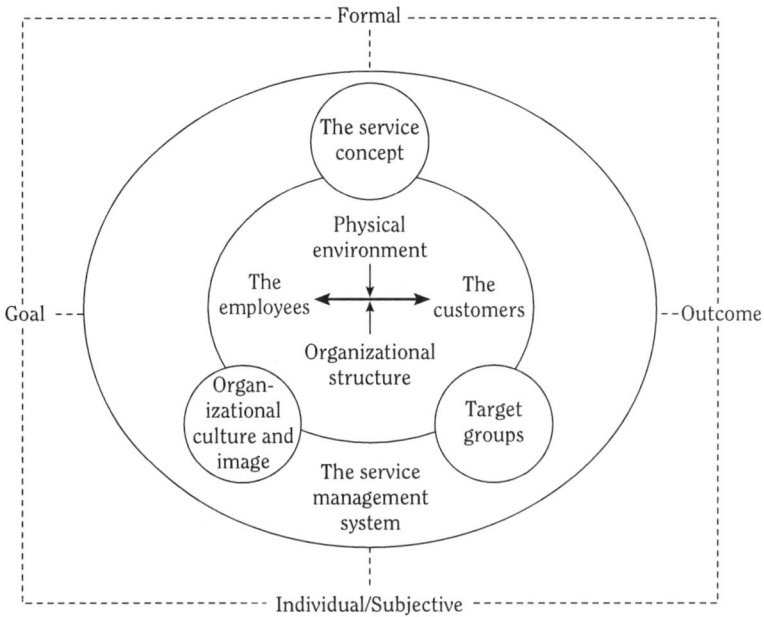

FIGURE 4.5   The Assessment Model
Source: Edvardsson and Gustavsson, 1990.

- *Formal outcome.* The aim of the analysis in this field is to gain insight into the organization's activities from various formal and official documents presenting results, such as systems for following up what has been done, appraisals, annual reports and annual accounts.
- *Subjective outcome.* Here the focus is on how employees perceive the outcome and results of the relationship between the organization and its customers. An important part of the analysis is to map the customers' perceptions of the quality of the service delivered and also to study employees' views about the service which they give and about various internal services. The data are collected by means of personal interviews with various employees and a questionnaire to customers.

A consistency analysis

Collecting data for these four areas gives the basis for a comprehensive consistency analysis, the aim being to identify the main inconsistencies within and between the four fields. There might, for instance, be faults in the support services because of a defective production system or equipment. The formal goals might have been 'incorrectly' understood, which affects implementation and the results as perceived by the customer.

The service management system not only includes the co-service system, but also the projected target groups in the market and a guideline for what core customer benefits should be offered, for which we use the term service concept. Finally, organizational culture and image are used as analytical components. Our research suggests that internal values and norms (organizational culture) and external values and perceptions (the customers' images), though different, have much in common and mirror one another. They are concerned with employees' and customers' basic frameworks and values in relation to the service and the service organization. They affect behaviour and the perception of the service outcome. When we speak of perception in action, we find it relevant to combine the internal and external values into one analytical component.

The chapter now turns to models for understanding how customers perceive quality, starting with an early and ground-breaking piece of research into service quality.

Expected and perceived quality

During the 1980s three American researchers, Leonard L. Berry, A. Parasuraman and Valerie A. Zeithaml, studied the quality of services. Their work has resulted in several reports and a book on service quality, how it arises and how it can be improved (e.g. Berry *et al.*, 1985, 1988; Parasuraman *et al.*, 1985, 1988; Zeithaml *et al.*, 1990).

Their early research was of customer-perceived quality in four service industries: banks, credit card companies, stockbrokers and service companies for household machines. They used focus group interviews with three groups in each industry, and analysed their findings into 10 factors or dimensions: tangibles, reliability, responsiveness, competence, courtesy, credibility, security, access, communication and understanding the customer (Berry *et al.*, 1985). In a later study (Parasuraman *et al.*, 1988) they reduced the number to five: tangibles, reliability, responsiveness, assurance and empathy.

Tangibles refers to the physical environment in the service organization: facilities, equipment, staff and their dress, i.e. concrete things that the customer can easily observe. Reliability is the company's ability to perform the promised service. Price agreements and other conditions should be fulfilled, time limits kept and the service performed accurately from the start. Responsiveness entails performing the services promptly and quickly, helping the customer and being available when he or she needs help. Assurance covers the knowledge and competence of the staff and their ability to elicit trust and confidence.

The three key points that arise from this research are:

- Service quality is more difficult for customers to evaluate than goods quality.
- Customers do not evaluate service quality solely on the outcome of a service; they also consider the process of service delivery.
- The only criteria that count in evaluating service quality are defined by the customer.

(Zeithaml *et al.*, 1990)

In the first study (Berry *et al.*, 1985) the authors draw four conclusions:

1 Customers' assessment of service quality is the result of a comparison between their expectations and experience of the service after delivery. If their expectations have been met, they are satisfied, if not, they are dissatisfied. If expectations have been exceeded, they are more than satisfied.

2 Customers' assessment of quality is affected both by the service process and by the outcome of the service.

3 Service quality is of two kinds: the quality of the normal service, and the quality with which 'critical incidents' are handled. Critical incidents are deviations from the 'normal': situations where the relationship between customer and company has 'gone wrong'.

4 When problems arise, companies have to increase their contacts with customers. Many service companies have few personal contacts with

customers, but when a critical incident arises, more and 'closer' contacts are needed to satisfy customers.

Figure 4.6 shows how the customer's expectations and perceptions of the various aspects of service quality affect the final quality assessment.

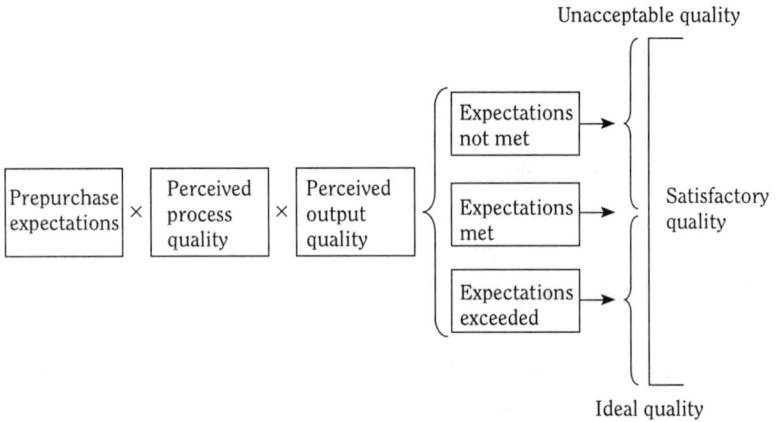

FIGURE 4.6   Expected and Perceived Service Quality
Source: *Berry et al.,* 1985.

In further studies of service quality the three authors found that there are two levels to the customer's expectations of the service, *adequate* and *desired* (Parasuraman *et al.,* 1991). The first level is what the customer finds acceptable and the second what he or she hopes to receive. The distance between the adequate level and desired level is the 'zone of tolerance' (Fig. 4.7). The zone expands and contracts like an accordion.

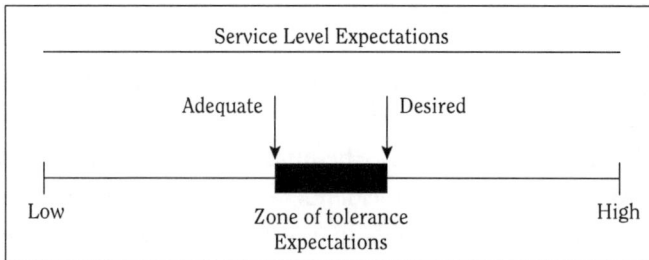

FIGURE 4.7   Zone of Tolerance
Source: Parasuraman *et al.,* 1991.

Like the zone of tolerance, the two levels may vary from customer to customer and from one situation to another for the same customer. Similarly they vary depending on the quality dimension involved.

The gap model

The same researchers, Zeithaml *et al.* (1990) developed a model which shows how various gaps in the co-service process may affect the consumer's assessment of the quality of the service. We have found this model to be useful to help managers and staff examine their own perceptions of quality, and to recognize how much they really understand customers' perceptions (Fig. 4.8).

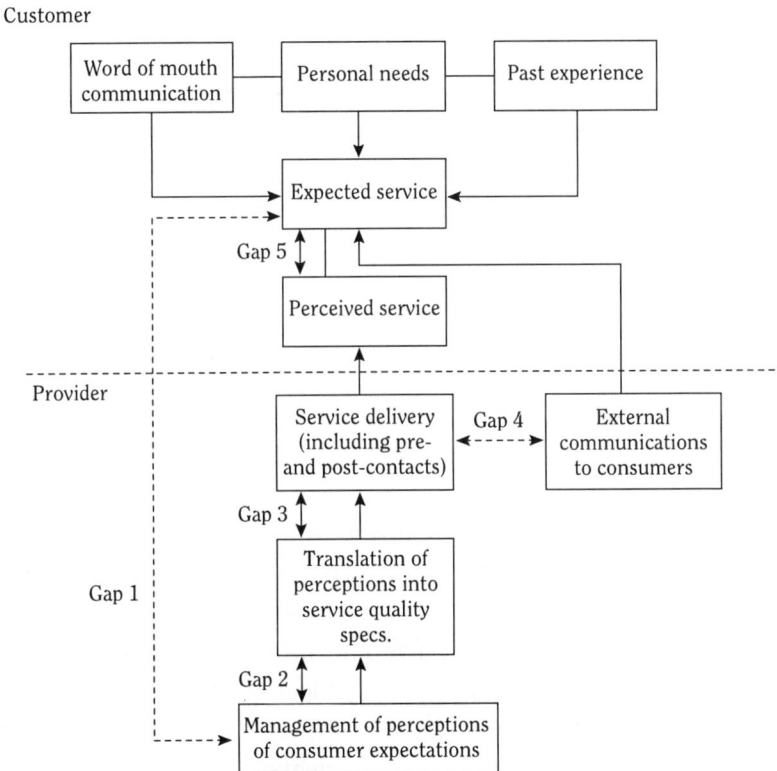

FIGURE 4.8   The Gap Model
Source: Zeithaml *et al.*, 1990.

Gap 1 is the difference between the consumer's expectations and management perceptions of consumer expectations. Management does not understand how the service should be designed, what support or secondary services the customer requires, etc., i.e. what the right quality for the customer is.

Gap 2 is the difference between the company's quality specifications and management perceptions of consumer expectations of the service and its quality. Often in an attempt to reduce costs, management places internal restrictions on how a service is to be performed, restrictions which deprive the staff of the opportunity to meet the customer's expectations of the service.

Gap 3 is the difference between the quality of the service delivery and quality specifications. Even if the quality of the service is carefully specified in a company, the result in practice may be different from what was intended. Service quality is difficult to standardize, since it is so often dependent on personal contact between the customer and company staff.

Gap 4 is the difference between the quality of the service delivery and the quality promised in marketing. It is important not to promise the customer more than the company can deliver. At the same time, it is important for the company to inform customers about the efforts being made to raise quality, which would otherwise not be visible to the customer.

Gap 5 indicates the difference between expected and perceived service quality. The gap is a function of the other four gaps, i.e. Gap 5 = f(gaps 1, 2, 3, 4).

The gap model, developed from empirical research, has been used as an instrument of analysis in several companies. The same researchers (Parasuraman *et al.*, 1988) have developed an instrument, Servqual, for measuring service quality in the five dimensions given above: tangibles, reliability, responsiveness, assurance and empathy. Servqual is described in more detail in Chapter 8.

The gap model is basically customer-oriented. Quality is realized by the customer in a comparison between expected and perceived quality after the customer has received the service. The model is also process-oriented in that it seeks the gaps that may arise in various parts of the co-service process, gaps which eventually affect the difference between the customer's expected and perceived quality, the final and most crucial gap.

Figure 4.9 shows a further development of the original gap model. The new model illustrates the inter-organizational factors which affect the different gaps. It thereby facilitates an analysis of what caused the gaps and how they can be reduced.

Quality in the service encounter

The final model we consider for analysing customer perceptions focuses on the encounter between the customer and the service provider (Bitner, 1991). Bitner believes that the customer's perception of these encounters is a crucial component in the evaluation of the total quality of a service. This is particularly true of repetitive services, where the long-term relations with customers depend on many 'moments of truth', and also for service with a high professional component. In order to improve quality and build up lasting customer relations, it is important, then, to understand what happens in these encounters and what affects the customer's perception of them.

Bitner makes a distinction between customer satisfaction with a service and the quality of the service. She sees customer satisfaction as something that is directly linked with the transaction, based on the customer's comparison between expected service and his or her perception of the service actually received. Quality, on the other hand, is a more global attitude towards a company or service. Bitner discusses the 'marketing-mix' approach to marketing which is based on the four Ps of product, price, place and promotion. This traditional approach to marketing proposes a set of controllable variables which a company should use in a coordinated manner to communicate with and satisfy its target group. According to Bitner, service companies need to consider an additional three Ps: physical evidence refers to the environment in which the service is produced and the equipment used; participants refers to the actors who participate in the delivery of the service and thus influence customers; process indicates the activities and procedures by which the service is produced.

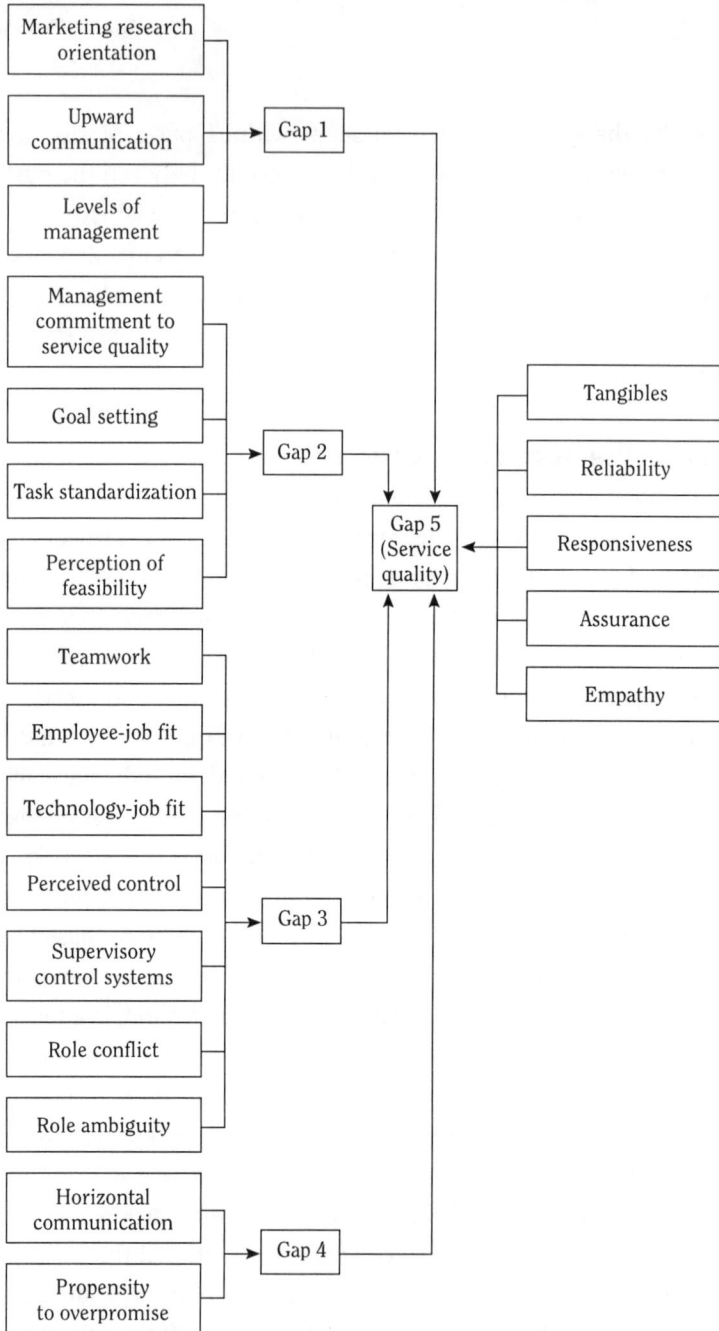

FIGURE 4.9 Further Development of the Gap Model

Source: Zeithaml *et al.*, 1990.

Bitner's criticism of the marketing-mix approach for services is well founded in our view. A new approach needs to emphasize customer interaction and personal relations where the customer is an active, contributing partner, not a passive, external 'target' made to react to stimuli. Such an approach has been developed by Gummesson (1987), Grönroos (1990), and in public health and social services by Øvretveit (1992a, 1993b).

As with other models we described above, Bitner's model shows that the customer may have certain preconceived ideas, a 'preattitude' about a service provider, which affect his or her expectations of the service. If the difference between the expectations of a service and the way in which the service is performed is sufficiently large, the customer becomes dissatisfied with the service. However, there are several factors that affect the customer's final assessment of the service, termed 'attributions' by Bitner. Bitner bases her argumentation on social psychological theories, which state that when the result is not what was expected, people tend to look for reasons and, we might add, tend to blame other people not systems. Their idea about 'why' will affect their final perception of a certain service. Apart from the traditional marketing mix, the model includes the physical environment, actors and processes (contextual cues) as influential factors.

The other parts of the model illustrate how perceived quality can be affected by previous experience, information from others and the company's image, apart from 'moments of truth'. The implications for managers which Bitner points out include the following:

- The link between quality in the moment of truth and the customer's total quality perception. It is important to understand fully what happens at the moment of truth. As regards repetitive services, the accumulated experience of many moments of truth can be crucial for the customer's total assessment of quality.
- Since the customer seeks the answer to 'why', it may be possible to solve critical situations to the satisfaction of the customer by means of logical explanation. This presupposes an understanding of how customers understand why things go wrong: their 'attribution process'.

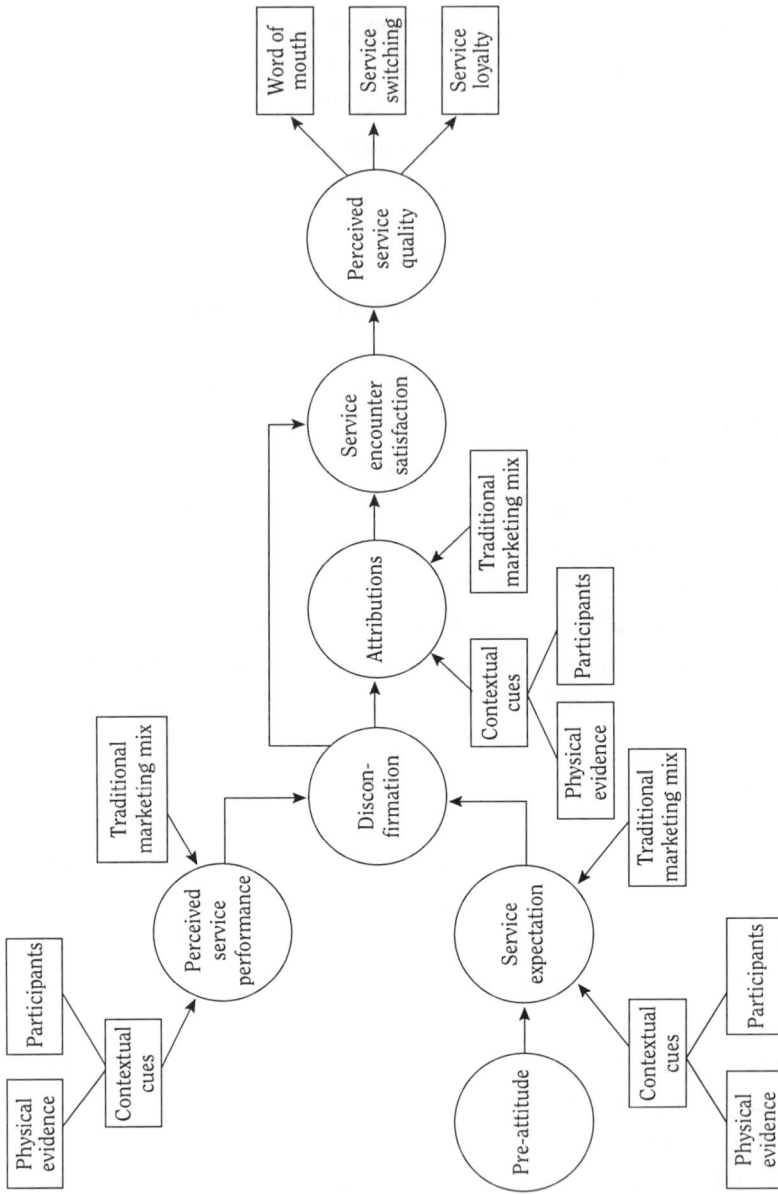

FIGURE 4.10 Evaluation of Quality in the Service Encounter

Source: Bitner, 1988.

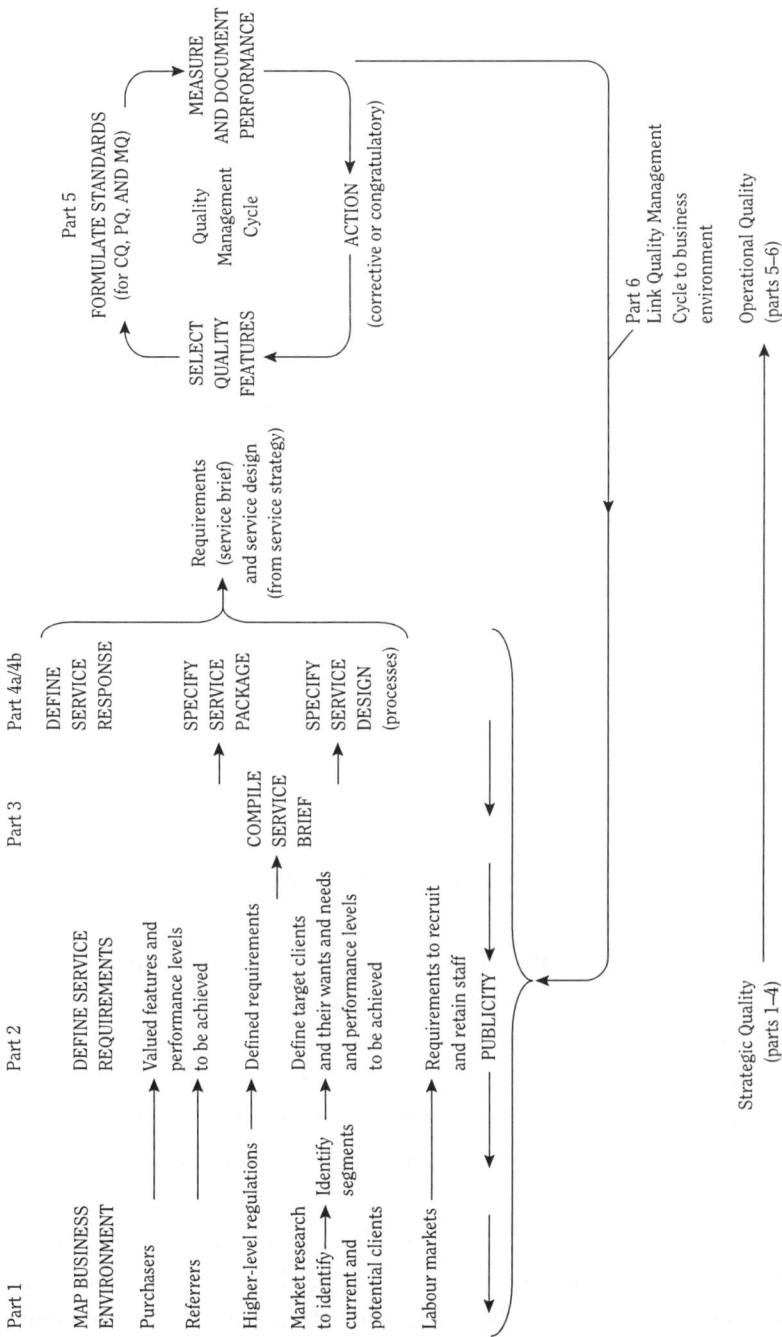

FIGURE 4.11 Diagram of the Wel-Qual Framework
Source: Øvretveit, 1992a.

Part 1

MAP BUSINESS ENVIRONMENT

Purchasers ⟶ Valued features and performance levels to be achieved

Referrers ⟶

Higher-level regulations ⟶ Defined requirements

Market research to identify ⟶ Identify segments ⟶ Define target clients and their wants and needs and performance levels to be achieved
current and potential clients

Labour markets ⟶ Requirements to recruit and retain staff

PUBLICITY

Part 2

DEFINE SERVICE REQUIREMENTS

Part 3

COMPILE SERVICE BRIEF

Part 4a/4b

DEFINE SERVICE RESPONSE

SPECIFY SERVICE PACKAGE

SPECIFY SERVICE DESIGN (processes)

Requirements (service brief) and service design (from service strategy)

Part 5

FORMULATE STANDARDS (for CQ, PQ, AND MQ)

SELECT QUALITY FEATURES

Quality Management Cycle

MEASURE AND DOCUMENT PERFORMANCE

ACTION (corrective or congratulatory)

Part 6

Link Quality Management Cycle to business environment

Strategic Quality (parts 1–4)

Operational Quality (parts 5–6)

● To attain the right level of quality, the decisions of different functions must be coordinated so as to support rather than contradict each other. The model is both customer- and process-oriented. It deals with microprocesses in customer relations and emphasizes their major, and often neglected, importance (see Fig. 4.10).

The Wel-Qual framework

The final model we consider shows a way to link some of the market considerations we noted above with an organization's definition of quality, and this to a quality system for setting standards and measuring service. It shows how key features of the 'business environment' can be linked to the service concept and to the design brief for the service – we consider the latter in Chapter 7. This framework was developed for health services but has proved a useful integrating model in other services, especially those taking a TQM perspective or using quality awards for self-diagnosis. The diagram (Fig. 4.11) is self-explanatory – for more details on the different parts and the links between them, see Øvretveit (1992a).

OUR VIEW OF QUALITY ANALYSIS

The start of any quality improvement is work to clarify what an organization means by quality, both in general and in detail for each type of service. Quality must be defined on the basis of detailed surveys of what existing and potential customers think. However, quality issues concern not only customers, but also staff and owners. In this chapter we proposed that an organization also decide the concepts and models to use to describe the company's intended quality and to develop a common view of quality and a common 'quality language' which everybody understands. Such concepts and models help to prioritize the quality factors that are particularly important for the service at the time.

The models we described are all relatively easy to use for practical quality improvement programmes. Each has a different emphasis and highlights different aspects, so how does one decide which to use? Our advice is to work with two or three models which together cover the three aspects of:

- customer-perceived quality
- the processes in service 'production'
- the whole, and thus adopt a system approach.

Using one model may give quick results, but will have gradually diminishing effects. Quality improvements should link the service concept, the co-service process and the system. The concept must be adapted to the customers' needs, all the parts of the process must be analysed, as too must the system which is built up to produce the service. We also noted quality from the perspective of the three main interest groups: customers, staff and owners. Figure 4.12 shows how the various aspects of quality improvement relate to each other. The figure helps to understand the connections and, at the same time, helps to choose a model for quality improvement, depending on the aspects of service production to be studied or which interest group perspective is to be adopted.

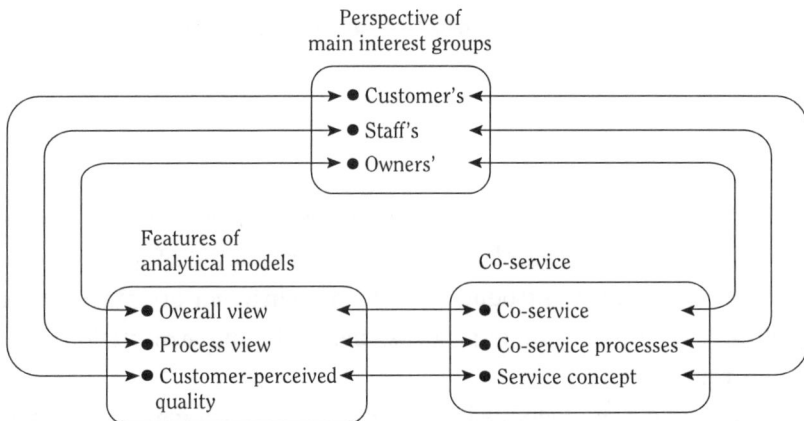

FIGURE 4.12 **The Connection Between Models, Interested Parties and 'Servuction' or 'Co-service'**

CHAPTER

5

Customer orientation and customer care

Market conditions are changing so rapidly today that keeping up to date with customers is a matter of life or death. What are they thinking? What are their plans? What decisions have they taken?
(Peter Drucker)

Both public and private organizations now view customer care as a central concern, regardless of their understanding of quality methods and TQM. Most aim to introduce or extend a customer orientation to their activities, with the customer's needs, demands and expectations as the guiding principles.

Because of an ill-defined concept of 'the customer', some service organizations do not have a sufficiently sharp customer orientation. Every manager has a variety of customers: the TQM approach emphasizes internal as well as external customers. In this chapter we consider the concept of 'customer', how managers can build a customer orientation on their concept of customer, and we give practical examples. In the third and fourth sections we consider quality factors seen from the customer's perspective, and how managers can develop a customer orientation in their area. We finish by discussing critical incidents in service and customer care.

Most companies say that customer orientation is an overriding concern, but in practice it rarely penetrates far into the company beyond a person or unit 'responsible for customer care'. Our experience in service companies is similar to Crosby's:

> Certainly the customer comes first ... This is one of the great myths of our time. In reality everyone else comes first if we are thinking of a customer in terms of the one who lays down the money for what it is we are selling. There are many other customers along the way who drain off the intensity of devotion to the final user ... . Staff are primarily concerned about themselves and what is happening to make their world successful.
>
> (Crosby, 1988, p.49)

Our research indicates major structural changes in many markets and in the public sector: suppliers and customers, producers and consumers are developing both closer relations and more of them: the boundaries are blurring. Benson Shapiro, professor at Harvard, uses the term 'the new intimacy'. Relations with the customer, an ongoing dialogue with the customer, active listening and respect for the customer's views are all central aspects of corporate development strategy. Kanter (1991) asks how companies can get even closer links with customers, and describes five challenges:

- Understanding who the customer is.
- Making the customer a member of one's own organization.
- Making the customer visible to all employees.
- Rewarding faithful customers.
- Having the ability to handle critical incidents by being flexible.

Since quality is realized in the customer and the customer is the ultimate judge of the quality of the service, managers need to make customer orientation the starting point for all quality improvement. Although customer orientation means placing customers at the centre, it does not mean being completely governed by them. It means that the service provider understands and respects the customer's wishes, needs and demands, and because of this is better able to use the available resources to best serve the customer. The customer-oriented service company has gained insight into the customer's assessment criteria and staff listen to the customers intently, but they are not always governed by what the customers say. We will explain this apparent contradiction, and show how, for example, that only with a customer orientation can we refuse service that a customer asks for in order to give customers a quality service.

THE CUSTOMER

Few companies and organizations have a clear idea of what 'customer' stands for in their business. They have a very indistinct picture of the customer and how he or she is to be served. This is in part because the term 'customer' is ambiguous. In our work we have used the expression 'multi-customer' to underline the fact that a company frequently serves different customers. The customer might, for instance, be a business traveller who travels by SAS, but also the person who books the ticket for the traveller. Sometimes the customer is often a purchasing group of different people with perhaps different views and values. There are also different purchasing roles: the initiator, the influencer, the decision maker and the user. Who has the greatest influence in the purchasing process? On what grounds is the service provider selected? Øvretveit (1993a) proposes a framework for 'mapping the business environment' to identify, in reality, how purchasing decisions are made and who influences these decisions and on what critieria. These considerations are important when developing a quality measurement system (discussed in Chapter 7). Øvretveit (1993a, p.17) proposes distinguishing,

> services to the public in terms of whether the service is a for-profit organisation purchased by the public (e.g. many shops, travel and financial services); a not-for-profit service, and financed by the public, the government or private organisations; or publicly-owned and publicly-financed, privately financed, or a mixture ... we need to distinguish between a service to customer-purchasers,

and a service financed by a third-party for users who do not pay directly. Customers' attitudes and behaviour are different in each type of service.

The concept of 'customer' in public services is useful to emphasize a service rather than provider-orientation, but can also be misleading. Public services operate in a complex 'business environment' and have to meet a variety of requirements other than the needs of a particular individual at one time (see Part 1 of the 'Wel-Qual' framework in Fig. 4.11). The immediate beneficiary of the service is not a 'customer-purchaser' who pays directly for the service, but part of a triangle with a purchaser/financing authority at one corner and the service at the other. In health services, rather than 'customer', Øvretveit (1992a) proposes a combination of patient, carer (e.g. relatives), referrer (e.g. a doctor deciding that a person needs a hospital service), and purchaser or financing authority. Each party has needs and expectations which the service provider must understand, and reconcile when they are different – this is only possible if the service provider has a good relationship with each.

To help identify their customers, managers can use different classifications. Customers are classified as internal or external, the latter being divided into existing and potential customers. We saw in Chapter 2 how to further divide customers into segments, each segment containing customers who are 'similar' in essential respects, and different from customers in other segments. Other instances are private customers and company customers. We may also distinguish image-creating customers, profitable and unprofitable customers, commission-generating customers, and demanding customers, whom we view as valuable stimulants to business development. These groups often have different needs, demands and expectations.

Customers can also be classified according to their relations with the company. Customer relations may be strong or weak, and customers may be 'whole customers' or 'partial customers'. A 'whole' customer may, for instance, have all his or her insurance policies with one and the same insurance company while a 'partial' customer has relations with at least two insurance companies.

To understand the customer's perspective, his or her needs and wishes must be placed in context. An example of context is the customer's business logic, that is, the logic or trends in the business run by the customer; another is the individual customer's household or family. Focusing on the customer means understanding the world, the values and the context in which the individual customer lives.

Albrecht and Bradford (1990, p.20) take the following view:

> A customer is a human being. He or she comes in all sizes and in all colors. A customer is a child asking for help in reaching a toy on a tall shelf, or an elderly man who has lost his way in a maze of hospital halls. A customer is a woman who does not speak English very well and who is trying to make her needs known in the only way she can. A customer is a co-worker asking for your assistance so he or she can serve the paying public. Tax-payer, patient, client, member, rate-payer, guest, card-member – all are synonyms for the most valuable asset a business has i.e. the customer, who comes to you and pays money for your service or product. What is a customer? A customer is the reason your business exists.

The customer, then, is the person or persons receiving the results of the business. The quality of the service is realized in the customer and is interpreted and perceived by him or her. Without customers there would be no income and thus no business. The main task of quality improvement is to create the conditions for services which the customer perceives as having the right quality in relation to their price. This presupposes that the company has a thorough understanding of the customer's needs and expectations.

Needs, wishes and expectations

Let us say more about what we mean by needs, wishes and expectations. Needs often underlie wishes and expectations. We do not always know what our needs are or the best way to satisfy them: sometimes other people understand them better, for example a professional person making an assessment such as a doctor. However, they are always our needs and we are the final judge of whether we accept the service or not. Wishes refer to the way in which the customer would like to satisfy a specific need, but there may not be the resources to meet these wishes. Expectations spring from the customer's needs and wishes, but are also influenced – often to a considerable extent – by the company's image or reputation in the market, the customer's previous perceptions and experience of the company, and by the company's current marketing. Expectations concern the relationship between the customer and the service company, and change over time.

To gain a real understanding of the customer's needs, wishes and expectations, it is necessary to go beyond traditional market surveys, and involve the customer in developing new services. Customer-friendly services with the right quality emerge from a dialogue with demanding customers: both in design and in provision. This means including customers in development projects, and helping them to articulate their needs, demands and wishes. This relationship is closer to counselling and psychotherapy than a survey questionnaire or interview. Customers are able to define the factors that are important to them, and their relative importance. We believe that this customer-active paradigm and working interactively with customers is the best way to develop the service concept and the service processes.

In defining their 'customer', managers also need to understand their service process. Tracing a 'customer's journey' or their order over time and through the organization shows the internal services needed at different times to serve the customer. It shows the internal services to internal customers at different stages which result in the external service to customers in the market. One of the principles of TQM is that everyone in the organization has a customer, and many have internal customers. Internal customer relations are as important as external ones, as are the internal customer's needs, wishes and expectations. To produce a service with the right quality, the whole chain of customer relations has to be organized.

Our general point is that, to give a quality service, a business and each manager in it has to define who their customers are, and understand their needs, wishes and expectations. The latter means getting into a dialogue with customers to develop an understanding. To ensure that people in the organization understand their customers and respond, a business has to develop a customer orientation.

'CUSTOMER-ORIENTATING' A BUSINESS

How often do you hear staff in a business that you know ask, 'How will this change help us to give a better service to our customers?' A customer orientation is where staff have a real concern for the customer and where all business decisions are made with a view to improving customer service. To orientate a business's activities successfully towards its customers, both staff and managers must:

- listen to the customers with the greatest attention
- understand and use customers' needs, wishes and expectations as a basis for their activities
- understand the logic of the customer's business (when the customer has a company)
- have insight into the customer's assessment criteria and act on them
- know and understand how and why the customer gives priority to a certain supplier
- make decisions and act on the basis of the customer's motives, needs and expectations
- avoid being guided only by internal limitations and conditions.

A customer orientation comes from the top, as several well-known chief executives have understood: 'The market/customer-oriented company lets the market steer every investment, every measure, every change' (Carlzon, 1989). '... the world is full of the sort of customer who deserves the consideration and attention which I advocate, and I am prepared to tie myself in knots to conquer and keep them' (Rogers, 1987).

Ingvar Kamprad, former chief executive of IKEA, concludes that:

- the consumer must derive lasting pleasure from his purchase
- quality must be adapted to the consumer's needs

- most people often have only small resources – the basic condition must then be an extremely low price.

'Customer-orientating' a business means wearing customer spectacles and seeing with the customer's eyes. It is a matter of listening actively both to what the customer says and to what he or she does not say. This is not just a job for the marketing department and a few other selected people: in a customer-oriented company everyone is a 'customer listener' – looking for customer feedback, noting it and sharing it with others to decide what action to take. It is up-to-date and relevant facts about the customer and understanding which underpin all quality improvement.

A customer orientation is necessary to develop new products and services. One example of how this may be done comes from Garvin's (1988, p.208) description of product development in a number of Japanese companies. Like some Western companies, they incorporated consumers' views into their products and did extensive market research on quality. In addition they used a novel approach which helped to develop a customer orientation in their employees:

> Several Japanese companies had even created internal consumer review boards. These were groups of employees, without technical training or QC skills, whose primary function was to act as typical consumers and test and evaluate new products ... all such groups had final authority over new product release. If they were dissatisfied, redesign was inevitable. The message here was unmistakable: Customers – not the design staff, the marketing team, or the production group – had the final say in determining acceptable product quality.

Far too few companies really understand the customers, both in terms of their needs, purchasing behaviour, etc., and know them as individuals through close cooperation and dialogue. Not understanding the customer is a common reason for the complete or partial failure of quality projects.

Customer orientation in the service chain

Service management in a TQM perspective involves not only quality in relations with external customers but also quality in the internal service chains and in relation to suppliers and other partners. All involved in the parts of the chain need to have a customer orientation, but this can be difficult to achieve. One way is to create a group or 'chain manager' with overview across the services in the chain, and with a responsibility for ensuring a shared customer orientation.

One way of understanding quality in such chains and of creating a customer orientation is to consider the core and support services offered to the customers, and their primary and secondary needs. A primary customer need might be to travel from Stockholm to Oslo and back. In the course of satisfying this need, a number of other needs arise, for example, how do I purchase a plane ticket, how do I get to and from the airport? Can I get in touch with customers during the journey? The offering or service system must be designed to satisfy both the primary and secondary needs (Fig. 5.1). The core service is the flight. Support services in this example might be sending the ticket by post to the traveller or preparing it for him or her to pick up at the airport. Payment might be made by credit card. An airport bus, taxi or SAS limousine is needed to get to and from the airport, and access to a telephone or telefax enables the traveller to contact customers or his or her own company.

Customer orientation and quality are not just a question of ensuring that the content of the service offering satisfies the customer's needs. The manner in which the service is delivered and the customer's relations with the company must also meet customer expectations.

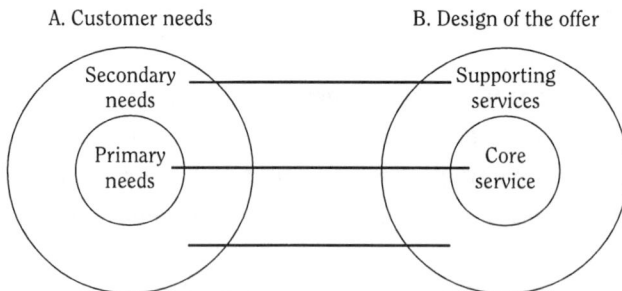

FIGURE 5.1   Customer Needs and the Design of the Service Offering
Source: Development of figure in Edvardsson, 1986.

Quality improvement is a matter of helping the customers, of adapting to them, of keeping them informed and of showing them how their needs can best be satisfied. This helps to develop a long-term trusting relationship with the customers: the customers become collaborators or business partners in co-service.

All staff have a role in and a responsibility for customer orientation. Service managers have to make sure that staff understand that they are part-time marketers, and help them to market the service appropriately. In order to do their job, staff need to know what others in the company are doing, and the links in the service chain – the service process not the company management structure.

Customer orientation is illustrated in the attitudes of different companies towards their customers. Stew Leonard Ltd, a well-known quality company in the retail food industry in the United States has the following quality policy:

Rule 1: The customer is always right.
Rule 2: If the customer is ever wrong, reread rule 1.

The way a company refers to its customers reveals its attitude towards them, especially the terms which staff use 'off-the-record' for different types of customers. In advertising it is customary to refer to customers as accounts. The customer is a bag of money and the object is to get as large a share of it as possible. How does this fit with customer satisfaction through quality? Is the focus really on the customer – perhaps it is on the account? The Disney Corporation refers to its customers as guests and its staff are hosts with particular roles. In the SAS quality book from 1987 we find the following:

> We shall never refer to our customers as anything else but customers, passengers or travellers. Every form of slang expression in this context is a rust attack on our service spirit. Nonchalant comments behind the scenes affect behaviour when meeting the customer.

Doctors call their customers patients, and assume that people are passive and do not mind waiting. Some doctors, nurses and other professions also use terms to describe different types of customer, which we will not refer to here. What are the terms used to describe different types of customers in your business, and do these terms show a respect which arises from a true customer orientation? Do staff hold the following attitude?

> A customer is the most important visitor on our premises. He is not dependent on us. We are dependent on him. He is not an interruption to our work. He is the purpose of it. He is not an outsider to our business. He is a part of it. We are not doing him a favour by serving him. He is doing us a favour by giving us an opportunity to do so.

Some might find the following extreme, but it coveys the attitude which led SAS to major successes in the early 1990s:

> To be a winner in the 90s, we must be where the customers are. But we must also deliver what the customers want. And do it so well, that we are paid what it costs. So we shall give the men and women in European industry and commerce superior travel service wherever they go.
>
> Perhaps this sounds presumptuous. For, of course, the whole industry has always adapted to people. But the point of departure has always been the products, technology, and aircraft. Now we start with people. Each individual's personal needs will take precedence. This will lead to major changes for our customers.
>
> (SAS, 1990)

Behind successful service companies there are discerning and demanding customers. These companies have chief executives and staff who are sensitive and listen actively to their customers. Service companies, which are geared to quality, seek out a dialogue with their customers. It is through such a dialogue that managers can understand the customer's context and the logic of the business, and also build a closer and more lasting relationship.

QUALITY FACTORS FROM THE CUSTOMER'S PERSPECTIVE

Understanding the customers involves teasing-out and defining with them the elements or factors of service that are of particular importance to them: what they value and do not value. Most studies, irrespective of the type of business investigated, have reached similar conclusions. In Chapter 4 we showed that the customer's perception of the service company's staff is often central to his or her perception of quality. Staff competence, motivation, commitment and interest in the customers and their problems are crucial: they must be both able and willing to help customers (Chapter 6).

In most services the most important quality factors are reliability and confidence. This means that the service does provide what was implicitly or explicitly agreed, and that the customer's expectations are fulfilled. The staff must inspire confidence, give the customer the feeling that they are trustworthy and reliable as providers, and that they have the competence and capacity to provide the desired service. Managers and staff working in services often forget how sensitive customers are to signs which might suggest unreliability or untrustworthiness in the service. A third common factor relates to interest in the customer. Personal attention and consideration, and empathy are essential clues to quality for many customers.

A fourth factor is how critical incidents and customer complaints are handled. This is how quickly the service recognizes that a customer is dissatisfied, and how quickly and effectively – from the customer's point of view – the situation is dealt with and 'put right'. In these situations the service provider has an opportunity to communicate what sort of a person he or she is. There is evidence that professional handling of critical incidents and customer complaints strengthens customer relations and heightens the customer's perception of quality. Poor handling of these situations adds insult to injury, and so dissatisfies many customers that they, and anyone they tell do not use the service again. The cost of this 'demarketing' is incalculable, especially on staff morale when, in fact, good service recovery can prove substance behind the quality statements of a service. Because of the importance of these issues we return to them later in the chapter.

There is some evidence that top managers recognize the importance of different quality factors in their service. In a 1988 study, 1055 top executives in 14 European countries were asked about service quality, among other things. The study summarized their views as a 'service priority index' based on 'buying influence' and on 'room for improvement'. The results were as shown in Table 5.1.

TABLE 5.1   Service priority index

RANK	FACTOR	PRIORITY INDEX
1	Fitness for use (as perceived by the customer)	56
2	Problem solving (a systematic and committed effort to understand the true needs and difficulties of the customer)	48
3	Reliability ('a promise made is a promise kept')	47
4	After-sales service	44
5	Speed of delivery	43
6	Courtesy	36
7	Price	31

Source: Gummesson, 1989a.

In a study from 1989 (Table 5.2), the American Society for Quality Control (ASQC) gives quality factors for services and their respective importance for quality (Chapter 1 gives more details).

TABLE 5.2   Service priority index

Behaviour, attitude and competence of staff	65%
Satisfying needs	15%
Rapid service	11%
Price	9%

Source: ASQC, 1989.

One interpretation of the ASQC results is that it is no longer sufficient merely to satisfy the customer's needs – just to provide services of an acceptable technical quality. Over and above that, the staff must be competent and, not least, have the right attitude and give the customer the feeling they are interested in him or her. This is difficult to fake.

PROBLEMS FACING CUSTOMERS OF SERVICE COMPANIES

An article in Sweden's *Dagens Industri* (Daily Industry) on 1 December 1989 presented the results of a number of problem detection studies (PDS), carried out by PDS Research AB in Sweden. We mention this study because it gives evidence from an extensive survey of customers of a number of service firms, and insights into the nature of their problems. The studies identified the problems which customers experience as the most serious with regard to a product, company or type of business (Thams, 1985). The first phase is a survey to make an inventory of the problems, by interviewing customers and company employees such as salespeople, and service and marketing staff. In the second phase the problems are listed without priority. Two questions are added to each problem:

1 How big a problem is this for you?
2 How anxious are you to have the problem solved?

Respondents answer on a scale of 0 to 3.

In the studies at least 200 customers are asked by letter to answer these two questions on a list of 100 to 200 problems. The answers are processed on a computer and the problems ranked according to the points they have received for the two questions.

PDS research has compiled data from the 100 latest studies, carried out from 1987 to 1989. We list below the 10 most serious problems found for service companies. Readers might think about whether any could apply to a service they know:

1 Difficulties in contacting customer service staff and salespeople. Understaffing makes it difficult to purchase services. Furthermore,

the staff in the organization hide: they are on courses, sitting in meetings or dealing with unimportant administrative business. The salespeople quite simply do not want to meet the customer.

2 Lack of information about the services offered by the company over and above the basic service. A powerful message to advertising agencies: media noise creates confusion. It is difficult for advertising to combine attention and facts and it is directed more to potential than to existing customers.

3 Problems with day-to-day running.

4 Unclear or incomplete price information/tenders. Services in the building industry, for instance, intentionally provided unclear tenders.

5 Physical accessibility.

6 Unclear or incomplete product catalogues, company representation: too many fine pictures and too little action.

7 Company presentations lack substance, the customer wants objective information but cannot find it anywhere.

8 Handling of complaints. Complaints are still seen as a threat rather than an opportunity. Unfortunately, companies are aggressive even if the customer is right.

9 Lack of reward for faithful customers. This point is rapidly increasing in importance.

10 The content and form of the invoice. Clear invoices lead to quicker payment. Invoices are becoming a more important information source and database.

Most of these 10 customer-perceived problems, and those we have found in our research concern the customer's relationship with the service company, and communication, information and accessibility.

ORGANIZATION FOR CUSTOMER ORIENTATION

Many managers say that they are creating a customer orientation, but the evidence, even from internal surveys of staff, shows little success. Why is that? Our view is that organizational structure and corporate culture exclude the customer in essential respects, and that many managers fail to change to a customer-orientated structure and culture. Instead of including the customer in the co-service system, the service company, often unconsciously, shuts itself off from the customer. We considered service culture in Chapter 3, and structure in relation to design in other chapters: here we consider why there is this difficulty.

Part of the problem is that organizational theory lacks relevant descriptions and working models for a customer orientation. 'The customer-in-perspective' – the customer as a participating and controlling element in the organization – is conspicuous by his or her absence in academic and practising managers' theories. Research on networks, symbolism, organizational culture, business ideas, market orientation and other approaches to organization tends towards placing the customer in the centre, but managers have not been able to use these ideas, for a number of reasons. It is true that there are models for decentralization, dismantling the pyramids, or for turning them upside down. But few of these organizational forms are based on the customer-in-perspective and build on the co-service process, which we have argued is central to service quality.

This is demonstrated in a book on organizational theory which has attracted much attention, *Images of Organization*. In it Morgan (1986) describes eight different pictures of organizations. None of them is based on the customer-in-perspective or customer-controlled systems. The tendency for organizational theory and managers to focus on the inner world often blocks new thinking, both in business and in research. Open systems and models which include external interested parties have never really succeeded in penetrating and influencing the fundamental principles of business organization. It is a major and urgent task for both researchers and practitioners to develop theories and organizational models which are based on the customer-in-perspective and which can provide the necessary breakthrough for this approach at all levels.

At the practical level, the customer still comes second, and is outside and marginalized when it comes to organizing a business. The customer in the centre is a notion of how things perhaps ideally ought to be, but the customer still has to take second place to internal interests or rather self-interest. In practice, defining the customer is subordinate to defining the business idea, internal goals and strategies. The inner life of the company and how it is to be organized are still the overriding concerns. The organization of customer relations is perhaps included in the work of the sales and marketing department but it does not permeate the company as a whole.

Rather than 'top–down' or 'bottom–up' perspectives, we propose in this book and elsewhere an 'in–out' or 'co-service process' perspective. This involves defining activities externally – for the customer and other interested parties/actors in the market – and focusing on the service process in relationship with the customer. A TQM framework helps to bridge external with internal, but, for services, has to be complemented with theory of organizational structure and culture related to the co-service process. By 'theory' we put the emphasis on managers' theories-in-action: their assumptions about structure and culture which inform their business decisions.

CUSTOMER CARE

It seems to me that most companies are much better at getting new customers and selling to them than they are at retaining their old customers.

(Rogers, 1987)

If you place the customer at the centre, then customer care and handling complaints are central to all service managers' work and to improving quality. However, in many companies, service managers view this to be the work of other departments, rather than other departments assisting them in this work. In addition, marketing is to identify and attract new customers. It is only recently that researchers and some service managers have recognized the importance of taking care of existing customers in the first place. Service managers need to take responsibility for both customer care and marketing. It is they who have the main relationship with the key customers who place large orders or create a positive image for the company. The latter is important for other potential customers, as we showed in an earlier section on reliability and confidence.

Look after customers as an investment in the future! says Professor Claes Fornell of the University of Michigan in the Swedish Post Office's customer magazine, *Kunddialog* (dialogue with the customer) (1990b), and we could cite many other examples. Increasing international competition in shrinking markets has led to a greater interest in 'defensive marketing', says Claes Fornell. When, for instance, a garage loses a customer, it is both difficult and expensive to get him back. On average, it is much cheaper to retain an old customer than to get a new one.

Why do companies lose customers? A study reported by the Swedish Post Office shows that it is not primarily a price issue but the following:

TABLE 5.3   Why do companies lose customers?

Death	1%
The customer moves to another town	3%
Competitors have won him over	5%
Lower prices elsewhere	9%
Unsatisfactory handling of complaints	14%
Lack of interest on the part of the supplier	68%

Source: Swedish Post Office, 1990a.

> Goods and services are becoming increasingly similar – all competitors offer the same basic product. What is decisive is the extra, what is over and above the basic product: Advice, customer service, user training, guarantees, credit, customer care.
>
> (Swedish Post Office, 1990a)

It is profitable to look after one's customers. Attracting new customers is perhaps more exciting, but it is often costly. Estimates show that on average it costs six times as much to sell goods or services for a certain figure to a new customer than to an existing one.

Reichheld and Sasser (1990) report the costs of losing customers in various service industries. One of the services studied was credit cards. They found that on average it cost £30 to get a new customer. The net income in the first year is £18, in the second year £24, in the third £26, in the fourth £29 and in the fifth £33. With time, then, the customer becomes more and more valuable for the service company. The cost of losing a customer can be calculated by discounting future net income at the current value. It turns out that the costs are extremely high. This means that services should see customer care as an investment and not as a direct cost, as using resources today to create the conditions for future returns. Unfortunately, traditional accounting and financial reports to managers do not show the costs of lost customers or investments in customer care.

One of the first books to draw this issue to the attention of ordinary managers was Peters and Austin's (1986) well-known, *A passion for excellence*. They considered how two categories of company reacted to dissatisfied customers. The first and most typical sees complaints as a disease to be free from so that the pain can be rapidly forgotten. The second category sees complaints as a golden opportunity, an opportunity possibly to make a friend for life. 'We find time and again that even terrible failures can be turned into something positive. The dissatisfied customer can become a top customer and a better friend than ever if only you ring and apologise' (p.141). This tallies with the results of our own and others' research.

Customer dissatisfaction is often emotionally charged, but when customers are asked why they are dissatisfied, they can generally provide a rational explanation, even if it is not the real reason. Claus Möller, president of Time Management International, writes in *Harvard Business Review* (Möller *et al.*, 1990, p.24)

> When I worked with SAS years ago to improve the company's service, we asked flight attendants to distribute forms asking customers to rate the service. I

observed that the process itself was flawed: attendants did not make eye contact, and when customers asked, the attendants what they did, they commented on what I call service quality: material aspects such as space between the seats, waiting time, punctuality of flights, even the fact that champagne was served in plastic glasses.

In summary, customer care is profitable for several reasons:

- Firstly, it is easier to serve existing customers. Relations and trust between people are already present.
- Secondly, existing customers represent a continuous source of income. When you lose customers there is a gap in income. It costs money to build up trust, new routines, etc.
- Thirdly, old customers are a major source of ideas for developing the service company.
- Fourthly, satisfied customers speak well of your company and its services. This is the best marketing.

ACTIVE CUSTOMER CARE

Active customer care is a matter of managers and their staff establishing a dialogue with customers and a long-term relationship with them. Zemke and Shaaf (1991) have studied 101 companies to find common denominators for companies which are considered to be leaders in customer care. They found the following five areas:

1 *They listen carefully to customers and try to comply with customer requests.* Companies have many channels for listening to customer requests because traditional customer and market surveys are not sufficient. They allow complaining customers to have their say, as well as customers with suggestions for improvements. They maintain that making it easy for customers to say what they think is important, irrespective of whether it is negative or positive. The best 'listening channels' are the staff who are in continuous contact with the customers. Øvretveit (1993a) describes systems which make it easy for staff to pass on or record customer views.

Apart from listening, the companies which Zemke and Shaaf studied were also good at making rapid changes in response to the information they gathered about customer requests.

2 *They have a vision of what customer care entails.* Visions are needed which are communicated throughout the organization in a simple manner so that everybody can understand them. This is not a once-only event, but a continuous process.

3 *On the basis of the visions, they define customer care in concrete terms. Following up in the form of monitoring and evaluation is also part of the success formula.* Zemke and Shaaf found that these companies further defined their visions in the form of goals or undertakings towards customers. This is a prerequisite for monitoring and following up customer care.

4 *They are careful to employ service-minded staff and they provide staff with the necessary training and authority to use their knowledge and skill.* The companies studied spend a lot of time and care on recruitment. They hold many and long interviews. Education and school certificates, although not without importance, are not decisive. Attitudes to work and to customers are often more important than education. Staff are trained as and when necessary. Recommendations from employees carry great weight but so do recommendations from customers.

All the companies emphasize the value of giving staff the necessary authority. Managers must rely on their staff but they must also allow failures. Not being allowed to make a mistake will result in nobody daring to try anything new.

5 *They reward staff who make an extra effort in connection with customer care.* The importance of designing the reward system to encourage customer care is something the companies studied were well aware of. Rewarding even what may seem a trifle in contacts with customers increases the employees' pride in their own work even when it is a question of low status tasks. In our experience this is more a question of managers recognizing and showing appreciation than financial rewards.

Zemke and Shaaf selected the 101 companies because they had achieved much in customer care. Furthermore, they were very profitable companies, which was largely a result of their listening to, looking after and complying with customers. The book also highlights what we have found: the crucial importance of the employees for the customers' perception of quality in contacts with the company. This is valid not only for those with direct customer contacts or just for service companies, but also manufacturing companies are generally just as dependent on good relations between their customers and the company's contact staff.

Below we give illustrations of customer care from two Swedish companies. The first, Solifer Caravan, shows how a company can set up an effective dialogue with its customers in a novel way. The second gives an example of how not to care: Old books are of no interest to X-bank, reveals a frightening attitude towards customers and their needs. We then turn to a useful method for managers seeking to improve customer care: critical incident analysis.

Solifer Caravan

The year is 1983. Sales of caravans in Sweden have been decreasing for three years. Solifer has 10 per cent of the market and, with this, lies in fourth place. The company feels that this is totally unsatisfactory for such a good product. 'Our marketing was virtually wholly geared to finding new customers and this search was increasingly expensive, so something had to be done.' Market surveys found that 75 per cent of all caravans were purchased by previous owners. They realized that if all Solifer owners changed to the same make, sales would increase considerably. Together with their consultants, EBC, they decided to change course and concentrate their resources on existing customers.

An intensive dialogue with the customers – by post, personal contact and via retailers – was essential if they were to devise successful measures for customer care. A customer magazine was started with a name to underline the idea of two-way communication: *Answers to Solifer Owners*. They now print 17 000 copies three times a year. It often publishes surveys with answers from Solifer owners and a lot of letters – caravan-owners have a lot to say about various matters.

One suggestion was the idea of starting a club, and a number of Solifer owners formed 'Club Solifer', independent of the company. There are now 1500 members and it is an important 'discussion partner' for Solifer, for the retailers and even for the tourist industry. Contacts with and between members of Club Solifer go via a club magazine. Moreover there are regular meetings – not just during the summer. Solifer has its own 'caravan village' at the caravan exhibitions in Jönköping every year, which is open to club members and others. It has become an excellent meeting place for makers, retailers and customers.

The intensive dialogue leads to many customers contacting the company by letter. It is a golden rule that everybody who writes gets a personal answer. Letters arrive at Solifer beginning, for instance, 'Hi all you at Solifer' with three pages about using the space in the caravan more efficiently. Erik S. Forselius, the Managing Director, observes that one of the ways of maintaining the competitive edge is continued active customer care. 'It is profitable', he says, 'but you must realize that it takes a lot of hard work and perseverance'.

His message to retailers is clear: There are three ways of increasing sales:
1 Sell more frequently to existing customers.
2 Sell more to existing customers.
3 Get new customers.
The first two ways are the cheapest and we have your present customers on our computerized customer register.

This new customer register is a step in the process of refining the strategy that was initiated in 1983. All retailers can concentrate their efforts on, for instance, those who plan to change caravans within a year. 'You get more out of every crown you spend on advertising if the message is directed towards just those who are likely to purchase', says Erik Forselius. Selling more to existing customers is a good form of customer care.

Lack of customer adaptation

We now turn to an illustration of another kind of customer care, which shows the cost of poor customer care in bad publicity. An article in *Svenska Dagbladet* (a major Swedish newspaper) for 10 February 1989 began as follows: 'After 40 years as a customer in the bank, Ragnar Jones, who has an antiquarian bookshop on Norrtullsgatan in Stockholm, has been told that his routines do not suit the bank. He should therefore change banks.'

Together with his wife Siri, Ragnar Jones runs a renowned antiquarian bookshop. His customers often pay by cheque. At the same time the Joneses need cash to purchase books and to give change. Therefore they visit the bank several times a week to cash the cheques. But this is not popular with the bank because Jones is an unprofitable customer, according to the deputy branch manager of 'X-bank'. This bank saw Jones as old-fashioned.

The bank's attitude was that Jones is a small customer who causes the bank a lot trouble. An uncooperative customer who would not open a cheque account and leave the day's takings in a bank box. Ragnar Jones, like many other of the bank's customers, is a peaceful businessman who does not show when he is annoyed. 'We have always used X-bank and we cannot understand why we must change to suit the bank. It is the bank that introduced the cheques and not we businessmen. Why should they now refuse to cash them when we come into the bank?'

His anger led to the article in a national newspaper, and also to the opportunity for 'X-bank' to respond and to gain publicity for its customer care. Did it?

'We have offered him alternatives but he will not accept them. In any case, we do not really want retailers as customers with their daily takings and need for change.' Could X-bank not make an exception for customers like the Joneses? 'No, we reckon that the system we have proposed is good for both the bank and the customer', replies JG. 'We do not know what to do now', says Siri Jones, 'shall we accept this in silence? Surely they cannot treat small businesses like this?'

There are many other examples which we could have taken, which cannot be discounted by saying that the media are only concerned with making stories rather than reporting. It is because cases like these sum-up the dissatisfaction of many customers that they are reported: they are not news because they are unusual, but because they are common. Managers might consider whether an article like this could appear about their service, and what they are doing to avoid 'free advertising' for their competitors.

CRITICAL INCIDENTS

In this section we look at a simple and cost-effective technique which managers and their staff can use to improve their customer care. In one project, one of us trained staff to use it successfully in a health service where we did not have time and money to do expensive surveys (Øvretveit, 1991a). We describe one study in detail to illustrate the concept and to give managers some ideas about how they might use the technique, and we give two more personal illustrations of the concept.

A 'critical incident' is a special, problematic, delicate or unpleasant incident which affects a customer's perception of the quality of the service. It is something that 'crystallises a customer's perception of the quality of a service – something which they can "put their finger-on" and remember and which, for them symbolises the service' (Øvretveit, 1992a). A 'critical incident' is often the result of special demands on the resources of the service-producing company, particularly the staff. 'Critical incidents' are often encounters with the customer which go wrong, but they can also be encounters which 'delight the customer' because staff give higher service than expected, especially in difficult circumstances.

Critical incidents are the high and low spots in an otherwise unremarkable or unnoticeable service. A critical incident is often the final trigger which causes a customer to complain. We have studied critical incidents in customer relations and our results suggest that even if the company only responds with recognition and apology, dissatisfaction can be removed in 90 per cent of the cases. More important is that these events are used to make substantive changes to prevent similar situations arising. As many as 70–95 per cent of the customers who experience problems with their supplier do not complain. They remain dissatisfied, spread negative comments and perhaps change supplier. Market surveys made at TARP in Washington DC show that only 4 per cent of those who are dissatisfied actually convey this to the service supplier. Further, these studies show that dissatisfied customers tell 10 other people on average how bad the service/ service provider is.

Since few customers complain, managers who only listen to complaints are missing most of the problems. The company must actively seek out dissatisfied customers and make it easy for the customer to lodge a complaint and then listen actively to the complaints. We use five quick indicators to get a sense of current quality before starting a quality project with a service: one is how much trouble does the service take to seek out complaints. One reason for the generally poor quality of UK and Nordic services in comparison to US services is the cultural attitude to complaining, and that it is sometimes better to seek out 'could do better' advice than 'complaints' to ensure feedback from 'the silent majority experiencing service mediocrity'. Part of the dialogue we have emphasized is discussing with the customer the best way to resolve the situation and prevent the problem for other customers – the latter being something that many customers want to do, especially in health services.

The customer's perception of quality is often affected more by how staff deal with their dissatisfaction and complaint than by the incident itself. It is the service's response to the customer's complaint which reveals the reality of a quality service. What managers and staff do or do not do in such situations remains in the customer's memory. The normal encounters – moments of truth – with the service company do not always leave a lasting impression in the way abnormal situations do. It is important to handle critical incidents professionally and turn them into something positive. Critical incidents offer unique marketing and quality improvement opportunities.

Every complaint against SAS is an opportunity to sell SAS. Customers who are well compensated often attach more importance to the compensation than to our mistakes. We must handle complaints quickly, flexibly and generously. It is even more important to put things right and provide compensation before the customers complain. Saving SAS' face is a task for everybody working in direct contact with customers.

The customer should feel that we are generous. The customer should feel that we are not suspicious of him. Our attitude is different from that of the insurance company when it comes to settling claims. In the balance between what is legally correct and what the customer thinks is reasonable, the customer's view carries most weight. It is the keynote of our service when mishaps occur.

(SAS, 1987, p.169)

Apart from prevention, the manager's task is to ensure that staff have sufficient authority to deal with customer complaints and critical incidents at the time. From a quality viewpoint it is absolutely essential that the customer is compensated rapidly and on the spot. The way to turn the incident into a perception of bad quality, rather than the reverse, is to make staff refer to higher ranking managers and the customer wait before hearing whether he or she will be compensated. This does not communicate to the customer real 'care'. The importance of sufficient authority on the front-line cannot be overestimated.

Many companies believe that silent customers are satisfied customers. Our research shows that in one sense it is profitable for companies to increase rather than decrease the number of complaints or 'could do betters'. Then they can do something about the dissatisfaction and increase their chances of retaining customers. It is here the real profit lies since it costs on average six times as much to get a new customer as to retain an old one. Companies with many complaints need not be bad companies. Instead they may be good at conducting a dialogue with their customers. Yet manager and staff performance is often assessed on a crude rating of complaints.

Achieving reconciliation with the customer

A critical incident, even when it leads to the loss of a customer to a competitor, can be turned into something positive. One can and should seek dialogue and reconciliation with the customer.

> As in all failed relationships, the first step towards reconciliation is to find out what went wrong. There may have been a misunderstanding between the customer and IBM's service organization. There may be a conflict of personality between the customer's contact person and the salesman. There may be a power struggle in progress at the customer's – a new manager who wants to make his presence felt. Or the competitor's salesman succeeded in convincing the customer that he could supply a superior product. When you understand the reasons for the failure, you can seek a solution.

> (Rogers, 1987, p.163)

Reconciliation involves apologizing, expressing regret at what happened, compensating, empathizing and showing in various ways that 'one cares'. This only works, as we have emphasized, if manager and staff really do care. Personal consideration – meeting the customer halfway – is crucial. Companies with this basic attitude have a good chance of being able to turn even the worst critical incidents into something positive for both the customer and the service company. Consider two illustrations of what we mean.

Examples of good and bad 'service recovery'

We could take an example from the research, but we give one which managers may recognize in the experience. One of the large hotel chains in Sweden had advertisements in the daily papers emphasizing their good quality. One of the messages was: 'Our motto is personal service and quality.' The advertisements were placed in both the national and local press on several occasions. One of the authors (Edvardsson) was going to Uppsala (a major university city in Sweden) to take part in a course and needed to stay overnight. Naturally he chose the 'quality-oriented' hotel, for professional reasons of course.

Having reached Uppsala at 5 p.m. on Sunday, I checked into the hotel. I had booked a room and everything was in order. In the lobby there were a number of posters underlining the quality drive - 'Our motto is personal service and quality.' I was given the key to room 203 ... . The room looked all right, everything seemed to be in order. On the table there was a nice card with the following text: 'I am responsible for ensuring that everything in your room is all right.' It was signed Sara ...

... After taking some exercise, I went to the sauna which was shut off and cold although it should have been hot. I pointed this out to the receptionist, who was sitting reading the evening paper. The answer I got was 'I suppose one of the guests shut it off'. I was able to reach that conclusion myself. I was somewhat annoyed but understood that such things could happen. But I felt that she was not interested, that she could not care. She seemed completely indifferent to the fact that the sauna was cold - no expression of regret, no apologies, no offer of compensation. Instead she picked up her newspaper, sat down and went on reading.

I had expectations of personal service and quality and I felt that I was not getting that service. It was the body-language of all the staff which communicated indifference.

Back in my room, I took a shower. When I took the towel to dry myself I found it was wet. Now I was really annoyed, and on reflection, this was the first real thing which I could point to which crystallized my experience so far. After drying myself as well as I could on toilet paper, I went down to the reception desk and pointed out what had happened. The same girl was behind the desk.

I looked at her and said, 'My room has not been cleaned.' She did not answer but went over to the cupboard on the wall, opened it and took out a key. She said, 'Here you are, the key to room 205.' She then sat down and went on reading the newspaper. I felt things had gone too far. I had been treated in an impersonal manner, or even rudely by Nordic standards. I asked, probably in a fairly irritated tone, 'What's the meaning of this - is this personal service and quality for you?' No answer again. Instead she referred to the building work in progress in the hotel and that, 'we have absolutely no control over the cleaning staff'. I asked her if she really meant what she said, 'no control over the staff'. Again no answer. I felt that she was unable to handle the situation.

Although I did not want to cause trouble, I thought it worth pursuing the matter, even though many guests would have left the matter at that. I took up the question of compensation. 'Quality-oriented hotels usually compensate their customers when something goes wrong. What do you do?' She looked bewildered. I said I was going into the restaurant to eat and would be back in half an hour. By then I expected her to suggest some suitable compensation.

When I came back and asked for compensation, I got the answer that she was not authorized to compensate me. 'Who is?' 'The hotel manager', she replied. 'Why have you not asked him?' 'He is at home and we are not to disturb unless it is urgent.' This was obviously not an important or urgent matter. I felt even less important and badly treated. When I checked out the next day, I asked the hotel manager to ring me.

Three days later he phoned. He sounded rather annoyed. 'I heard you were given a room that had not been cleaned, but were given a new one instead, wasn't that all right?' Even then I felt he did not really 'care' and he did not do anything to meet me halfway. I had booked a further four nights but I asked him to cancel them. Then he woke up. I was sent two coupons worth Swedish Kronor 20 each to be used in the hotel. I have not used them and do not intend to.

This example is not an isolated incident but all too common, and similar in many respects to the experience of another of the authors in a study done for a UK hotel chain (Øvretveit, 1993a). The second example is, unfortunately, less common. It concerns an airline and it was recounted by a couple of old-aged pensioners. They had been on holiday in Ireland. On the journey home their plane was late into Copenhagen, which meant they missed their connection to Stockholm. They were very upset and did not know what to do as this was only the second time they had flown abroad.

As they stood at Kastrup wondering what to do, a stewardess came up to them and asked if they had any trouble, which gave them an opportunity to describe their situation. They were very angry and were convinced that the airline had made a mistake. The answer they received was:

'Please accept our sincere apologies. We must be able to do something about this. Wait here and I shall help.' A few minutes later the stewardess returned and said, 'There is a plane to Stockholm in two hours and there are three seats available. Shall I book you on the flight?' The couple thought that sounded fine and accepted. Then the stewardess asked, 'What can we do for you while you are waiting?'

The couple were so surprised at the unexpected question that they had nothing to say. Then came the suggestion: 'Can we offer you dinner?' They thought that sounded excellent. In a few minutes the situation had changed from something very negative to something positive.

They were transported across the airport to the restaurant, ate a good dinner and took the evening plane to Stockholm. They felt satisfied. A few days later when they were looking through their travel documents, they realized that it was not the airline that had failed but it was they who had misunderstood the departure time from Dublin. It was not the airline but they themselves who had made a mistake. This reinforced their positive impression of the airline.

What would have happened if the stewardess at Kastrup had begun by analysing who was in the wrong in order to distribute blame and then returned a few days later with an opinion. Or if she had had to ask her boss first what she should do? Would that have been placing the customer at the centre?

What do the old couple remember best from their holiday trip, the fault or the friendly treatment, that someone cared about them and helped them? What they told one of the authors, and many others, was how well they had been looked after. Their view of the airline was formed in the situation. Their experiences at Kastrup on a Sunday evening at the end of July will remain with them for ever. There are studies that show that a positive experience is perhaps passed on to seven other people while a negative experience is passed on to thirteen on average. This publicity is much more effective than 'ordinary' advertising.

Theodore Levitt (1984) puts it in these terms, 'It is in a situation where you do not get what you expect, that you become aware of what you in fact get.' It is in these critical incidents that service companies create and change customers' perceptions of their quality. Below we present two more systematic studies of critical incidents in customer relations.

Breakdowns: a study of critical incidents in an airline

We have emphasized co-service and the service process, and have found that the critical incident technique (CIT) captures part of the process, although it is a 'snapshot'. The method is also useful for managers and staff to investigate and gain a greater understanding of situations where quality fails. We describe the studies below because they show ways in which managers and staff can use the method in their own service, or help them to understand the kind of information they might get from others using this approach in their service.

The main advantage of CIT is that it generates detailed process descriptions of critical incidents as the customer perceives them. The customer has the opportunity of describing the situation in his or her own words. The weakness of the method is primarily that the interviewer can filter, misrepresent or unconsciously misunderstand the respondent, which is true of all 'verbal' methods.

The main aim of the study was to describe and analyse critical incidents from the customers' point of view and thus create a basis for 'crisis management' (Edvardsson, 1992). The study involved interviews with 320 business customers and 80 airline employees in Linjeflyg, the domestic airline in Sweden. For an incident to be defined as critical, it had to be described in detail and deviate significantly, either positively or negatively, from what business passengers thought normal or expected.

Data collection and analytical model

The study involved collecting data about the cause, course and result of these critical incidents (Fig. 5.2).

CAUSE ————————————> COURSE ————————————>OUTCOME

FIGURE 5.2   Model of a Critical Incident

The study selected respondents and critical incidents according to:
- negative incidents
- passengers had experienced the incident themselves during the last two years while they were travelling on business
- the respondents were selected at random at four different airports

- two critical incidents from each respondent
- airline staff respondents had worked in the front office for at least six months
- the critical incident was to be seen from the perspective of the business passenger.

The study method was a personal interview where the respondent was asked to recount in detail in his or her own words a critical incident personally experienced. The interviews were conducted at four airports with two students acting as interviewers and two others keeping a record. The accounts were between a half and one page in length.

Analysis of critical incidence interview data is more difficult than for traditional survey studies. It involves a scan of the accounts to reveal any patterns which could be used to classify the incidents in accordance with the above model. The causes of the critical incidents could be divided into source (= where) and type (= what). During the course of the critical incident it is possible to distinguish passivity or activity on the part of the two parties, the customer and the service provider. The result for customer relations could be classified as a strengthened, unchanged, weakened or broken relation with the airline.

The critical incidents were classified into main categories and sub-categories. An example of a main category is air transport, which concerns critical incidents occurring at the airport or on board the aircraft; the sub-categories here are: delayed flight, cancelled flight, delayed luggage, overbooking and lack of information.

Results – Business Passengers

Cause
The study found that the most common source of critical incidents for business passengers was related to what happens at the airport or on board the aircraft (air transport). The conditions causing the critical incident were: delays (114), cancelled flights (112), delayed or damaged luggage (26), overbookings (14) and other sources (8). When it came to ground transport,

the critical incidents are often the result of the airport taxi being late or not coming at all – another example of what we have said earlier about the service chain.

TABLE 5.4   Business passengers' perception of the source of critical incidents

	NUMBER	PROPORTION
Air transport	274	85.6%
Ground transport	32	10.0%
Other incidents	14	4.4%

Course

TABLE 5.5   The actions of the business passengers

	NUMBER	PROPORTION
Active	76	23.8%
Passive	244	76.2 %

Table 5.5 shows that, in most cases, the business passengers said that they were passive – they did not do anything to try and resolve the problems resulting from the critical incident. They appeared to have confidence in the employees, expecting them to sort out the problems. This seems quite natural. Most people deem it impossible to do anything about the weather or technical problems with an aircraft.

Outcome

TABLE 5.6 The effect of the critical incident on the business passengers' relations with the airline

	NUMBER	PROPORTION
Relation broken	8	2.5 %
Relation weakened	42	13.1 %
Relation unchanged	256	80.0 %
Relation strengthened	14	4.4.%

Table 5.6 shows that in 80 per cent of the cases the critical incidents studied resulted in unchanged customer relations. In 16 per cent of the cases the critical incidents resulted in a weakened relationship, and in 4 per cent of the cases in a strengthened relationship as perceived by the business passengers. Thus the airline was in many cases able to deal with the situation in a satisfactory manner from the customer's viewpoint.

One value of studies of this type is that they give industry-specific examples which are useful in staff training, and which powerfully convey what customer care and quality services mean for what staff have to do. Below we give incidents which illustrate the problems facing an airline, and which are common in other services. The low proportion of broken relations is in part because the airline at that time had a monopoly.

Delay

Delays are the most frequent causes of critical incidents in air transport, and are common in other services. In one instance a business passenger was delayed by a 'technical fault'. The staff were alert and exercised their authority to give vouchers. However, the passenger's dissatisfaction was because of insufficient information about the delay – again a common finding in other studies. The passenger explained that 'technical fault' was diffuse and not good enough. (It is perhaps better than the British Rail explanation of, 'apologize for lateness which was due to a delay in arrival of the service on time'.) However, the business passenger claimed that 'if the airline explained why the plane was delayed, it would increase the passengers' willingness to accept the situation'.

Cancelled flight

The next most common cause of critical incidents after delays was cancelled flights, and again, managers in other services might consider how they handle cancellations. Cancellation is often due to technical faults or bad weather. The situation described below occurred when a business passenger's flight was cancelled because of a technical fault. The passenger was convinced that the reason for the cancellation was that there were too few passengers booked on the flight. There was little information about the cause of the delay, and when the flight was later cancelled, the businessman was very annoyed. He had lost valuable time for work and the staff 'did not care' and their attitude was 'disgraceful'. As in many services, time is important to customers. In this case : 'If the airline cancels too many planes, in the end you lose patience and take the train instead.'

Other services in the chain: the airport taxi

The airline provides ground transportation such as airport buses and taxis for its passengers. In this example the passenger missed his flight because the taxi that had been ordered earlier did not come. The result was that the businessman was unable to attend an important meeting with a customer. The staff did not attempt to assist him resolve the problem by arranging alternative transport. The airline did not accept responsibility for the situation, and the passenger received no compensation for the inconvenience.

Below we present critical incidents recounted by airline staff in the study, because these are also common in other services.

Cause

TABLE 5.7   Staff perception of the source of critical incidents

	NUMBER	PROPORTION
Air transport	58	72.5%
Ground transport	12	15.0%
Other incidents	10	12.5%

The staff believed that 72 per cent of the critical incidents (Table 5.7) arose in connection with air transport: delayed or damaged luggage (26), cancelled flights (14), delays (12), overbookings (4) and other sources (2). The first two factors account for 69 per cent of the dissatisfaction.

Course

TABLE 5.8   The staff view of their actions

	NUMBER	PROPORTION
Active	68	85.0%
Passive	12	15.0%

Table 5.8 indicates that 85 per cent of the staff said they were active in trying to resolve the critical incidents. They felt they were helpful and tried to reduce irritation by compensating business passengers with vouchers.

Outcome

TABLE 5.9 The effect of the critical incident on the business passengers' relations with the airline (according to staff)

	NUMBER	PROPORTION
Relation broken	0	0%
Relation weakened	16	20%
Relation unchanged	48	60%
Relation strengthened	16	20%

Table 5.9 shows that as many as 20 per cent of the critical incidents were seen – by the staff interviewed – as resulting in a strengthened relationship between the business passengers and the airline. This may be compared with the customers' view (Table 5.6) where we find that only 4 per cent perceived the relationship to be strengthened.

Luggage

Lost luggage was the factor which many staff thought created most critical incidents for business passengers. In one incident a passenger became extremely annoyed, and started to abuse the staff. The staff felt that the result of the incident was a very dissatisfied passenger, with weakened relations with the airline, even though the staff recovered the suitcase and took it to the owner by taxi.

Cancelled flight

Staff also thought that cancelled flights were a common cause of irritation among business passengers. In one incident the cancellation was due to bad weather. Four planes were due to depart at the same time but only one could take off. The passengers were informed via loudspeakers that those who had international connecting flights were to go on board first. Chaos broke out and several business passengers who did not have international tickets rushed to the counter and the tumult resulted in a VDU falling to the floor. However, the passengers received no information and they finally realized that they had no chance of getting on the flight. The staff learnt, among other things, the importance of a well-organized queue system.

Summary
This survey found that, although there were similarities, there were also considerable differences between the ways business passengers and staff perceived the causes and handling of critical incidents. The former saw delays and cancellations as the most common problems, while the latter thought that the majority of the critical incidents were caused by delayed or damaged luggage.

We also find a statistically significant difference between the business passengers' and the staff's perception of the effect of the critical incidents on the customers' relationship with the airline (broken, weakened, unchanged or strengthened). The staff are more positive than the business passengers. This study shows, along with others, that collecting information from the front-line staff does not give us a proper insight into the customers' perceptions of quality failures. This does not mean, however, that information from front staff is valueless. Several researchers (e.g. Schneider and Bowen) and CEOs such as Carlzon of SAS maintain that the 'psychological closeness' between staff and customers means that there is much valuable information about customer needs, wishes and expectations to be gathered from the service company's contact staff.

The study also shows that staff are not aware of the importance of clear and correct information when critical incidents occur. The customer needs to know why there is a problem and what the likely outcome is in order to be able to decide how to act. Customers need to feel that they have some control and are being treated with respect. Would the following turn a 'quality risk incident' into a positive incident? The captain or another credible person goes into the departure lounge and meets the passengers. He apologizes for the delay and explains what has happened: a punctured nose-wheel, or electrical fault. He gives his estimate of how long it is likely to take to repair the damage, informs passengers of alternative means of transport: changing flights, bus or train, etc. and perhaps provides some form of compensation for the delay: a cup of coffee for instance.

One of the conclusions to be drawn from the study is that the airline should train its own staff in the techniques of communication and how to relate to customers when critical incidents occur. Several of those interviewed did not believe the information they received. 'They're lying again when they say it is a technical fault. There are in fact too few passengers, and the flight will lose money. But they won't admit that.'

Further, several of those interviewed felt the information to be insufficient and late. Credible, clear and rapid information emerges as an important source of customer-perceived quality. The study shows that the most important quality-creating resources are reliable core services, and confidence-inspiring, knowledgeable and motivated staff who show empathy and are able to look after customers, and deal with complaints in non-routine situations.

The moment of truth: positive and negative critical incidents

Another study using the critical incident technique (CIT) arrived at similar conclusions (Bitner *et al.*, 1990). We note here how the study was done because it shows other ways in which managers and staff may use the method. This study took data from 700 incidents from customers in three service industries – airlines, hotels and restaurants. The study distinguished the special occasions (and how they were handled by the company employees) that led customers to characterize an encounter with the service company as very satisfactory or very unsatisfactory.

Customers were asked the following questions:
- What specific incidents resulted in the customer being satisfied? How did the contact staff act and behave in these situations?
- What specific incidents resulted in the customer being dissatisfied? How did the contact staff act and behave in these situations?
- Are the underlying incidents and behaviour which led to the customer being satisfied or dissatisfied similar?

● Are there patterns in the actions and behaviour which are common to different service companies and which may be considered the underlying causes of satisfaction or dissatisfaction?

Critical incidents, moments of truth and customer care

In recent years the concept of 'moment of truth' has been used widely in marketing and service research. Surprenant and Solomon (1987) define the 'moment of truth' as 'the dyadic interaction between a customer and a service company'. This definition is based on their previous work where they suggest that 'the moment of truth is a role play' (Solomon *et al.*, 1985), in which both the customer and the service provider play their roles. 'Moment of truth' in this sense focuses on the person-intensive element in the actions of the service company.

Shostack (1985) defines the moment of truth in somewhat broader terms as 'a period of time during which a customer interacts directly with a service'. Her definition covers all the aspects of the service company with which the customer can conceivably interact, including its staff and physical environment. Shostack's definition does not limit the encounter to the interaction between the customer and the company but suggests that the 'moment of truth' can occur without human interaction. We concentrate on the personal interaction between the customer and staff although we are aware that, as Shostack indicates, the moment of truth covers more.

A critical incident is one moment of truth that becomes a monument in the mind of the customer of the quality of a service. In the airline study we used these concepts to group types of critical incidents, and these groupings might suggest ways in which managers and their staff could analyse critical incident data for the purposes of deciding improvements.

Group 1   The employees' handling of faults in the service delivery system

When the service system fails, the service company's employees must accept and react to the complaints or disappointment of the customers. The way in which the employee treats the customer and the content of this treatment determine the customer's perception of satisfaction or dissatisfaction. Group 1 concerns failures in the delivery of the core service (hotel room, meals in the restaurant, flight), and unavoidable mistakes that occur even in the best of companies. More than the mistake itself, the ability and willingness of staff to accept and handle such complaints decide how the customer perceives the quality of the service.

Group 2   The employees' handling of special customer needs and wishes

When a customer asks for the service system to be adapted to his or her unique needs, the employee's answer determines whether the customer will feel satisfied or not. To be included in Group 2, the incident has to include either an explicit or implicit demand for adapted service. 'Adapted' is from the customer's viewpoint, since much of what the customer sees as 'special needs/desires' can be routine (or even statutory) from the company's viewpoint. What is important is the customer's perception of how his 'special' wishes or needs have been met.

Group 3   Spontaneous action/behaviour of the employee

Service quality is not only carefully controlled and designed processes: there must be room for employees to seize an opportunity to excel. Group 3 incidents are actions and behaviour on the part of employees which are completely unexpected for customers. Satisfactory incidents include pleasant surprises (special consideration, being treated royally, receiving something that had not been ordered). In contrast, unsatisfactory incidents include unfriendliness, theft, discrimination, neglect of the customer. Table 5.10 shows how we grouped the incidents in the airline study.

TABLE 5.10   Group and category depending on the type of incident

| GROUP AND CATEGORY | TYPE OF INCIDENT | | | | | |
| | SATISFACTION | | DISSATISFACTION | | TOTAL | |
	No.	%	No.	%	No.	%
The response of the employee to fault in service delivery system Group 1	81	23.3	151	42.9	232	33.2
The response of the employee to the customer's needs and wishes Group 2	114	32.9	55	15.6	169	24.2
Spontaneous actions on the part of the employee Group 3	152	43.8	146	41.5	298	42.6

CUSTOMER ORIENTATION AND CUSTOMER CARE FOR QUALITY IMPROVEMENT

In this chapter we considered customer orientation, customer care and complaint management. We emphasized the importance of:

- defining and understanding the customer's needs and expectations, in terms of factors that are important to them and aspects of service that they value
- designing the co-service and systems on the basis of data from and about customers
- being actively considerate to existing customers

- being sensitive to signals of discontent
- making it easy for the customer to complain
- looking after the customer, correcting faults and giving reasonable compensation.

Services can use various methods to find out about customer preferences and to improve customer care. We emphasized more interactive methods and dialogue, and describe one method in detail. Critical incident technique is suited to the 'co-service process' nature of service, is comparatively cost-effective, directs managers towards sources of quality problems and how to resolve them, and gives useful material for training. It is easy to train staff in how to use the method, which also helps them to become more customer-orientated.

For continual quality improvement managers need to take a systematic approach to customer care and to developing a customer orientation. Below we suggest some examples of what might be included in a programme for customer care.

- Design and implement suitable activities to reinforce the relationship with existing customers.
- Ensure that each co-service process is followed up by having the employee(s) of the service company who have provided the service interview the customer.
- Give benefits to key customers, e.g. major or image-creating customers.
- Systematize critical incidents and customer complaints and learn from them. Decide how you will avoid repeating them. Decide how critical situations should be handled when they arise and prepare staff to handle them.
- Train staff in customer care.
- Give staff the authority and resources to make quick decisions and act to handle dissatisfaction or reward faithful customers.
- Stimulate employees to be creative in developing customer care activities.
- Invest in meetings and regular contacts with customers via newsletters or customer magazines.

- Increase information about individual customers by setting up a customer database. This should include details of the customer's purchasing behaviour, complaints, activities directed towards the customer and plans for what should be done during the coming year to care for the individual customer.

Competence for service quality

Many companies are now realising that quality is not the sole responsibility of any one department. To be truly successful, a company needs to employ the creativity and enthusiasm for continuous improvement of all its people.

(Roger Atkinson, Director of Quality Management, Air Products PLC)

Have you ever stayed in a hotel or been to a restaurant which proudly proclaims its recent 'extensive upgrading' of buildings and facilities? Did this make you notice the newness and decoration more than otherwise, and the taste (or lack of it) of the 'no expense spared' renovations? We suspect that you also became more aware of the quality of the service. Perhaps you noticed a discrepancy between the high quality of the physical surroundings, and the service given by staff – staff not knowing how the new systems worked, and generally not as customer friendly as one would expect.

We tend to avoid 'newly upgraded' services for a time, not because we find modern service decoration lacking in taste, but because it is likely that staff were ignored as all the money, planning and energy went into the physical changes. Planning frequently fails to consider how to ensure that the staff can use the new systems, and how to improve the ability of staff to give a quality service and solve quality problems. The building and system work has to be fast for the business to re-open as quickly as possible, the budget goes over limit, and staff are ignored in the chaos, wondering if they will have a job when it is all finished.

This is one example which highlights the lack of attention given to staff competence to give service, and to staff development to carry out quality improvement. Texts on quality and quality strategies often do consider staff competence, but seldom describe it in any detail. Competence is a person's theoretical and practical knowledge and his or her capacity to utilize this knowledge. This includes the ability to learn and to adapt old knowledge. Competence also includes the contact networks individuals have at their disposal and the way they perceive their work. Competent service depends on people's motivation to use their competence, and on their attitude. The chapter considers these points in more detail and shows how to analyse the elements of staff competence called for in different service organizations. It is the competences of different individuals which together can produce the right quality. In this respect services are more sensitive than goods because they are generally produced in the interaction between two or more individuals. Quality is created in these human relations.

The customer-perceived quality of a service depends on the competence of the staff to handle their relations with customers. These staff depend on the competence of other staff to provide them with what they need to serve the customer. All rely on competent management to be able to do their job: 'Service is a social process, and management is the ability to direct social processes. And service organizations are more sensitive to the quality of their management than probably any other kind of organizations' (Normann, 1984).

We start by pointing out two obstacles to quality improvement. Then we describe how social values have changed, making it more difficult to recruit, develop and keep quality-conscious employees. We consider how the 'staff concept' gives the conditions for realizing the company's business concept. The chapter shows that the staff concept depends on developing staff competence and motivation, both of which are needed to improve the quality of services. Staff need support and encouragement to improve, and opportunities for personal development at work. We finish with guidance for giving staff opportunities for the kind of development which will improve service quality.

OBSTACLES TO QUALITY IMPROVEMENT

Many service companies accept that it is the people in the organization who create quality service. However, few have found it possible to achieve the right quality despite the best of intentions. Our research suggests that this is because managers have not paid sufficient attention to two obstacles:

- Staff do not have a full understanding of the business, and do not understand the consequences of their actions for others. Staff in support services do not see the importance of their work for the final quality of service to the end customer, and do not fully recognize other internal staff to be customers.
- Staff want to change and develop with support, and want more than monetary rewards. If they do not feel that they are growing as people, then their motivation and commitment are diminished and the quality of their work suffers.

Managers in service industries, where pay is low and where the work is repetitive, may feel that this is fine in theory but impossible in practice. We do not underestimate the difficulties of removing these obstacles, but we would argue that in these types of service removing these obstacles is even more important. The way out of the vicious circle we described in Chapter 4 is for managers to help staff giving service to grow as people, and get more satisfaction from serving other people – internal or external customers. To the view held by some managers in these industries, that they are unskilled and only do it for the money, which is low, because we cannot pay more in this industry', we ask: what are you going to do to change things to improve quality? We aim below to give some ideas that are relevant for all types of service.

CHANGES IN VALUES

In most modern service companies, producing standardized services is not sufficient. It is essential to understand the customers' needs and, if they have one, their business, and to adapt the services accordingly. Staff are expected to make decisions which suit the customers and the service company. All this requires employees who respond to conflicts and each new situation as a challenge, rather than withdrawing. It means selecting staff with the capacity to carry the responsibility which arises in these situations, and recognizing that their capacity will develop naturally (Jaques, 1989; Stamp, 1989). It also calls for a high level of motivation, which is where we start.

Maccoby (1989) believes that employees are best motivated when the demands placed on them correspond to their own values. However, values are continually changing in society, not least because the level of education is rising. Values can be grouped into three categories: maintenance values, outer values and inner values (Zetterberg, 1983). Maintenance values relate to people's efforts to get something to eat, clothes to wear and somewhere to live. Outer values have to do with belonging to the 'right' social group, living in the 'right' area and striving to be noticed in various contexts. For people with these values, social status is primarily marked by material things. Inner values concern personal development and the attempt to create a better quality of life both for oneself and for others.

These three kinds of values in society have changed dramatically during the twentieth century, and even in the last 10 years. For instance, during economic recessions inner values are less prominent. There are more sophisticated ways of looking at values, for example recognizing 'ecological values', but our point here is to argue that continual changes in values have consequences for both the business concept and the company staff concept. The staff concept has to be adapted not only to the business concept but also to developments in society.

There is also reason to ask whether the values of the managers and directors in a company correspond to those of the employees. Edström *et al.* (1989) classified directors and managers on the basis of their attitude to work which, in its turn, depends on the values formed in their childhood. Differences in basic values can lead to different interpretations of visions, goals and strategies and prevent change or, at least, make it more difficult. Managers often make assumptions about staff values which can wreck quality improvement projects, for example about how staff will value and respond to performance-related pay. Because people's values are difficult to change, service managers need to understand them and take them into account, especially in a more multicultural society. People develop in line with their values, not against them.

Managers' attitudes to work also affect recruitment and selection of employees. Managers tend to employ and promote employees who are similar to themselves. Therefore there should be people with different attitudes to work, who stand for different basic values, in the 'inner circles' which influence decisions about whom to employ. It is not the basic values themselves that are the problem, it is managers not understanding their significance which makes change difficult. Edström *et al.* (1989, p.233) hold that, 'It is important to create a productive integration between the different sets of basic values. If this is successful, the organization's full competence and commitment will be liberated for strategic renewal.'

Values are relevant to the formal employment contract but also to the implicit contract between employer and employee. The latter is something which we formulate within ourselves when we take a job and stay with it. One part of the implicit contract is the demands and expectations we have of our employer. A second part is what we as an employee are prepared to 'give' our employer in return. Good implicit contracts are a prerequisite for the employee to be motivated to become involved in and take responsibility for the business of the organization, and depend on similar values.

BUSINESS CONCEPT AND STAFF CONCEPT

> We believe that customer satisfaction begins with employee satisfaction. That is why we so strongly adhere to our People–Service–Profit' philosophy. Simply stated, if we put our employees first, they will deliver impeccable service and profit will be the natural outcome.
>
> (Fred Smith, founder of Federal Express)

In Chapter 2 we discussed the terms business concept and staff concept. We develop these notions here, and underline the importance of linking them together in order to get quality improvements.

The term business concept is often used to describe the totality of a business system. According to Normann (1980), business concept is not an ideal or vision, but summarizes the business that already operates. Normann describes the business concept as a system which is made up of three subsystems: the market, the product system and the organization. In turn, each subsystem consists of a number of elements: the market consists of different groups of customers and the products can be distributed via different channels. The products may be goods or services, or a combination of both. An effective business concept is characterized by a harmony between the elements which enables the whole to work.

In the same way as the business concept gives an holistic description of the business, the staff concept describes how an organization uses and develops its people. The business concept and staff concept should be in harmony and together form the basis of the company's 'competence strategy'. We represent this in Fig. 6.1.

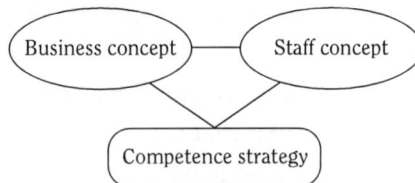

FIGURE 6.1   Business Concept, Staff Concept and Competence Strategy
Source: Thomasson, 1990.

Bergstedt's view of the way of linking the two is that:

> Harmony between staff concept and business concept implies that the staff concept must be designed to achieve correspondence between the life situation, competence and demands for development of a group of individuals, and the environment and context which the business concept can offer this group.
>
> (Bergstedt, 1983, p.66 [our translation])

Bergstedt holds that the staff concept must be designed to mobilize and channel human energy with the aim of supporting the company's business concept. In this respect, the staff concept means:

- recruiting, developing and retaining the 'right' people
- motivating and rewarding for efforts and performance which are congruent with the business concept, the strategic goals and the corporate culture
- planning development paths for people in the organization
- having instruments and channels to disseminate the company's philosophy, goals and values throughout the organization.

Bergstedt underlines the special situation of service companies, where the customer sees the front-line staff as representatives of the whole company and its operations. This makes it more important for staff in services to understand the business concept than in manufacturing companies. A well-designed and used staff concept is of great value to the company and its employees. People of different ages, at different stages in life, from different social groups have different demands, needs and expectations of their work. If the company can offer the 'right' opportunities, people will respond and give their energy and both parties will gain.

An example of the staff concept in practice

An example of a company with a well-planned and consistently applied staff concept, which complements the business concept, is Federal Express, founded in 1973 by Frederick Smith. The business concept is the rapid and reliable distribution of parcels and letters 'overnight' by road and air. From the start, Smith, had a 'different' staff concept. For both top and middle management he wanted people who were creative and could think along unconventional lines. They should preferably be considered 'a little mad'. His philosophy is that whoever wants to be a leader must look after his staff and lead them, and also be humble and respect each individual. Smith's belief, which is carried through in practice, is that if you give people challenges and responsibility they will be able to handle them. His management philosophy focuses on three things: people, service and profit in that order. Federal Express is ranked as one of the 10 best companies in the United States to work for and it has a greater proportion of women and blacks in managerial positions than most other American companies. In 1990 Federal Express was the first service company to receive the Malcolm Baldrige National Quality Award.

COMPETENCE

The main resource for quality and quality improvement in services is all the employees in a company. It is they who use the systems, and apply the new tools and techniques of quality improvement. To give customers the right quality, staff not only need to be aware of the importance of quality but also experience quality in their work. A good 'quality climate', which generates and sustains commitment and willingness, is a precondition for achieving the right quality for the customer.

In service companies quality is realized in the contacts between staff and customers. It is during each 'moment of truth' that poor external and internal quality is revealed. A poor internal quality climate will affect relations with external customers. Everybody with customer contact is an ambassador for the service company and influences the customer's perception of quality to a greater or lesser extent. Staff behaviour and attitude affect how the customer perceives the service. Service managers have to make sure that their staff get the training that they need to deal with the situations that may arise. We have emphasized the co-service nature of the staff–customer relationship. Customer participation in producing service makes it difficult to predict every situation that may arise. Staff need training to work with customers to create service, and this calls for special skills (Øvretveit, 1993b; see also this volume, Chapter 9).

Staff competence in a TQM perspective means that they need the competence to be able to give service, but also to contribute to continual improvements to the quality of the service. Managers need to recognize that staff competence for service is more than the skills to do one job. Sandberg (1989) describes five elements of competence: theoretical knowledge, practical knowledge, networks, capacity and conception. A person's competence to carry out a task depends not only on the individual parts but also on the person's ability to integrate these parts. Sandberg illustrates this in 'the competence circle' (Fig. 6.2).

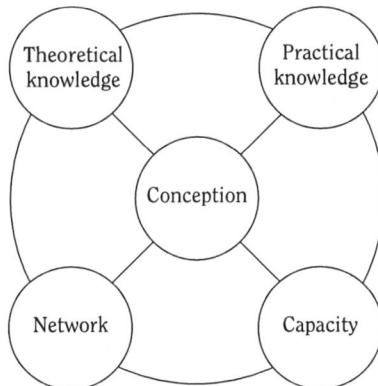

FIGURE 6.2   The Competence Circle
Source: Sandberg, 1989.

Staff can gain theoretical knowledge from books and lectures. This is knowledge that can be transmitted and shared by several people. Practical knowledge is proficiency and skill, which eventually becomes automatic for the person performing a task. It is knowledge that is difficult to transmit. A description or picture of how something is done helps learning, but before a person has practised the skill, his or her proficiency is both low and very uncertain. Reading books, looking at pictures or listening to lectures is not enough to become a competent dancer, driver or manager. Practice is also required.

Capacity can be both physical and mental. Physical capacity is being able to perform a certain amount of physical work within a certain time. Mental capacity relates to self-confidence, daring to try but also knowledge of oneself and self-criticism. Part of competence is having access to a network, which consists of both personal contacts and access to databases, manuals and other resources. In many cases, the network exists within the individual's own organization, but certain tasks call for access to external contacts to complete them. With increasing complexity, the right quality service depends on people's ability to access and use network resources quickly.

Conception is the fifth element to this general competence model. The way in which we perceive the world around us underpins the way we act. The way people perceive their duties underpins the way they solve them. People's perception of their duties depends on their personality, but also on how these duties are defined and explained. In a strongly centralized organization management details how it wishes the tasks to be performed. In a decentralized organization there is often more scope to define independently and interpret how the tasks are best performed. How staff perceive their responsibilities influences how they integrate their theoretical and practical knowledge, their capacity and the resource network.

People who have the same jobs in an organization may have similar education, the same experience of the work, and similar values. Nevertheless, their competence to perform the task may differ since every individual in a given situation combines personal qualities and abilities in a unique manner. But this does not mean that managers cannot give a general description of the competence individuals working on similar tasks should have. An analysis and description of competence requirements is a prerequisite for being able to find a suitable person for a job.

To be able to offer the right quality a company needs a competence strategy, linked to a quality strategy. Both must be in line with the company's overall development strategy. Competence strategy refers to long-term planning of the current and future competence requirements in the company. The strategy involves mapping and analysing the availability and need of competence, and deciding on how to develop staff competence. Getting competent staff is a necessary, though insufficient, prerequisite for service quality. If selecting staff is the most important thing which managers do, the second is developing staff. Staff will have to adapt to new circumstances and contribute to continual improvement, and without development good staff will leave.

Developing competence

For managers to develop staff competence, it helps to recognize first, that the capability of their staff develops naturally and second, that they can do as much to develop competence by delegating the right tasks and giving the right work opportunities as by training.

A systematic approach to developing competence calls for a description of the goal and of how it should be achieved. Service companies need these descriptions at a general, collective organizational level, at a departmental level, at the work team level and at the level of the individual. The natural point of departure is a clearly-formulated staff concept, which defines what is required of employees, and what the company can offer in return. A competence strategy then becomes part of the staff concept.

An opportunity to utilize and develop their competence in their work is important not only for people's commitment and ability to do a good job, but also for their well-being and health. However, people's demand for development does not always match the needs of the organization. A competence strategy also needs to take into account the way in which people's capability develops, and to assess and predict the path in which staff capability will develop, with or without training and other development opportunities. It is likely that some staff will outgrow their level of work quite quickly, especially with development opportunities, and other staff at the same level will only seek a change in type of work rather than level of work. Jaques (1989) and Stamp (1989) discuss these issues in more detail.

Developing competence calls for attention to a number of elements.

First and foremost, competence consists of theoretical and practical knowledge, but knowledge in itself is not sufficient. It is motivation that drives service quality. The company cannot count on people maintaining their ambition, will and motivation unless something is done to develop them. Managers have a key part in rewarding and encouraging staff. The third condition for individuals to produce good work is that the organization gives them the necessary authority, resources and support to carry out the task. Figure 6.3 shows the link between the conditions that must be present for the staff to perform their tasks well and the way the company creates these conditions.

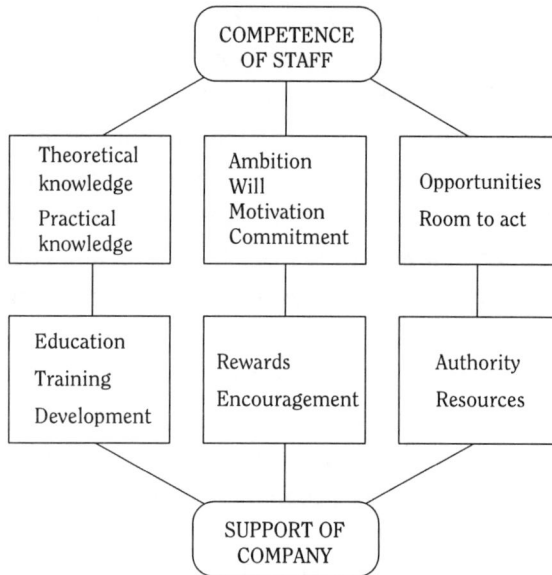

FIGURE 6.3   The Interplay Between Staff and Company as a Condition for High Quality Improvement
Source: Thomasson, 1990.

Basic and specific competences

So far, we have talked about competence at a general level and defined its components in general terms. When we attempt to specify the competence requirements for quality improvement, we soon find that general terms are

not good enough. Different tasks require different types of competence, but staff in a company also need common or core competences, irrespective of profession, position or task – a basic competence which includes:
- knowledge of the company's history
- knowledge of the company's business concept and overarching goals
- knowledge of the company's market and customers
- basic knowledge of the four components of the service management system, target groups, service concept, co-service system and organizational culture and image
- awareness of the importance of quality, both external and internal, for the long-term development and survival of the company
- competence to handle critical incidents for internal and external customers, i.e. 'critical competence' (see Chapter 5).

We can term the fourth component business competence. It consists of understanding the company's financial situation and what may affect it. Not least important is an understanding of the significance of one's own performance for the total result. It is a managerial task not only to convey cost awareness to everybody in the organization but also to introduce 'result thinking' at all levels, which includes results other than financial ones.

Business competence also includes understanding customers and their needs, having the ability to see and assist them solve their problems. In many cases it is also a matter of identifying the customers, of understanding that customers may, in their turn, have customers to serve or that the customers one sees may have an employer who is also a customer of one's own company.

In describing competence in terms of a number of components, we have refrained from pointing to any particular component as being linked with quality. Instead, we believe that quality thinking must permeate all the components.

Methods for raising competence
There are various ways to develop individual and group competence. Conventional educational methods are not usually cost effective, especially if they are not closely connected with everyday work. Since competence

consists of several components, competence-raising methods are needed which we term Learning, Training and Development (LTD). A development strategy involves basic LTD which, in principle, is the same for everybody, and special LTD for the professional group and team. Critical competence can be raised by means of situation-adapted LTD, based on known critical incidents, both internal and external.

Figure 6.4 shows how various types of education, training and development can be linked to competence.

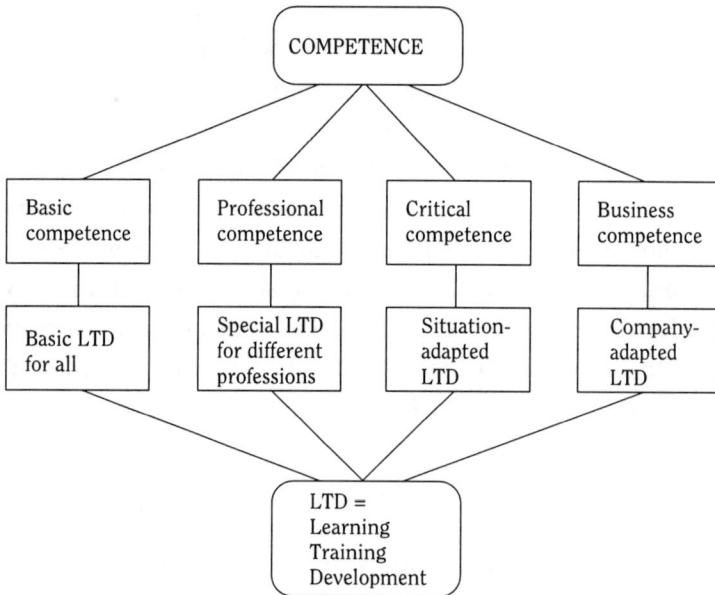

FIGURE 6.4   Model for the Development of Competence
Source: Thomasson, 1990.

Analysing competence for service quality

Analysing 'competence requirements' means listing the competences called for to do certain tasks. It should precede 'competence analysis', which maps the existing competence available within the organization and the potential for development. A simple model (see Fig. 6.5) can be used in both cases. First we define five 'basic forms' but there may be other, specific needs in an organization. The five forms of competence can also be broken down into sub-components.

Note that individual and team competence determine service quality. If well structured, teams readily produce synergy: the total competence is greater than the sum of the individuals' competence. Furthermore, with good team dynamics, people continually gain competence from each other. For example, basic competence might be that all are aware of the business concept and the overarching goals. Demands for professional competence vary a great deal, but they may include the requirement of a certain type of education and experience in a certain profession. Social competence may be a matter of handling customer relations but also being able to work in a team. Critical competence is being able to deal with customers in situations that go wrong. Business competence is a matter of understanding the economic consequences of one's actions. A competence requirements analysis based on this model indicates the demands that are placed on the individual and the group: a demand profile.

The same chart can be used to analyse people's existing competence in relation to the criteria established in the demand analysis. The competence analysis produces a competence profile, which in its turn may be compared with the demand profile for the given tasks.

	INDIVIDUAL	GROUP
BASIC COMPETENCE		
PROFESSIONAL COMPETENCE		
SOCIAL COMPETENCE		
CRITICAL COMPETENCE		
BUSINESS COMPETENCE		

FIGURE 6.5   Model for Analysing Competence
Source: Thomasson, 1990.

Although some managers might view this as over-lengthy, the value is that it helps people and teams to assess themselves objectively. It helps to depersonalize what could be the threatening task of recognizing deficiencies. Often managers hand over analyses of this type to personnel departments, and they and their team lose an understanding and ownership of their development process. We have outlined this approach because it is reasonably quick and easy to use for self-diagnosis and development.

THE DEVELOPMENT AND MOTIVATION OF THE INDIVIDUAL

> Who knows, we can perhaps create workplaces where people appreciate and enjoy learning new things, both as a basic part of their work and as a step in their development as individuals. This would be the opposite of how we are educated in school – where the system is a cross between controlling the masses and punishment.
>
> (John Cleese)

Many people lose their motivation unless they are given the opportunity to develop in their work. In a recession companies often cut back on staff development. Although staff are pleased to have a job, without development opportunities they become demotivated, just when the company needs to make the greatest efforts to improve quality. The following is all too common in service organizations:

> When you get a job, you expect a lot from it and, while you are training, your expectations grow, but after a while you find that the expectations have not been fulfilled and you get disappointed.
>
> (From an interview with an airline employee)

A person's demand for, or what many see as a right to self-development calls for job- or task-mobility in the organization. New people or new tasks bring enthusiasm and ambition to improve and increase the efficiency and quality of the job. People often get better and better at their work over a period of several years. But we all need a new challenge, where we can use our experience as a basis for further development, and we will change company if the company does not offer these opportunities.

Just as companies need a 'kick' now and again to renew and develop, individuals also need change to feel the right motivation to work. Three well-known methods are job enlargement, job enrichment and job rotation. Job enlargement means that an individual is given more tasks – that the work cycle is lengthened. The idea of job enrichment is to provide greater opportunity for the individual to exert influence over his or her own work and work situation. Job rotation is based on the notion of organizing work in a way that makes it possible to change jobs with other people in the team for the sake of variation. The person who wishes to change jobs is often both curious and performance-oriented. He or she wants to expand the limits of personal ability. Such a person can see things in new ways and this is extremely valuable to the organization.

As is shown in Fig. 6.6, the development process can be seen as a rising spiral which eventually turns downward again. The upward part of the spiral illustrates positive development, where the individual perceives work as instructive, exciting and interesting and works with enthusiasm and pleasure. The downward part shows how tasks that were interesting to begin with become routine and how this can lead to boredom and dissatisfaction with one's work situation.

The spiral may be different for different professional categories and different individuals but it has a certain generality over time. Managers need to recognize the point in the spiral when a person feels that work is beginning to become boring and routine since, at that point, they have to 'choose a path' with their staff. Development discussions should start earlier, but if no alternatives are open, it is better to help an employee out of the organization than to prevent or delay his or her departure: ex-employees can be ambassadors for the company on the market.

Managers should recognize that 'over-competence' in a company has risks and disadvantages. Frustration can spead poor morale among staff.

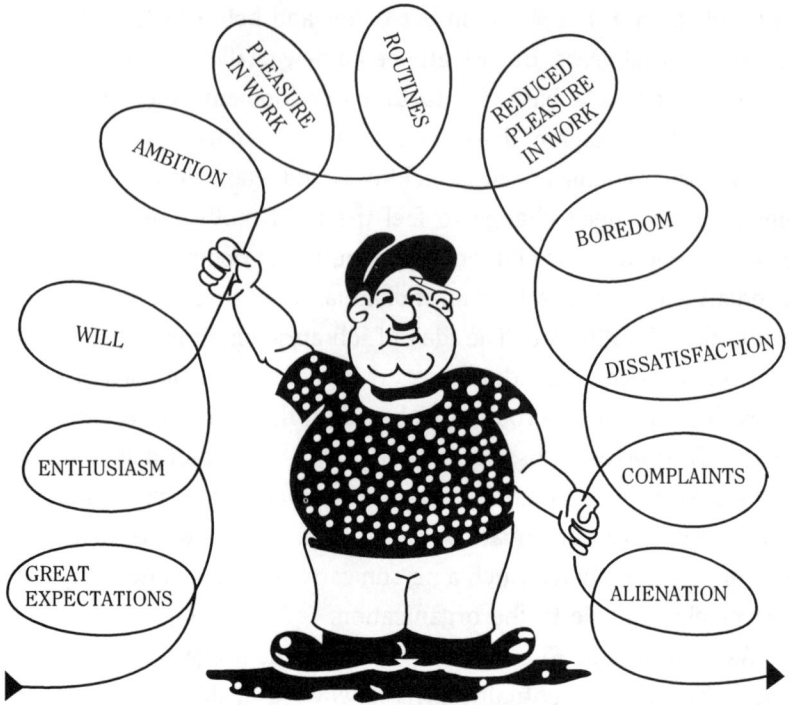

FIGURE 6.6   The Individual's Development and Motivation Spiral
Source: Thomasson, 1990.

Figure 6.6 shows how the people get into a spiral which at first has a positive effect on work motivation, but which eventually becomes negative.

The first of four ways of dealing with this is at source: at the recruitment stage. In some job markets managers are tempted to recruit over-qualified and over-educated people. The second way is to continue with 'over-recruitment' but at the same time plan for greater mobility in the organization. The traditional career proceeds 'upwards', but here the prospects are limited, particularly if the structure of the organization is shifting towards fewer levels. Moreover, in an organization moving towards decentralization and 'tearing down the pyramids', the levels in the hierarchy will be fewer and the opportunities for advancement fewer. Making a career may then involve moving to a new sphere of work, without it necessarily being promotion.

A third way is to broaden opportunities for staff to use their 'over-competence' for the job by giving them other tasks for part of their time – it may be possible to sell various kinds of service externally. A fourth way is to plan for 'beautiful exits', an unfortunate term, but it does convey the idea that both manager and staff can work towards a positive departure.

In summary, a carefully devised staff concept, adapted to the business concept, should form the basis of what we have here called competence strategy. Managers at all levels need to draw up development plans for their staff which relate to the overarching strategy. Competence analysis is a useful way to decide how to develop both individuals and teams. We now turn to staff attitude, an outward sign of competence and motivation.

CUSTOMER INTERACTION AND ATTITUDE TO WORK

We have noted that the 'moment of truth', when the employee comes face to face with the customer, is important for the customer's judgement of the quality of a service. It is at that moment that critical incidents can occur or be avoided, and the vicious or virtuous circles start. If the employee is to have a chance of acting in the right way, he or she must have the authority and scope to take rapid decisions. As Gummesson (1989b, p.85) puts it: 'You can stupefy your front line service personnel by making them robots with discretion to handle only a limited number of standard operations. Or you can empower them to handle deviations and to be more efficient.'

People's total competence also includes their attitude to work and to customers. In the early 1980s, SAS implemented its famous changeover from a production-oriented company to a market-oriented one. The company was successful in changing staff attitudes towards customers, and passengers experienced staff as friendlier and more pleasant. In turn staff thought that customers were happier and more satisfied, and their morale increased: customers really were human and important. A virtuous circle arose in the relationship between staff and customers.

A key point is that you cannot fake caring. Superficial behavioural changes are easy, but customers know the difference between genuine concern and rote actions or gestures. Real attitude change on the part of staff is the key. If the measure of quality is the difference between expectations and perceptions, then 'caring' becomes important. The 'little extra' is often easy to achieve in services, at no cost: the nurse coming with an extra pillow, or the taxi-driver not only lifting the heavy suitcase out of the boot but carrying it into the house. For the customer these small tokens of thoughtfulness enhance quality: they are unexpected and stand out as different from similar services.

CONCLUDING REMARKS

The basis of service quality is competent, committed and motivated staff. In this chapter we considered how to analyse competence and how to develop it. We indicated two obstacles to quality improvement: lack of under-standing of the whole, and the lack of opportunity for renewal and change. Changes in social values mean that people want self-development and satisfaction in their work. To retain and motivate staff, the company must offer them corresponding opportunities – especially in economic recessions.

Below we summarize some of these and other points of the chapter in terms of suggestions for service managers.

1 Map internal competence before recruiting new staff. Find out whether your organization already has staff with the required competence. Be aware that there may be hidden potential competence in your own staff and in other managers' staff which can be developed. Both the company and employees profit from developing rather than employing new competence.

2 Take into account at recruitment both the likely opportunities in the organization and the person's development potential for giving or managing service. People often need variety and new challenges to give their best. They may fall into a descending motivation spiral if their job does not change. Some claim that the limit is six to seven years in the same field; after that one must change jobs to regain commitment.

3 Invest in people and team development planning. A development strategy should be based on, and form part of the organization's staff concept. It should include development discussions between staff and their manager, which involves relating a person's view of own development needs to those of the company.

4 Help staff understand the whole. This involves understanding the business idea and goals, and their part in the service chain. Everyone is in some way responsible for quality in their relations with internal or external customers. Staff in internal support services need to understand how what they do affects the end customer. Developing their sense of service to internal customers makes quality more immediate, and helps to create a company-wide quality culture.

Quality measurement

**Count what is countable, measure what is measurable,
and what is not measurable make measurable.**
Galileo Galilei

S ustained and continuous quality improvement is not possible without measures of quality. Quality measurement is probably the most important technique for a service aiming for more than a superficial improvement. In our experience, choosing and using cost-effective measures is one thing which differentiates the successful long-term quality programmes from those which lose their way. To know where to start and to set priorities, managers have to measure the quality of their service. To work systematically to find and resolve the causes of priority problems, managers and their staff have to use quality measures. Really to know the effect of changes over time, managers need measures to compare the quality performance of the service.

In the TQM perspective of this book we could have described a number of methods, techniques and tools for quality improvement, which distinguish a TQM approach from a short-term crisis problem-solving approach. We chose to focus on measurement because this is the least well understood technique for services. Managers can use most other quality methods and techniques as they are described in the many guides and books on quality in manufacturing. However, managers and specialists have to develop and use special methods to measure quality in services – they need a measurement system which is 'company unique'. The way in which the methods are developed is also important – with customer and staff involvement. Without understanding the issues, managers can waste a lot of time and money using inappropriate measures: consequently we describe a variety of approaches and how to decide which to use.

The term quality measurement covers both quantitative measurement, expressed in figures, tables or diagrams, and qualitative measurement, where the results are usually presented in the form of verbal descriptions. In other words, we use the term 'measurement' in a wider sense than is usual. We discuss the aims and applications of both methods in the chapter. We demonstrate ways to define what is to be measured – in the form of quality factors – and give examples of techniques for collecting data.

Quality measurement in services is a growing subject, and here we aim only to provide an introduction. For more details we refer the reader to three texts. The first is a practical approach for managers, which shows how to develop a quality measurement system which integrates with other performance measures, and to link the system to the market, business strategy and reward systems. In this book Øvretveit (1993a) describes measures of three dimensions of service: customer quality, professional quality and management quality, and gives a guide to customer feedback measures which we draw on in our discussion in this chapter.

The second is an article by Gummesson (1992a) which gives details from the specialist literature about methods, question design, and attitude surveys. Gummesson's view is that, 'Measuring can only be efficient if managers know *what* to measure before asking *how* to measure. Therefore, it is imperative that a service organization understand the specific quality dimensions of its business.'

The third text is of growing importance in Europe, and managers will need to become familiar with it: the new international system set up in 1990 for the standardization of the quality descriptions and measurements of services, ISO 9004-2, *Quality management and quality system elements: Guidelines for services*. There is an equivalent in the United Kingdom for services: the British Standard 5750.

MEASURING QUALITY IN SERVICES

Measurement in manufacturing

Quality measurement has a long tradition in manufacturing industries, which use 'physical measures' to describe size, shape and deviations from standards. Advanced and also low-cost measures have been developed over the years, in part because of a general acceptance of the importance and usefulness of such measures. Manufacturers use these techniques to discover deviations from standards and to quantify the quality of their product. These measures make it possible to specify quality requirements in manufacturing, to describe the technical quality of product to customers in an unambiguous manner, and enable customers to compare products from different suppliers.

Yet product-oriented methods eventually proved insufficient for defining and measuring service quality. From the consumer's viewpoint the measurable quality features of a physical product are only part of the product's total quality. The quality of a house does not only lie in technical parameters. Its exterior and location may be crucial factors in the owner's assessment of its quality. The quality of a car may lie partly in the prestige it gives (or which the owner thinks it gives) him. Another type of product where quality is difficult to measure is food. The volume, weight and nutritive value can be defined and declared but what about taste?

More importantly, the conditions under which services are produced in the co-service process differs from those for goods production. We need to measure service quality in different ways. Although research emphasizes the 'moment of truth' as the most important quality-generating moment in services, we maintain that there are many other critical points which it is important to measure. The customer's perceptions and experiences of quality depend on many factors which a service must measure. Some are general to all services, others specific to the organization. Our experience is that knowledge of general factors helps, but measures need to be based on research into specific factors to be of most use to managers. In addition, managers should limit the number of factors which they and their staff measure when they start.

Two types of measures for services

Quantitative and qualitative methods complement each other. Quantitative methods aim for 'objective facts' and unambiguous measures, for instance how long patients have to wait for a certain operation, how many times the telephone rings before it is answered or how long customers have to wait in the cash point queue. They can be used to measure service availability (opening hours and waiting times), and precision (number of errors per 1000 transactions, number of delays, and time delays), and may be used at different times of the day, week, or year.

Qualitative measurements do not have the same precision, but give managers information that they cannot get from quantitative methods. Qualitative methods help us to understand people's expectations and requirements: they are 'meaning-rich' and can direct attention to causes of or solutions to quality problems. Service managers need both types of methods because customers' assessment of the quality of services depends on relations between people, as well as more easily measured factors such as waiting time.

Qualitative measurement involves listening, studying, analysing and interpreting customers' statements. Customers often do not have readily-formed views about quality and need help to reflect on and to articulate what is important to them. Qualitative measures help to understand customer expectations and perceptions of the quality of services. Later in the chapter we give examples of both qualitative and quantitative studies.

An increasingly common method of quality measurement is the focus group interview. This entails gathering a number of people, usually between six and ten, to discuss and ask questions about a particular field. The idea is that the members of the group will inspire and stimulate each other so that different views of the same phenomenon will emerge. The method has the advantage over traditional interviews of reaching several people at the same time. People find it easier to give and explore their views in a group. A disadvantage is that there may be people who find it easier to express themselves in an individual interview. Although skilful leadership is called for to use this method, we have found that managers and their staff can use it with benefit as part of a service development programme.

Steps for developing measures

Defining quality is the starting point for measuring it. To measure customer-perceived quality, the customers must give content to the concept of quality. This is best done by clarifying with customers the key quality factors for them, expressed in the customers' own words as far as possible. Examples of quality factors are *reliability, trust* and *recovery*. A cost-effective way to ascertain these customer-based quality factors is from focus group interviews. We have found it possible for service staff to use a combination of focus group interviews and critical incident technique to define quality factors.

The next step is to get customers to specify the quality factors in terms of 'variables'. In practice four to five variables per quality factor are needed to give specific aspects for designing a questionnaire. The variables should be formulated as far as possible in the customers' own words. Again, focus group interviews are useful for collecting data for this purpose.

The third phase is to get customers to indicate the importance of the different variables, for example on a scale of one to five. This helps to understand the customers' view of the 'ideal service'. The fourth phase is to get the customers to rate the service at present. One way is to use a questionnaire based on the variables that emerged in phase two. The results of this measurement give the information for setting quality goals grounded in the customer-based quality factors and variables. More practical details and examples of these phases may be found in Øvretveit (1993a).

In some services it is appropriate to formulate quality goals once a year at the same time as preparing the company's annual budget. This helps to control and evaluate both quality and financial results for the same period (e.g. two-monthly) and to integrate quality and financial data, which in turn helps managers to take a cost-conscious approach to quality and decide investment priorities.

We now turn to some of the pitfalls and problems which managers need to know about in using measures, in developing them, and in commissioning others to develop measurement systems.

DIFFICULTIES IN MEASURING QUALITY

Many measures of service quality are too-costly, too-complicated or too-late for most managers. Many are worse than useless because they direct attention to the wrong things – often the service survives because managers and staff ignore the measures.

(Øvretveit, 1993a)

In our experience, many service measurement systems are flawed and often not used by managers and staff. This is often because those designing the system and carrying out measurement do not know enough about what is to be measured, the purpose, and how the results are to be used. A common example is questionnaires based on wrong assumptions about which quality factors are the most important for the customers. The survey may be technically impeccable but be measuring the 'wrong things'. In the Appendix we give examples of customer-perceived quality measures which focus on the most central quality factors from the customer's viewpoint.

A second problem is that managers do not measure quality throughout the service chain. Internal services should be measured as well as the quality of services and goods purchased from suppliers and other partners. Quality problems may be 'imported' and they are not noticeable unless the quality of the input is measured.

A third difficulty is that measuring customer perceptions may of itself increase expectations. Measurement entails risks. In Chapter 4 we showed how the customer relates the expected quality to the perceived quality of a service. For this and other reasons managers should not measure quality unless they are really prepared to take action on the findings. Too often measurement is seen as an end in itself, and as a way of avoiding making real changes but of giving the impression of doing something about quality.

A fourth pitfall is too much measurement. There is a danger of tiring both customers and staff with too frequent questionnaires. Asking the same people to answer the same questions on repeated occasions reduces their motivation to answer correctly. The most common mistake is asking too many questions, which also make analysis and interpretation over-complex: the important gets lost in the detail. It is better to investigate what is important first, using focus groups or other techniques, rather than using a questionnaire for this purpose. The worst example we have encountered is a questionnaire from a company selling oil-drilling equipment. The form was 30 pages long with several hundred questions. The company also required the respondents to climb up the drilling rig to note the make and serial number of a large number of parts. Customers confirmed our view that the message this questionnaire sent was not that the company was eager for feedback, but that it had no idea what was important to customers, no respect for them, no sense of the value of their time, and that managers had given up all responsibility for measurement to specialists who had never met a customer.

QUALITY GOALS

Many service companies lay down standards and frequently measure their performance against them. Standards are reference points for measurement, but are also goals to be attained. Defining usable standards is a difficult and skilled task, as is setting the level. They should be clearly defined so that they are not misunderstood and they should be easy to measure. Standards must be based on knowledge of customer utility. If they are lacking or unclear, measurements may be the first step in establishing them.

Formulating measurable quality standards and goals and achieving them is not always enough to satisfy the customer. A large company regularly measured the length of time customers had to wait before the switchboard answered. The results showed that the goal of short minimal waiting times for customers had been achieved. The company could have revised the time standard, but fortunately it conducted a survey of the customers: customers were indeed satisfied with the short waiting times at the switchboard but the problems lay elsewhere. The person they sought did not answer, nobody knew where he was or when he would be back, and they were not connected with the right person when they explained their business to the switchboard. Simply noting that standards are being adhered to is not enough.

The following are examples of easily measurable standards and goals drawn up by an airline:

- 90 per cent of all telephone calls are to be answered within 30 seconds
- 90 per cent of the passengers are to be checked in within three minutes after their arrival
- 80 per cent of the flights are to be no more than 15 minutes late
- waiting times for luggage are to be no longer than 10 minutes between the first and last passenger
- complaints about the food should be no more than 3 per cent
- complaints about the staff should be no more than 1 per cent.

A goal of zero faults is often given for procedure standards. An example is air traffic control at an airport, where the goal is 100 per cent of take-offs and landings should be accident-free, or in health services where the goal is zero poor outcomes. In other businesses where deviations do not have such dramatic effects, a zero fault strategy can have positive effects for attitudes to the quality of the work. Although some TQM experts would disagree with us, we believe that managers need to decide whether, for some areas in their service, zero fault standards would be unattainable and demoralizing. It may be better to establish attainable standards so long as everyone accepts that these are to be frequently revised.

QUALITY MEASUREMENT: A NEVER-ENDING PROCESS

Measuring quality is not repeating a questionnaire every year, but a frequent and changing activity. In addition to different routine measures, managers and their staff need to use special measures at different times when investigating the causes of quality problems. The questions which service managers need to ask are :

- Why should we measure quality?
- What should we measure?
- How should we measure it?
- When should we measure it?
- Who should measure quality?
- How should we use the results?

We have emphasized two issues in particular: identifying what should be measured, i.e. determining what quality factors are most important, and designing the measuring instrument for gathering and analysing the data.

Answering the first question, why measure quality, entails clarifying the purpose of the measurement. The purpose may simply be to discover the quality level of the company's services, before or after making changes. Another purpose is to help establish clear goals and standards for quality. The higher order purpose is to offer customers the right quality: to do this we may need to measure not only the quality level of the service, but also the level which customers expect and desire. Another purpose of quality measurement is to identify and localize recurrent quality problems. Managers will also find that measurement gives staff feedback about their efforts and shows that quality improvement produces results.

The question of how measurements are to be made depends on what is to be measured. For certain measurements quantitative methods are most useful, whereas other measurements require qualitative methods. Many quality factors, such as waiting times, number of faults or complaints, can be measured by means of simple, quantitative methods. But to gain an understanding of customers' quality perceptions, sophisticated qualitative methods may be necessary.

The question of when to measure has to be decided from case to case.

Sometimes, measurements must be spread to reflect fluctuating numbers, such as varying waiting times. Sometimes, it is a matter of measuring the quality perceptions of different groups of customers at a time when they are willing to talk or complete questionnaires. In general, measurement must be as early as possible so that the results can be used for improving quality or preventing poor quality.

When considering who should do the measuring, there are advantages to those using the measures doing the measurement, and perhaps designing the measures with specialist help. Again it depends on the purpose, but we have found that involving staff in designing and carrying-out measurement increases the accuracy and use of the measures. Note also that information technology makes it possible to programme-in automatic data capture for routine collection and reporting: for example switchboard response times, and health service electronic patient records.

For measurements to have an effect on the business the information must be fed back to where it belongs, to those who can use the information to improve quality, and in a form which they can understand. Quality measures also need to be used to assess and reward staff performance.

The following checklist can be used by managers to judge their service quality measurement system.

CHECKLIST – Does your system meet these requirements?

A cost-effective service measurement system will:
- focus staff attention on a few critical measures which they can influence
- give regular feedback to staff at each level of organization to enable them to make ongoing corrections before problems arise
- take little staff or management time to record data, or draw on existing data collection methods
- suggest or direct attention on aspects of service activity which need to be changed or adjusted to improve quality
- be linked to staff performance appraisal, incentives and rewards
- balance customer, professional and management quality measures of input process and output in ways that are appropriate for the type of service at its stage of quality evolution

- be developed and revised with the involvement of staff
- be reviewed and revised to meet changing business conditions
- measure aspects of quality which are important to the business strategy.

From Øvretveit (1993a, p.76)

EXAMPLES OF QUALITY MEASUREMENT

In this section we give practical examples of the principles which we outlined above. We summarize two studies carried out by CTF (Thomasson, 1989; Olsen, 1992). We give an account of the 'Servqual Instrument' (Zeithaml *et al.*, 1990) and Linjeflyg's (Swedish domestic airline) service barometer and SIPU's (National Swedish Staff Training Institute) quality barometers. We also provide a brief description of benchmarking as a method of measuring oneself against others. In addition we show how the Malcolm Baldridge National Quality Award criteria can be used to diagnose the current quality status of a service.

Total Quality Index (TQIX)

In Chapters 1 and 4 we described quality in terms of satisfied customers, satisfied staff and satisfied owners. Øvretveit (1992a, 1993a) and others also emphasize assessing and measuring quality from different perspectives, not just from the customer's perspective. Telia (Swedish Telecom) has devised a quality measurement system – Total Quality Index, TQIX – which is based on satisfying these three groups. Figure 7.1 shows how TQIX is constructed.

TQIX is based on six factors which are linked with the three interest groups. Two factors, *return on capital* and *income*, concern the economy and are linked to the owners. Two factors, *customer service* and *network performance*, concern service and are linked to the customers and two factors, *leadership* and *involvement*, concern job satisfaction and are linked to the staff. Each factor is divided into a number of performance indicators, 36 in all. In their turn, these are weighted from 1 to 12.

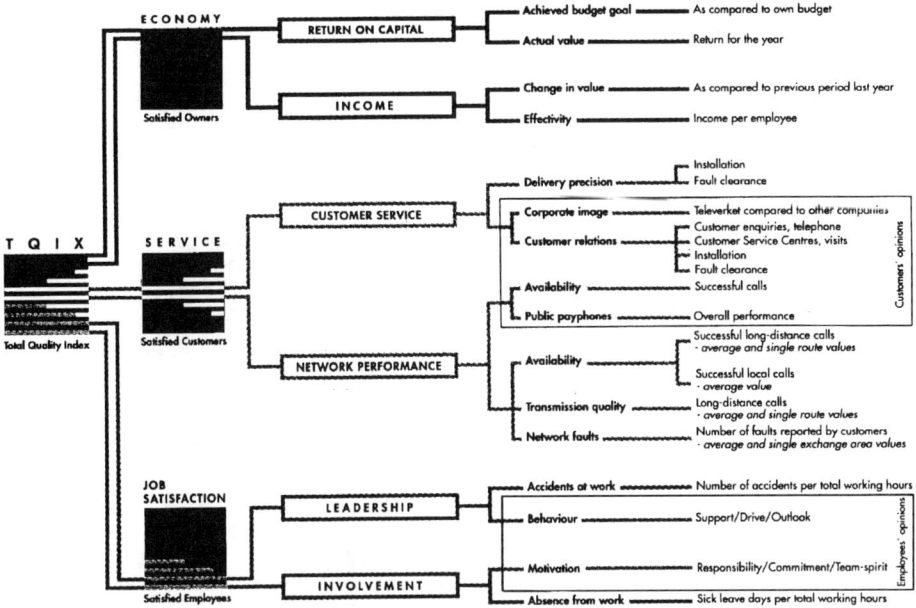

FIGURE 7.1   Total Quality Index used by Telia

TQIX is intended for use in each of Telia's 20 regions. The results are given in points according to the formula given below. The weight of each area (economy, service and job satisfaction) is its total number of awardable quality points, i.e. the sum of the maximum number of awardable quality points for each of its performance indicators. Each performance indicator is given a maximum number of points. Together the points for each indicator give the total value for each area: economy (30 points), service (45 points) and job satisfaction (25 points). That service has the highest number of points indicates that the customers are valued most highly of the three groups.

Figure 7.2 shows how to calculate the quality points awarded. The three areas of economy, service and job satisfaction correspond to the three main goals, satisfied owners, satisfied customers and satisfied staff. These are the targets of Swedish Telecom's concept of total quality. The three areas are interconnected and interdependent. The distribution of weights between the areas reflects Swedish Telecom's current priorities.

Example:

Measured value = 78%
Points-awarding interval = 50 - 100%
Weight = 4

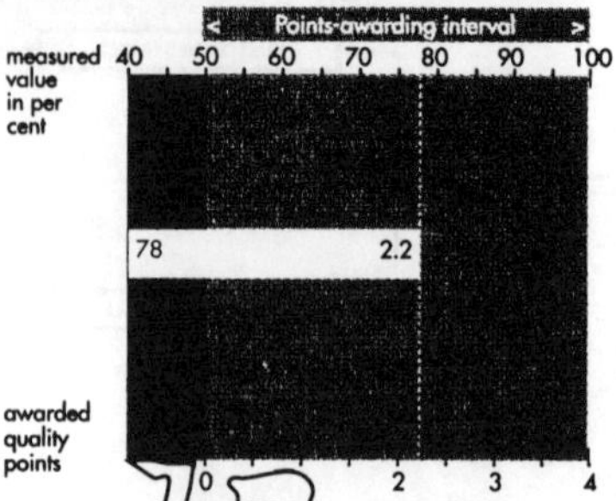

By inserting these values in the formula, the calculated number of quality points awarded = 2.2

The dotted line in the graph shows the relation between the measured value and the corresponding number of quality points awarded.

All measured values that fall within the points-awarding interval score quality points

$$\text{Awarded Quality Points} = \frac{a-b}{c-b} \times d = \frac{78-50}{100-50} \times 4 = \frac{28}{50} \times 4 = 2.2$$

(a) = measured value   (c) = upper limit of the points-awarding interval
(b) = lower limit of the points-awarding interval   (d) = weight

FIGURE 7.2   TQIX – How to Calculate the Quality Points

Other companies use similar quality measurement systems. They are generally based on a number of quality factors, which are then divided into a number of variables, each of which is weighted. Some companies define the quality factors themselves. Our experience suggests that the three interested parties, customers, staff and owners, should be allowed to express the factors and variables in their own words and determine the weightings.

A similar approach was taken by Øvretveit (1991a) in developing a quality system for primary health and social services care teams in the United Kingdom. In this case the customers were clients, patients and carers, the staff were professionals defining professional quality factors, and the 'owners' were managers who incorporated public regulations and requirements into their key factors. The system is now in everyday use and routinely revised, according to changes in priorities for each group.

Customers' perception of quality in the services offered by garages

One service industry which has been at the centre of media attention is the garage or car repair shop. In Sweden this industry has been scrutinized and tested and the results published in the press and broadcast on the radio and television. Reasons for this public interest is that customers find it difficult to assess some aspects of the service 'offering', and suspect that the quality of work is not as high as it should be. Faulty or poor repairs may not become apparent until the car has been driven some distance.

One reason for our interest in this sector is the combination of service and product quality. The material components are the parts to be replaced or installed. In addition the garage provides conventional services in answering the initial request from the customer, diagnosing the fault, agreeing the work, setting the price, and finally delivering the car or dealing with the complaint.

We have carried out quality measurement studies in Sweden and the United Kingdom in this sector. We describe below a Swedish study of customers' perceptions of the quality of repair and maintenance (*core service*) and in other less central activities (*peripheral service*) Thomasson (1989). The UK studies are described in Øvretveit (1993a), and are concerned with measurement systems which include customer perceptions, but also measure professional quality and payment systems linked to a composite quality index. We note general points from both sets of research.

The aim of the Swedish study was to describe how customers perceive the service offer made by garages. Service quality is a multi-faceted concept, and the customers' perception is one aspect of quality. The empirical part of the study involved interviews with customers, selected via cars left for repair or maintenance at three garages: a specialist garage (dealing with only one make of car), a general garage with some specialization and an independent garage located at a petrol station. Customers with privately registered cars and company cars were selected.

Method

The study illustrates a qualitative approach, using a 'phenomenographic method', which aims to describe how people perceive the world around them (Marton, 1978). This approach distinguishes between how things are and how they are perceived by an individual, but does not assume that there is true or false, or right or wrong perception. The interview technique used is an open one, in that the respondent is allowed to develop a personal view of the phenomenon studied.

The selection of respondents was carried out in two stages to get a broad spectrum of garage customers' views on quality. In the first stage different types of garage were selected in order to reach different customers. This resulted in the choice of the three garages indicated above, based on Karlsson *et al.* (1985). The second stage was to select a number of customers at each of the three garages, using a set of variables. The selection of customers was crucial for the results since the aim was to obtain a large number of variations in customers' perception of quality (Eneroth, 1984; Glaser and Strauss, 1967).

Analysis and results

The aim of the phenomenographic method is not to generalize the perceptions which a number of individuals have of a certain phenomenon. The analysis is geared rather to finding variations in these perceptions and to systematizing and categorizing them. This requires several very close examinations of the material. The categories that are initially established must be subjected to scrutiny and related to the material, and as a result perhaps reformulated. The analysis is integrated with the material and both aspects interact in an ongoing dialogue. It is a question of describing the multiplicity of conceptions but also of indicating the common ground in customers' perceptions of quality.

Customers' perception of quality

The analysis was intended to show variations in customers' perception of what is quality in the repair and maintenance of cars and in customers' contacts with the garage. Looking for variations in the way a phenomenon is perceived has an educational purpose. The number of people holding such and such a view is of less interest; the value lies rather in a clearer understanding of the fact that the phenomenon may be perceived in different ways.

Findings

The overall category for describing quality was CONFIDENCE. Quality means that the customer has confidence in the garage. This overall category is based on five sub-categories:

1 *Honesty/reliability/responsibility.* Quality means that the customer can rely on the garage to do what it is paid for, to keep its promises and to rectify any mistakes it may have made.
2 *Personal contact.* Quality means having contact with one person at the garage, a person who is able to accept responsibility for solving the customer's difficulties with his or her car.
3 *Accessibility/willingness.* Quality means that the garage is accessible, both regards location and hours of business, and that the staff are willing and able to help the customer when necessary.
4 *Attitude.* Quality means that the customer is treated in the manner he or she expects.
5 *Competence.* Quality means that the garage is competent enough to repair and maintain the customer's car and to handle customer relations well.

Further details

To illustrate the method and the type of data it can provide, the following

QUALITY OF SERVICE ●

gives a more detailed description of the five categories. We also give these descriptions because there is reason to believe that some items would be similar in other services with a professional component, and with a product/service mix.

Confidence

There are two explanations as to why confidence is given such a central position; firstly, every interview contained some form of statement implying that quality means having confidence in the garage. Secondly, confidence is built up over time with the help of the other categories. Confidence can be related to a particular individual or to the garage as a whole. Confidence is based on the ability of the garage to repair and maintain cars and to handle customer relations in a highly competent fashion. Confidence is gradually built up in contacts between the customer and the garage and it is reinforced reciprocally in that the customer's behaviour affects the way the company handles customer relations.

Honesty/reliability/responsibility

Honesty, reliability and responsibility may relate to different phenomena and have different meanings. In the interview material, the perceptions of the three concepts were very close to each other, the concepts sometimes overlapping. On occasion, different nuances appeared but the differences were so small that they did not justify separating the concepts.

The customer's lack of knowledge about the need for repair and maintenance and an inability to control what has been done on the car contribute to the feeling that he or she may be easily cheated. The customer's insecurity can be reduced by providing clear and detailed information about what needs to be done to the car and what has been done and why. Similarly, the individual items on the invoice have to be explained. It is also important for the customer to feel that he or she can come back and discuss any faults in the work, get them put right and be compensated for any inconvenience.

Personal contact

The customer wants contact with a person at the garage who knows both the customer and the car. This person then becomes a sort of 'family doctor' for the car to whom the customer can turn for help with both acute and chronic problems. The 'doctor' must be able to adjust the repairs to the car's condition and to the customer's financial situation. He must not discriminate against a customer or exploit a customer's ignorance. The less a customer knows about cars, the more important it is for the contact person to explain what needs to be done. Afterwards, he should go through what has been done and explain any discrepancies in relation to the original agreement.

There are some general lessons for other services in ensuring one contact person. The 'contact person' should be somebody who:

- knows the customer
- listens to and believes what the customer says
- knows the customer's car
- helps to make a diagnosis
- explains what needs to be done
- explains what has been done and why
- explains the various items on the invoice.

The contact person should, if possible, be the person who actually works on the car. If he is not that person, it is vitally important that he is able to communicate the customer's message to the mechanic.

Accessibility/willingness

There are many aspects to accessibility: that the garage has the 'right' location in relation to the customer's home or workplace; that the car can be left and picked up at times that suit the customer; that the customer can get in touch with the garage by telephone, to book a time, to discuss a problem, to obtain an estimate, etc; that there is someone for the customer to talk to when he gets to the garage. Good accessibility is often crucial if the customer is to have a high opinion of the garage's readiness to help, but it is not sufficient. Sometimes poor accessibility, in that the location of the garage is unsuitable from the customer's viewpoint, can be compensated by the fact that the staff are prepared to put themselves out for the customer.

Another important factor here is whether the staff are able and willing to help the customer in an emergency. It is in this type of situation that the company's willingness is really put to the test.

Attitude

The customer must not be discriminated against, for example, because of age or (lack of) knowledge. If the customer does not know how cars work, an explanation must be provided in language the customer understands. The reception a customer gets at a garage may be crucial for his or her decision whether to use the garage or not. It was clear from several of the interviews that customers decided to leave a garage and never come back purely because they felt the garage had a negative attitude towards them. For example, two respondents said that they felt they were 'invisible' to the staff at a large garage.

Competence

Competence relates to the knowledge and experience of the staff and their ability and willingness to use them in their relationship with the customer. There are two types of competence, *technical competence*, which covers the work to be done on the car, and *functional competence*, which has to do with the competence shown by the staff in customer relations (cf. Grönroos, 1983).

The image of small and large garages

Using this method we found that people linked their perception of quality to their attitude to large and small garages respectively. Again we think that there may be lessons for other services from our findings. The image of large garages is that they have, or at least are able to attain, a higher standard of technical quality than small garages. They are seen as less reliable, more expensive and less ready to put themselves out for the customer and solve any acute problems. Large garages are perceived as being impersonal and thus customers feel anonymous. Customers have much less confidence in large garages than in small ones.

The image of small garages is that they are less capable of attaining a high technical standard than large garages. They compensate for this to a certain extent with wider experience and greater responsibility in their work. Small garages are less negligent and cheat less than large garages and they put themselves out for their customers much more – according to the customers. Customers have much greater confidence in small garages than in large ones.

Concluding remarks

The study found that garages have a poor image. Customers' lack of confidence in large garages was based on the feeling that they can be cheated. The combination of not being able to check the work and the belief that they are paying a high price for the service gives customers the feeling of being manipulated. Good personal relations can minimize this suspicion. At a large garage the customer feels that both he and his car are anonymous, whereas at a small garage there is a greater chance of establishing personal relations with those working there, which results in a gradual increase in confidence.

Suspicion leads customers to want some assurance that they are not being cheated. They get this assurance from long-term personal contacts and through the willingness of the staff to treat customers in a manner they find acceptable and to put themselves out for customers and solve their problems. Customers perceive small garages to be better at this than large ones.

Quality in banking services

Background

Banking services have received much criticism in recent years, in the United Kingdom, and in many other countries. We describe a study of a Swedish bank below. We outline this study as an example of critical incident technique which we mentioned in Chapter 5. Critical incidents are situations which customers experience as particularly positive or particularly negative. The critical incident technique (CIT) is particularly suited to the co-service process and is discussed in Bitner *et al.* (1985, 1990), Andersson (1985), Edvardsson (1988c, 1992), Olsen (1992) and Øvretveit (1991a, 1993a). The method involves analysing critical incidents to reveal the cause, course and result of the incident.

Aim and method

The aim of the study was to understand better how private customers perceive problems in banking services. Olsen (1992) interviewed more than 300 bank customers and his report is based on 272 episodes which were seen as problematic by the customers.

Results

The study shows there is a clear link between problems the customer experiences, not least how they are handled, and the customer's perception of and relation to the bank. Olsen identified 17 overarching categories of core problems, which were linked to either the design, production or process of the service (Gummesson *et al.*, 1990; Gummesson, 1991d). These links gave the basis for ordering the problems as follows:

Design quality
- readiness
- communication, coordination with other banks
- mass communication, profile measures
- routines and policies, etc.
- system, technology
- education and training, recruitment
- conditions.

Production quality
- the meticulousness of the staff

- the competence, expert knowledge of the staff
- back-office
- customer (carelessness, lack of knowledge, etc.)
- external factors.

Process quality
- the ability of the staff to interact
- the ability of the staff to solve problems
- the customer's actions
- the behaviour of other customers.

The categories are presented in detail with the aid of illustrative examples and quotations from interviews with customers, etc. By studying these the reader can form an opinion of the breadth of variation in the critical incidents and how the various incidents are perceived by the customers.

Example 1 (negative outcome)
Concept class: design quality
Overarching category: readiness
Sub-category: prepared for computer breakdowns
The customer went to the bank at lunchtime when there were long queues and the computer system had broken down. It took a long time and people became impatient. After a while someone in the queue asked if people who wanted to make payments could do so and after a few minutes this was agreed. After further discussion it was agreed that people could take out small sums. The customer felt it was particularly irritating that the staff did not have any emergency measures in readiness.

Example 2 (neutral/positive and negative outcome respectively)
Concept class: production quality
Overarching category: back-office
Sub-category: transactions, etc.
The customer and her husband asked for a statement of account from the cash dispenser and it showed that the account was overdrawn by Swedish kronor 26 000, which was a complete shock to them. 'When we contacted

the bank, they checked the computer and found the error.' The bank had deducted payment of a loan twice. 'They were very obliging and pleasant and everything sorted itself out ... they thought it was embarrassing ... to compensate, they gave us a little present – a key ring, card game and small things like that.' The incident did not affect the customer's relationship with the bank.

Another customer received a statement which included two entries she did not understand. The first was a transfer to her account and the second a transfer from her account. The transfer from her account was somewhat larger. The customer called the bank and asked what it was, but they knew nothing about it. She had to contact another department. Eventually it appeared that the bank had wrongly credited the customer's account. This had been discovered but the wrong amount had been transferred. After this serious error and all the trouble it caused the customer, she did not even receive an apology and the incident had a negative effect on her relationship with the bank.

The aggregated material

Customers in the study felt they were responsible for the problem in one case out of ten. Most problems were related to the design of the service. More than half the customers obtained no solution to the problem they experienced. Only one person in five had a problem solved immediately or on first contact with the bank. The customer's relationship with the bank deteriorated as a result of the problem in more than half the episodes studied. More than one in five customers changed banks as a result of the incident. Only one case in twenty resulted in a reinforcement of the relationship with the bank. In all these cases the bank played an active role in solving the customer's problem.

Implications for other services

Negative critical incidents occur even in the best companies. The consequences may be serious, with a loss of customers and a deterioration in image. This study gives further support for our point in Chapter 5: if they are properly handled, the company's contact staff can still save the company's face and in certain cases even improve the customer's relationship with the company.

- Negative critical incidents must be avoided. The design of the service is particularly important for prevention.
- When problems do occur, everything must be done to satisfy the customer. It is important that front-line staff have the necessary knowledge to handle complaints and are authorized to put the fault right quickly. This must be done in a personal and professional manner. The worst possible scenario is for new faults to occur while the complaint is being dealt with.

Conclusions and experiences

With the aid of CIT, it is possible to collect data which capture aspects of the relationship with the customer and 'get inside' their understanding of service quality. In service blueprinting, negative critical incidents may be equated with failpoints, critical parts of the service. In other words, the service must be designed around them. In quality function deployment, the function of the critical incidents is first and foremost to identify the customer's needs and expectations. In the strategy and organization for services approach (Dale and Wooler, 1990), positive critical incidents may be used to identify various elements/features characterizing a well-performed service.

The study demonstrated one way of tailoring the critical incident technique to service quality research, to handle the rich information gained from interviews about concrete events. It is possible to use this method with success in most types of company, and staff can easily be trained to use it. It is possible to classify the accounts that have been collected in different ways, which permit both static and dynamic analysis. Apart from acting as input for the design of the service package, the data may be used in:

- gap analysis/inconsistency analysis
- training and education (role play, conflict handling, customer contacts, etc.)
- recruitment (critical staff characteristics)

- development of quality goals and policies
- design of a reward system.

Servqual

We noted in Chapter 4 some of the findings on which the Servqual method was based. It was developed by Leonard L. Berry, A. Parasuraman and Valerie A. Zeithaml, and is described in Zeithaml *et al.* (1990). We mention it here because it provides one way of measuring service with a ready-made instrument. We have argued for developing service-specific measures, but sometimes there is not the time or money to do this: in these situations managers should consider using Servqual. Detailed criticisms of the method are given in Øvretveit (1992b, 1993a), and an example of its use in health services is given in Babakus and Mangold (1992).

The method is based on the five quality dimensions *tangibles, reliability, responsiveness, assurance* and *empathy* (Parasuraman *et al.*, 1988). There are two parts to the measuring process: the first step is to establish the customers' perception of an ideal service and the second to measure the customers' perception of the services provided by a specific company. The measuring procedure requires the customers to react to 22 statements based on the above five quality dimensions. There are four or five statements for each quality dimension. The respondents are requested to react to the statements on a scale with seven intervals ranging from 'fully agree' to 'do not agree at all'. First, the expected quality is measured and, then, the perceived quality. In order to get more information, customers can also be asked to indicate which of the quality factors are most important, e.g. by selecting and ranking three in order of importance.

In the first measurement the seven-grade scale produces an 'ideal profile' for each dimension. The profile of customer-perceived quality obtained in the second measurement can then be contrasted with the 'ideal'. Deviations between expected quality and perceived quality can then be studied. The variables which show the biggest deviations and which the customers see as most important when assessing quality provide guidelines for quality improvement.

According to the authors, Servqual can be used in many different ways in various kinds of service industry. Servqual is most valuable if it is used periodically. In that way, changes in quality can be registered and measures taken to improve quality. Both customers and staff can be included. The main weakness is that its general quality factors are not relevant to all types of service. For further information about the design of Servqual and how it can be used, we refer readers to Zeithaml *et al.* (1990).

Linjeflyg's service barometer

An example of a simple quality measure is Linjeflyg's 'service barometer' (Linjeflyg used to be the major Swedish domestic airline company. It is now a part of SAS). It consists of regular measurements of customers' quality assessments of Linjeflyg as a whole and the service at various airports in the country. The measurements are taken several times a year by means of a questionnaire which is handed out to selected passengers on certain flights. The material is processed and analysed by an independent research institute, which also assisted in devising the questionnaire.

Passengers indicate on a scale of one to five how they perceive the service in 12 different areas, from the ticket office to the service-mindedness of the cabin crew. The customer barometer shows which airport is best according to the passengers and how they assess the various activities. The results of a particular measurement are distributed to the staff involved in the middle of the following week. The aim is to make rapid improvements, and give quick feedback on a questionnaire which staff were involved in distributing.

The material is easy to analyse with the results being shown for each airport and the different activities at each airport but also aggregated for the whole company. The distribution makes a form of internal benchmarking possible, in that each airport can be compared with the best airport on a number of points and also with the average for all airports.

Benchmarking

An increasingly common way of 'measuring' one's own quality achievements is to compare them with others. The method is called benchmarking and the idea is to measure oneself against someone else who is exceptionally good in a particular area. It is not just a matter of comparing oneself with competitors, in many cases it is better to find companies with other lines of business. Zairi's (1992) view is:

> there is a dual challenge facing senior managers:
> (1) To instigate benchmarking so that competitive targets can be achieved;
> (2) To ensure that the practice of benchmarking is spread throughout all the activities and business operations.

Zairi emphasizes the strong link between TQM and benchmarking. TQM is an internal ongoing process of improvement with zero defects as the ideal. Benchmarking is a way of achieving the best possible external performance in relation to one's competitors in a whole range of areas. In both cases the plan–do–check–act cycle is used in development work.

Xerox was a pioneer in using benchmarking. The company defines benchmarking as 'the continuous process of measuring products, services and practices against the company's toughest competitors and against companies recognized as industry leaders'. Xerox has a multi-stage approach to benchmarking. First, a decision about 'what' is to be compared: which products, services, or processes are relevant. Then, suitable companies for comparison are selected. They may be competitors or non-competitors. They may even be units within the same group. The main point is that they are considered leaders in the field in which the comparison is to be made. The next stage is data collection, and then, using comparisons between external and internal data, quality levels are set as targets within the chosen field. The analysis shows how big the differences are between one's own performance and those of the company selected for comparison.

When Xerox started to use benchmarking in 1984, 14 performance factors were involved; these have now been increased to 240. Some of the companies Xerox uses for comparison are American Express (invoicing and demand routines), Ford (production layout), General Electric (robots), Mary

Cay Cosmetic (stocks and distribution) and Florida Power & Light (the quality process) (see, 'How Xerox does benchmarking', *The Quality Executive*, No.10, February 1991). For a more detailed discussion of benchmarking we refer readers to Zairi (1992), Porter (1985) and Camp (1989).

MALCOLM BALDRIGE NATIONAL QUALITY AWARD

The improvement of quality in products and the improvement of quality in services – these are national priorities as never before.

(George Bush)

The Malcolm Baldrige National Quality Award is a prestigious quality prize given annually in the United States. The winners of the award use the fact in their marketing: it is regarded as a valuable asset as competition for the award is tough. We mention this award because we have found that the framework and criteria are useful for a variety of purposes, in particular for measuring quality producing activities in a company and the result of these. Øvretveit (1993a, 1993c) argues that the award criteria and measurement process help managers to focus on the key areas which produce long-term and sustained quality improvements. Øvretveit (1992c) describes computer software and a workshop process used for this purpose.

In assessing a company for an award a number of experienced and specially appointed examiners evaluate and measure, on the basis of a number of quality factors, the level of quality in various parts of the company. The companies competing for the award are awarded points for a number of variables which together reflect the individual company's total quality level. Points are awarded in seven examination categories (1992 Award Criteria):

		Points
1.	Leadership	90
2.	Information and Analysis	80
3.	Strategic Quality Planning	60
4.	Human Resource Development and Management	150
5.	Management of Process Quality	140
6.	Quality and Operational Result	180
7.	Customer Focus and Satisfaction	300
	Total:	1000

Each category is divided into a varying number of sub-categories. For instance, category 4, Human Resource Development and Management, has the following sub-categories:

		Points
4:1	Human Resource Management	20
4:2	Employee Involvement	40
4:3	Employee Education and Training	40
4:4	Employee Performance and Recognition	25
4:5	Employee Well-Being and Morale	25
	Total:	150

Øvretveit (1993a, 1993c) describes how the award framework can be used by a manager or management team to assess the current quality status of the organization, as a basis for developing and monitoring a quality strategy. In the United Kingdom IBM now uses the award framework for these purposes. In addition to internal measurement uses, Øvretveit (1993a, 1993c, 1993d) also compares a variety of award frameworks which purchasers of services can use to audit providers, including the European Foundation for Quality Management's (EFQM) European quality award (based on Baldridge), the British BS 5750, an adaptation of BS 5750 for health services, and the Brunel University SOS system (Dale and Wooler, 1988), and the WelQual system (Øvretveit, 1992a).

GUIDELINES FOR QUALITY MEASUREMENT

Quality measurement in service businesses has so far focused on customers' views. We believe that it is important to start quality measurement with the customer, but that this should be complemented with other internal measures. These include the quality of support services in the service chain, as well as professional and management quality.

Measurement serves several purposes. One is to provide guidelines for improvements. Measures need to give indications for managers and staff about the causes of quality problems and solutions. They also need to reveal where there are the greatest shortcomings in order to set priorities for improvement and investment. Another purpose is to measure the results of changes and give staff feedback on the effect of their actions.

The following summarizes key points to take into account when measuring quality in a service company:

1 Involve staff in designing measures and putting them into use. Explain to all those concerned why the measurements are being made and create acceptance for the methods; otherwise the measurements may be viewed as an instrument for management to control staff, rather than as an instrument for staff and managers to use to prevent poor quality.

2 Define exactly what is to be measured. Base measures on the company's definition of quality, and, for customer quality, find out from customers what they think are the key quality factors.

3 Start on a small scale and do not measure 'everything' at once. Keep it simple: complicated measures can cost more than the savings or extra income which they help to create.

4 Choose the methods of measurement according to what is to be measured. Use qualitative methods to understand and measure what people think and feel. Use both quantitative and qualitative data.

5 Appoint someone to be responsible for measurements, and for sharing with managers the responsibility for analysing, interpreting and turning the results into improvements in the company.

6 Measure both internal and external services. Do not measure something if you really cannot influence it.

7 Make frequent measurements so that the information is always up to date. A well-known chain of restaurants makes a survey of customer-perceived quality once a week. In one hotel chain at least five guests are interviewed at every hotel every day.

8 Make the results visible to the customers and the staff – graphs should be updated regularly. Present the results in a simple and comprehensible manner. Do not talk about median values, statistical significance or weighted mean values. It is easier to understand simple messages such as 'nine out of ten customers think that ...'.

9 Consider using quality award criteria like the Baldrige award to undertake a comprehensive assessment of quality. Awards can be used to decide where to make investments in the company to improve quality, and to compare the quality status of the company over time.

We give examples of questionnaires which can be used in various types of quality measurement in the Appendix. Øvretveit (1993a) reproduces a simple general-purpose questionnaire used by managers in different services to get feedback from their internal customers.

Service design for innovation and quality

One of the key service-quality challenges for the 1990s is service design. Service design is a form of architecture that involves processes rather than bricks and mortar. The idea is to design high quality into the service system from the outset, to consider and respond to customers' expectations in designing each element of the service.

The quality of virtually any service depends on how well myriad elements function together in the same service process to meet customers' expectations. These elements include people who perform various services that relate to the overall service, equipment that supports these performances, and the physical environment in which the services are performed.

(Zeithaml et al., 1990, pp.157–8)

This chapter shows that service design is critical for both quality and innovation, and describes techniques for design suited to services.

Quality by design is building in quality at the development and design stages. Quality defects are often caused by wrongly-designed production processes and delivery systems. According to Juran (1992), 92 per cent of the quality defects in manufacturing companies can be attributed to faults in the system. In the service sector, it is estimated that system-related quality defects account for 70–80 per cent of quality problems.

Many new services are not designed. Our experience is consistent with Scheuing and Johnson's (1989) conclusion that new services 'often come about as the result of intuition, personal fancy or inspiration, availability of capacity, or competitive action. Rarely are new product ideas subjected to careful, thorough scrutiny.' Our ability to design, or redesign services in a systematic way is far less developed than our ability to design both goods and goods production processes. Manufacturing companies have well-established concepts and methods for designing goods and manufacturing processes. Furthermore these methods are accepted in the business and used widely every day. However, these approaches do not take service characteristics into consideration – we need models and methods for designing co-services and service creation processes, and we need to make it easier for managers and specialists to use these methods to design and redesign services.

In this chapter we give a total quality service management approach to service design. We give examples of the approach, and illustrate it with a study from Swedish Telecom. The chapter starts by explaining why service design is important in TQM and defines some of the central terms of TQSM: service design, service concept and co-service system. Then we discuss strategies for service development and the process of service development itself. In the fifth section we summarize two techniques for designing services and in the sixth describe a process of phases for systematically designing a service.

WHY SERVICE DESIGN?

According to surveys conducted by Deming only an average of 6 per cent of all quality faults are caused by people in the organization – through carelessness, lack of knowledge, or bad temper – while 94 per cent are due to faulty, complicated or inappropriate systems for carrying out various tasks. Although we have not done systematic research into the subject, our experience from research and development work in services suggests that this is higher, especially, we regret to say, in public services in Europe. More importantly built-in faults corrode the source of quality – the staff. In services poor design affects staff and destroys their ability and motivation to give a quality service. Drawing on development work and a three-year evaluation of TQM programmes in the British Health Service, Øvretveit (1992a), notes that,

> Staff satisfaction in giving a quality service is the power-house for a service organisation. Staff satisfaction from helping a client is enhanced by the client's recognition of their proficiency. It is a proficiency that is possible because of the quality of the service process and organisation supporting staff. A major source of job dissatisfaction is being criticised by clients for poor treatment that a staff member knows was poor, but which they could not have given any better because of the system, the rules and other people's indifference. When the same problem and complaint keeps happening staff tend to ignore it to keep their self-respect. Staff know that clients think that they are less competent when they are handicapped by poor service design which condemn them to working with ineffectual systems and poor environments.

Built-in system faults continually put employees in unpleasant or impossible situations with customers. Staff lose their motivation because the system within which they work causes them and others to make errors, and they know it.

In goods manufacture, quality can be controlled when purchasing components, and by using and adjusting machines to assemble the components into products with a predetermined specific quality. Manufacturers have been developing and using these methods for many years. An example is the Norwegian company, Hydropower in Telavag, Bergen, which used 'modern' TQM manufacturing design and production based on Deming principles in the early 1950s to manufacture hydraulic winches, which have operated for 41 years with no maintenance. Manufacturers aim to prevent or correct faults throughout the process, from design to going to market, and before the customer receives the product. The opposite is frequently the case with services. Customers take part in a co-service production process. Their behaviour may be different at different times and will be different to other customers. If the customers are not actively involved in creating the service, they are often active observers, seeing and experiencing what takes place during the production process. They notice whether 'the service factory' is disorganized, they hear if the staff speak ill of other customers, and they know whether the staff are motivated or not. Customers also interact with each other – a further factor in co-service which is difficult to control.

How do we design something with an immaterial abstract core, and which is often produced and consumed simultaneously? We need concepts and frames of reference suited to co-service. Below we propose combining the design of product and the production process in service by analysing and mapping service processes and customer pathways (Øvretveit, 1993b). We also emphasize relating design to the business or service concept. A simple example is the Ohio-based Banc One Corporation, one of the emerging US super-regional banks, which are also doing well with private customers. The bank's information officer, John Russell, claims that it is because they offer superb service and that this is something people are willing to pay for. The bank's strength is most visible in the customer area with very advanced data processing. Each teller has access to information both about the customer and about the services he or she is likely to be interested in. Rather than windows, long counters and queues, one of the bank's branches has sofas, tables with magazines, newly-made coffee and a hostess to help customers find the right department under neon signs with 'home loans' or 'new accounts'. The bank is open from 9 a.m. to 7 p.m. on Mondays to Fridays, 9 a.m. to 5 p.m. on Saturdays and 12 p.m. to 5 p.m. on Sundays.

For many service companies, design is hampered by the lack of accurate data on customers' needs and expectations together with imprecise or unaccepted definitions of quality. We have considered these issues in other chapters – here we note the importance for design of understanding how expectations and perceptions are formed, and that they are not fixed. They can be described, from the service provider's point of view, in terms of tolerance zones delineated by the acceptable and desired levels of service (Parasuraman *et al.*, 1991). The nature of these tolerance zones is an important point of departure when designing and developing quality services.

SERVICE DESIGN

For many managers, designing a service is working with architects planning building layout or refurbishments. We do not want to minimize the importance of physical layout in the service offering, but even layout needs to be based on a sophisticated analysis of the co-service process. Service design involves understanding and planning the interaction of a variety of physical, electronic and human elements. We start with definitions of service design.

ISO definition of service design

The recent ISO standard gives a clear description of the meaning of 'designing a service' (ISO 9004-2:1991 (E) *Quality management and quality system elements: Guidelines for services*). The service version of the UK BS 5750 takes a similar approach. This definition is mostly appropriate for more standardized services – we summarize ISO's description and definition of service design below:

> The process of designing a service involves converting the service brief into specifications for both the service and its delivery and control, while reflecting the organization's options (i.e. aims, policies, and costs). Service specifications define the service to be provided, whereas the service delivery specification defines the means and methods used to deliver the service. The quality control specification defines the procedures for evaluating and checking on features of the service delivery. Design activities for the service specification, the service

delivery specification, and quality control specification are interdependent and interact throughout the design process. Flow charts are useful in depicting all the activities and their relationships and interdependences. The principles of quality control should be applied to the design process itself.

The 'Service brief' refers to the customer needs and expectations to be met by the service-producing organization: 'This brief defines the customers' needs and the related service organization's capabilities as a set of requirements and instructions that form the basis for the design of a service.'

The ISO description is similar to the service concept which we have introduced and used in our research (see below). However, ISO does not explicitly recognize the customer's involvement in the service process, which we have argued is central to service quality. We would also emphasize the importance of redesign: many businesses and managers do not have the often easier task of designing a new service, but need to be able to redesign their existing service at frequent intervals in a competitive market.

A model of the outcome of the service design process

We call the result of a service design process a 'service construct'. To design a service a company needs to formulate 'its service concept', and to design the co-service system and the co-service process.

The service concept

The service concept is a detailed description of a 'service offering' to match chosen customers' needs and expectations. We distinguish intended and realized 'service offering': the former is the intended outcome of the service process, while the latter is the actual outcome. The service concept is the starting point for and defines the requirements of the service process, and the system that provides the resources.

In defining the service concept it is helpful to distinguish between primary and secondary customer needs. Primary needs are those that are determined by the basic need, for instance making a trip. This can be done

A. Customer needs   B. Design of the offer

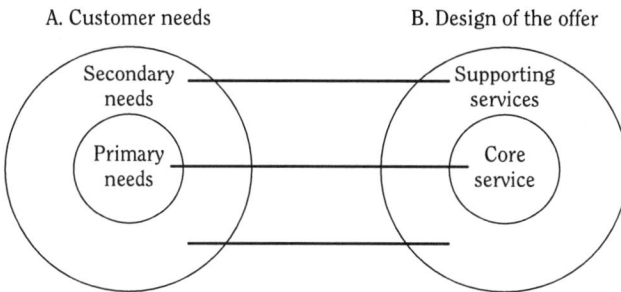

FIGURE 8.1   Model of the Service Concept
Source: Development of figure in Edvardsson, 1986.

in several ways: by taxi, train, airplane or car. If the choice is air travel, a number of other questions arise, such as how to order the ticket, how to get to the airport, and from the airport to the destination. These are secondary needs arising from the chosen service: different choices would have triggered other secondary needs.

Other additional support services are required to satisfy secondary needs. Examples are airport taxis, airport buses, and contracts between the airline and the travel bureau which make it possible to book several services at the same time. Figure 8.1 shows the relationship between a customer's needs and service design. Our studies show that unspoken expectations about the fulfilment of secondary needs are common. A good quality service contains a relevant set of support services of the right quality as well. What separates successful service companies from their less successful competitors is often the extent and quality of support services. The customer takes it for granted that a number of support services will be available. Before designing the service, it is therefore necessary to identify and understand these often unspoken needs for secondary services. This calls for dialogue with potential customers.

The co-service system

Services are often part of a larger system that includes other services. To realize the service concept, different resources or elements need to be organized as a system. We later consider how these resources form part of the co-service process – here we look at the elements of the system. These elements include: employees, customers, organizational structure and physical/technical environment. Examples of the latter are telephone services including switchboards, computers, and other technical systems used by both seller and buyer.

Employees

Studies we outlined in previous chapters show that customers' perception of service quality largely depends on how they evaluate the employees' knowledge and commitment. For many customers, the individual employee is in essence the service. Employees are more than a 'resource', they are the essential ingredient in the service, the critical and decisive bearers of good service quality. We have to adapt the technical systems, routines and other resources to 'human logic' or to the way people actually function. Service design does not just involve specifying requirements in terms of systems and processes, but must take account of how individuals and groups of staff can best contribute to the work and their ideas about design. Service design has to consider the needs, demands and wishes of staff to ensure competent, motivated and committed employees. The co-service system is a socio-technical system, with staff in a central position. Design should include staff selection, training/education and development, analysis of work content and job design as well as agreement on a reward system.

Customers

Customers are the second element in the co-service system. Design has to consider their role at different times in producing the service and how they interact with other elements of the system and other customers to do so. Involving potential customers in design helps to clarify the extent and nature of their involvement in producing the service. This is a delicate balance to achieve, not least because system design often prevents or forces involvement. Self-instruction co-service systems, which involve customer training, need careful design to be fast for frequent users and understandable for beginners. Services are interactions and service quality is largely the result of different interactions: interaction between customers; interaction between customers and staff; the customer's interaction with the physical environment such as equipment, furniture, computer systems and the premises and the customer's relationship with the organization, for example routines and opening hours.

Organization and management structure

The third element of a co-service system is how the organization assigns responsibilities to different roles that staff fill, and the relationships of accountability and authority between them. Organization and management for service is a large subject in its own right: here we wish only to emphasize that the management structure must mesh with other elements in the co-service system. Two aspects are of particular importance: first, ensuring the right balance between control and autonomy, by clearly defining limits and goals, devolving authority, and having effective accountability. This balance is critical for staff and their managers to handle critical incidents. The second is ensuring lateral structures, both permanent and temporary (quality circles, quality project teams), to get coordination between departments with staff who take part in the same process. Administrative routines are also important, for example, how informative and easy to understand the bill is for the customer.

Physical environment

> In judging a service we over-invest the tangible with a significance it often does not deserve, to compensate for our difficulty in judging the intangible and unassessable – this is true for some physical products: a heavy camera is bound to be reliable, even a Russian one.
>
> (Øvretveit, 1993d)

Because services are difficult to assess before using them, people are even more influenced by visible aspects of the service which might, for them, give a clue to the quality of the intangible. The physical environment – premises and equipment, and the technical systems – sends clear signals about quality; the location of a hotel, the design of the building, the layout of the lobby and the way the rooms are furnished are good examples of this. A high-quality physical environment is important for staff and for customers, but has to be designed as part of a co-service system. We have methods for quality physical design, but few which ensure it is part of the co-service system. Consequently many services set themselves up to fail by raising customer expectations with high-quality physical design, which they then cannot sustain: customers then experience continual dissonance between the physical environment and their experience of other aspects of the service.

The service management system

The co-service system forms part of a larger system, which we term the 'service management system'. This comprises the target customers, the service concept and the organizational culture and image (see Fig. 8.2, cf.

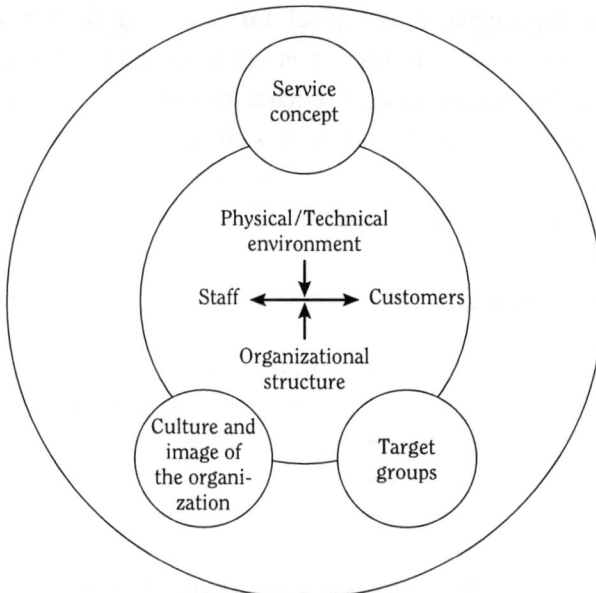

FIGURE 8.2   Service Management System
Source: Edvardsson and Gustavsson, 1990.

also Fig. 4.4 in Chapter 4). We term it the 'service management system' to emphasize that each part of the system and the whole has to be managed and designed to give a quality service. Image refers to customers' perception of the service company and its individual services. Organizational culture refers to the norms and values underlying management and decision style, behaviour and attitude.

The co-service process

> As the complexity of streams of processes increases, so does the probability that a company will lose control of the characteristics that are necessary to meet customer expectations, add value, and hold down costs. The result is the worst of two worlds: as the quality level falls below customer expectations, the cost of producing the product or service increases out of proportion to the value added.
>
> (Conti, 1989, p. 45)

The third design consideration is the co-service process, where the elements of the service system work together through time to create the service product. For design purposes there are two co-service processes. The first is the customer process or client pathway (Øvretveit, 1993b), which is the different phases that the customer passes through in receiving and co-producing the service. The second co-service process is wider and encompasses the variety of internal support services and their interaction with each other as internal customers and suppliers. In general terms, the co-service process is the chains (or streams) of activities for realizing the service. Some links in the chain are more problematic or critical than others, and need special attention at the design stage.

For a service to match the service concept in all respects, the process must be hammered out in detail. Quality and productivity must be built in from the beginning by designing the 'right' co-service process. Although necessary, involving many departments in design is quite difficult, especially as each department or function tends to optimize its 'own' processes and not take into account the whole. One management task in service design is to create an understanding of the service as a whole and of how co-service processes often cross departments, functions and professional groups, as well as requiring close inter-department cooperation.

It is in the co-service process that the different resources of the co-service system are utilized. The system is the stable elements, or resource prerequisites. The process, which consists of activities, has to be designed to make the best use of the service company's potential and its employees and to handle limitations in the best possible way. In practice, many managers are concerned with service redesign because they and their staff cannot produce a quality service with the existing design. Yet they still depend on elements of an existing system, and because of this need the full involvement of staff with a good knowledge of the co-service system's potential and limits.

Linking strategy, the business environment and service design

Before considering strategic issues in service design, it is useful to note how to link market issues with specifications for service design. Later sections of this chapter consider techniques for specification in more detail but the framework in Fig. 8.3 shows how different considerations are linked in design (see Chapter 4, Fig. 4.11 for complete framework).

The framework of Fig. 8.3 is used in health services, but is relevant to other service companies, whether or not their 'customer' is a third-party purchaser. The fifth part of the framework covers how the 'service brief' of requirements and service design are used in the operational quality management cycle for setting standards and measurement.

STRATEGIES FOR SERVICE DEVELOPMENT

Design has to be governed by the business strategy of the service, a subject which we now consider. Grönroos (1983, p.74) maintains that when developing a service it is essential to decide 'what level of quality one wishes to achieve and what profile, and the goal of the development process in terms of technical and functional quality'. The answers to these questions

Part 1	Part 2	Part 3	Part 4a/4b
MAP BUSINESS ENVIRONMENT	**DEFINE SERVICE REQUIREMENTS**		**DEFINE SERVICE RESPONSE**

- Purchasers → Valued features and performance levels
- Referrers → to be achieved

- Higher-level regulations → Defined requirements → **SPECIFY SERVICE PACKAGE**

- Market research to identify → Identify → Define target **COMPILE SERVICE BRIEF** → **SPECIFY SERVICE DESIGN** current and segments clients, their (Processes) potential wants and clients needs and performance levels to be achieved

- Labour markets → Requirements to recruit and retain staff

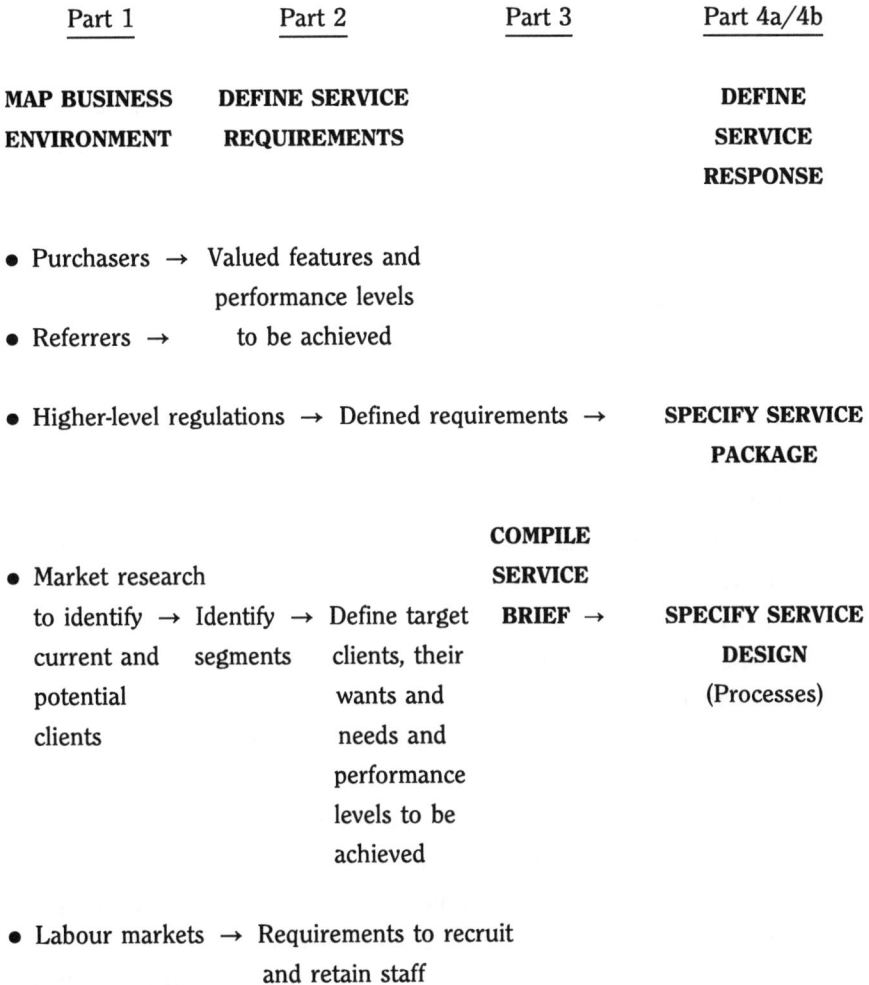

FIGURE 8.3 Four Parts of the Wel-Qual Framework
Source: Øvretveit, 1992a.

depend on the business strategy. Grönroos distinguishes three types of strategy: service-oriented, goods-oriented and price-oriented. He gives the Finnish Insurance Company Sampo's so-called 'Sampo agreement' as an example of the service-oriented strategy. The idea of the agreement is to solve all the consumer's insurance problems with the emphasis on giving a total service. McDonald's is an example of a company applying a goods-oriented strategy. It is the product itself, in this case a hamburger, which is the basis for the service. The price-oriented strategy focuses on price as a means of competition. In the airline industry there are a number of examples of lower prices helping to expand the market. With the aid of reduced ticket prices, aircraft can be filled at times of under-capacity. The airlines have thereby reached categories of customers who previously did not think they could afford to fly.

One of the central strategic decisions concerns which of the above strategies is to be the competitive core and thus the guiding principle for service design or redesign. Concentrating on price will lead to very different assessments and criteria for changing existing services compared with the situation where level of service lies at the heart of the strategy. The choice of strategy depends on the types of customer selected, the role one wishes to play for them, what it is that creates value for the customers and the customers' grounds for selecting the product and the supplier. It also depends on the competitive situation and the resources and capacity the company needs to carry out the strategy.

A further dimension to development strategy is whether the company is proactive or protective: interested in being ahead of most of its competitors or choosing to defend its present market position. Nyström (1979) makes a distinction between innovative and positional elements in a company's product development. Innovative companies seek to utilize and help change operational environments while positional companies seek to adapt to and maintain stable operational environments. The question is whether the company should generate changes – as, for instance, SAS and Citibank have done – or whether development should concentrate on reacting to changes with the aim of safeguarding and defending the position the company has on the market.

Success and failure in industrial services

Companies considering strategies for service development can learn from De Brentani's (1989) report of the results of a study, 'Success and failure in new industrial services'. She studied service development in 115 Canadian companies, including banks, insurance companies, management consultancies, auditing companies, transport companies and telecommunications companies. Altogether she interviewed 148 managers and analysed 276 development projects, 150 of which were successful and 126 failures. Among the indicators of success used were profitability and market position. De Brentani concluded that service companies need a more systematic methodology for developing new services:

> It is well known that service companies do not use a highly sophisticated new service development process ... . Active involvement by employees from different functional areas and use of a 'drawing board' approach to designing services clearly influences how well the new service meets customer needs .... Similarly, testing new services prior to launch and planning a detailed launch program that includes training and internal marketing for the frontline usually leads to a high level of sales and competitive performance.
>
> (p.255)

She also proposed a more systematic approach to quality in development:

> Customers care about quality but cannot easily assess whether a new service provides the desired outcome. Successful service development, therefore, requires that companies identify what buyers perceive as quality and incorporate these features into the service design. Moreover, service companies need to help clients evaluate quality by providing 'tangible' clues that describe the quality features being offered and by creating a high quality image for the new service.
>
> (p.256)

De Brentani observed that the need to develop innovative services is probably even greater in the service sector than in manufacturing:

> new services need to be unique and truly innovative to achieve a major
> advantage in the marketplace ... unless they are clearly differentiated, they tend
> to be viewed as generic and because new services are so easily imitated ...
> Focusing on new and superior ways to solve old problems, offering creative
> ways to solve old problems and offering creative ways to differentiate the service
> experience are important routes to achieving a strong competitive position.
>
> (p.256)

Finally a key development criterion which we also emphasize is designed for cost-effectiveness:

> Clearly, more direct efforts to reduce costs need to be made. Many business
> services could probably become more standardized, for example, insurance
> firms and banks have moved in this direction with a number of services they
> offer .... Certainly improving communication between the technical and the
> marketing functions within the firm can lead to new services which enhance
> cost efficiencies.
>
> (p.256)

Service guarantees

A further strategic issue in service development is whether to make use of service guarantees and how, in that case, they should be formulated. Service guarantees are becoming more and more common, perhaps primarily for more standardized or 'closed services' such as cleaning, security, travel and hotel services. Guarantees are becoming more common in 'open services' such as consultant and architectural services. One of the authors introduced a service guarantee in 1990 for educational workshops, consultancy, development research contracts, and publications produced by the programme he directs. Staff in the programme wondered whether it was such a good idea when he broke his arm and had to authorize them to refund £2600 for a cancelled workshop.

Although some guarantees are only 'money-back-if-not-satisfied', many involve making it clear to the customer what he or she can expect. The service provider communicates in concrete and detailed terms what the customer will receive and what will happen if what was promised is not delivered. This is useful both in marketing and in quality control from the service company's viewpoint. From the customer's perspective, the guarantee means that the value of the offering is concretized, that the customer's expectations will probably be more realistic and that the customer's uncertainty will be reduced. In the United Kingdom the government has imposed guarantee-like 'service charters' for different public services such as health sevices, taxation, customs, underground and British Rail. These, however, are not part of quality programmes in these services and were not formulated as part of the service design.

Unconditional service guarantees have proved to be a powerful tool for controlling customer expectations and creating competitive advantages and customer satisfaction (see, e.g. Hart, 1988). Formulating suitable service guarantees should be part of the process of designing a service. SAS International Hotels have introduced what they term 'No excuse for not being perfect'. Their guarantee is: 'If there is something wrong with this room and it is the fault of the hotel, we will put it right within 60 minutes of being notified; if necessary, we will try to provide you with a new room. If not, you will not have pay for this room. This is your guarantee for a perfect stay in our hotel.'

Service guarantees can and should be used not just externally to the customers but also internally. Internal service guarantees encourage quality improvement. They force companies to go through processes in detail to decide, for instance, who is responsible for what, and specify the demands on the internal service more precisely than previously. When what is promised is not delivered, the use of the guarantee is a powerful signal to the organization. The customer's voice is heard and this helps push the organization towards placing the customer in the centre. Hart (1990b, p.1) maintains that perhaps the greatest effect of service guarantees lies in stimulating internal development of the service process.

> Specifically, it forces an organization to explicitly define its customers' needs and to understand its service-delivery process, including controllable and

uncontrollable variables as well as possible failure points and weaknesses in the system.

SERVICE DEVELOPMENT

What can managers learn from product development to help develop and design quality services? The marketing literature describes product development in terms of successive stages. Bellenger and Greenberg (1978) distinguish between idea generation, idea evaluation, development and testing of product concepts, profitability analysis, product development and commercialization. Is this general model of product development applicable to developing services? Opinions differ. Rathmell (1974) maintains that there is in principle no difference between developing services and developing other products. Grönroos (1983) is more sceptical, because he believes that product development concepts are based on companies which produce and market goods: 'The product development issues arising in the service sector have been largely ignored' (p.71). Cowell (1984), however, maintains that service development and the development of physical products follow the same basic principles:

> While the terminology of new product development and the range and order of the steps included in the process varies, the underlying notions behind the use of systematic procedures does not. These are, first to create as many good ideas as possible, secondly to reduce the number of ideas by careful screening and analysis so ensuring that only those with the best chances of success get into the marketplace.
>
> (p.133)

In a TQM perspective, service development starts with ideas based on the specific needs of particular groups of customers in the market. These ideas are 'refined into a service concept and 'service offering' for the market. In our experience, few companies undertake systematic and target-oriented service development, even large manufacturing companies where services in combination with physical products play a central role for their competitive position. At present there is insufficient research into product development in services to justify rejecting existing models. Our view is that the general model of product development can contribute to developing new and competitive services. Crawford (1983) provides a useful and detailed discussion of phases in the process of product development in his book *New products management*. Below we outline one model for developing and designing services.

Scheuing's model of service development

Scheuing's (1989) model for developing new services was based on empirical research into how new services arise (see Fig. 8.4). The model describes a sequence of 15 steps, grouped in four stages: choice of direction, design, testing and introduction:

1 *Choice of direction*. Scheuing's (1989, p. 372) argue that a well-designed new service strategy drives and directs the entire service innovation effort. 'Whereas new service strategy development has to take environmental constraints and opportunities into account, idea generation, too, can draw on a number of external sources for inspiration.' The service concept is often produced in a haphazard and hurried fashion, and is often hazy as a result. The key to successful development work is a well-planned approach to development, based on market targets which, in their turn, should be derived from management goals and the purpose of the business. Ideas are then assessed in terms of such criteria as profit opportunities and practicability.

2 *Design*. This involves designing the new service, delivery system and marketing programme. The service idea is tested for its ability to satisfy needs and against the reason customers buy. If the concepts pass this stage then it is worth working-up a business case to recommend to management about which ideas to pursue.

3 *Testing*. Testing predicts how potential customers will receive the service, and how the service functions in practice. The aim is to be able to refine the service on the basis of customers' reactions before the offering is introduced on the market.

Marketing Objectives →	1 Formulation of New Service Objectives and Strategy	← Environment Analysis
Internal Sources →	2 Idea Generation	← External Sources
	3 Idea Screening	
Customer Contact Personnel →	4 Concept Development	← Prospects
	5 Concept Testing	
Budget Development →	6 Business Analysis	← Market Assessment
	7 Project Authorization	
Operations Personnel →	8 Service Design and Testing	← Users
→	9 Process and System Design and Testing	
	10 Marketing Program Design and Testing	← Users
All Personnel →	11 Personnel Training	
	12 Product Testing and Pilot Run	← Users
	13 Test Marketing	
	14 Full-Scale Launch	
	15 Postlaunch Review	

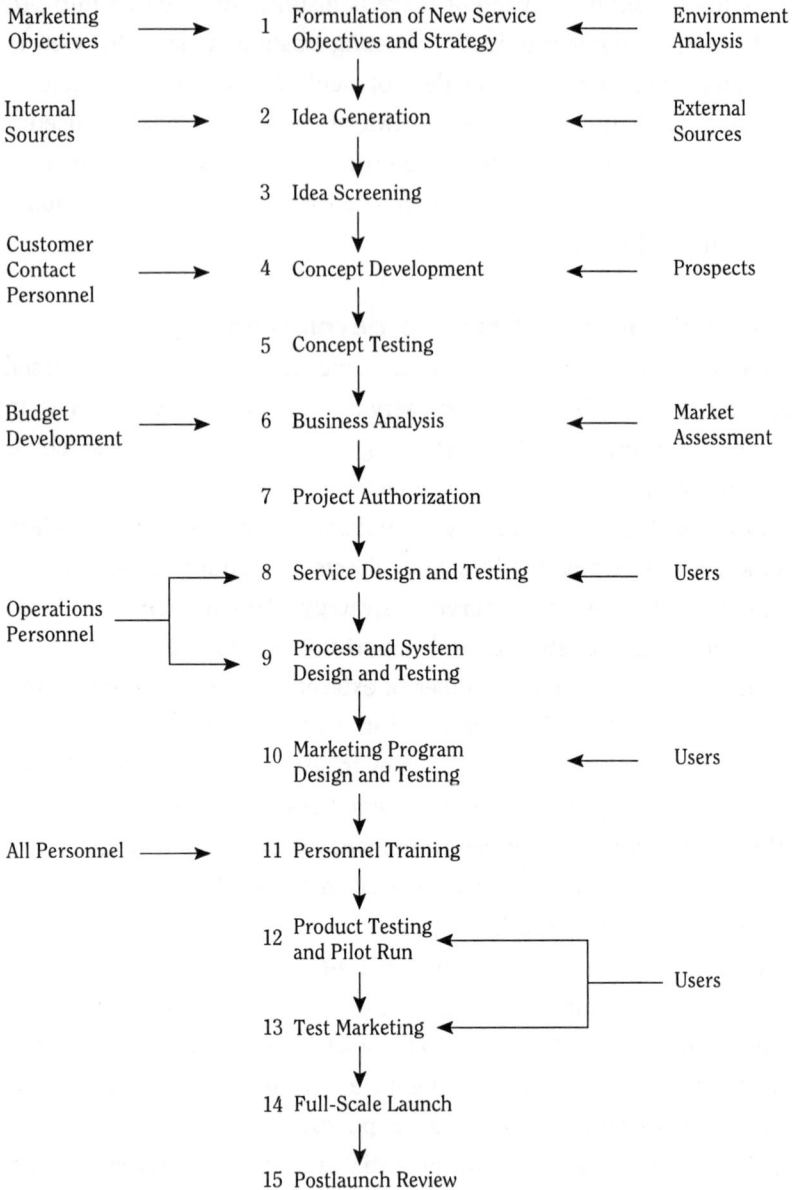

FIGURE 8.4   Normative Model of New Service Evolution
Source: Scheuing, 1989.

4 *Introduction.* The fourth and final stage of the model covers introducing the service to the market, and evaluating it to see whether the targets have been reached and to decide refinements.

We now turn to two specific techniques for service design before outlining our model for a systematic and planned approach to service design.

TWO TECHNIQUES FOR DESIGNING SERVICES

In this section we describe two of the new techniques which are proving useful for service design within a TQM perspective: service blueprinting or service mapping and quality function deployment (QFD) for services.

Blueprinting and service mapping

Blueprinting is a systematic method for analysing and representing the steps in a service process (Shostack, 1984, 1987; George and Gibson, 1991; Kingman-Brundage, 1988, 1989; Baum, 1989; Davis, 1990). The technique grew from systems analysis and flow charting for computer programs. Illustrating the service as a flow of processes enables us to understand better the mutual dependence between activities, people, products and other building blocks which together form the service. It helps to map, at the design stage, the critical points and potential failures in service. The method can be used to design a new service, to evaluate and redesign an existing one, and as an instrument for evaluating co-service. Simplified blueprinting can also be used for staff and service development, using frameworks such as those outlined by Øvretveit (1992a, p.54), and for patient-pathways in health teams in Øvretveit (1993b).

The bases of blueprinting are detailed drawings which take time to produce. These drawings make it possible to identify and avoid quality defects, and give a basis for dealing more effectively with problems, should they arise. The drawings mark events, activities and assignments with different symbols, placed in chronological order to describe in detail how the service is produced. In all services time is a factor which affects costs and quality. Blueprinting models make it possible to take time into account by calculating times which are acceptable to the customer, for the various stages in the service process. This makes it possible to control productivity as well, and thus profitability. Standard times are also important when it comes to measuring quality and allocating the company's resources properly. The time required is, in general, related to the complexity of the service.

In the blueprint, a 'line of visibility' separates the processes in the production of the service which are visible to the customer from those which are invisible to him or her. In the visible section the customer experiences the staff and various types of 'physical evidence' which contribute to customer-perceived quality. The size of the section of the blueprint above the line of visibility varies with the service involved, but generally the largest section of the blueprint lies below the line – most of the processes are invisible to the customer. Shostack compares the visible part with the tip of an iceberg, with the line of visibility being equivalent to the water-line. The visible part of the service process can be further divided by a 'line of interaction' which separates activities in which the customer participates from those carried out by the service company's staff in the 'back office'. This helps to focus on the most difficult part of the process to control, where the human factor creates a greater risk of variation in quality. The situations in which the customer and the service company interact – 'the moments of truth' – can be examined at the design stage using this technique. The blueprint helps to identify failpoints: the processes where failures may easily occur, either below or above the line of visibility.

Shostack (1984) describes how blueprinting can help a service company identify possible sources of problems before quality problems arise. The following summarizes the steps she describes:

1 *Map the course of events.* The first step is to map the various activities underpinning the service. For more complex services, with many decision situations and alternatives, this can be very demanding as the many events can be difficult to identify and define. Identifying the various components provides information about the input required in the service

process. It gives us better opportunities for analysing, controlling and improving the design of the service.

2 *Identify conceivable failpoints*. When the course of events is clear, it is easier to discover conceivable failpoints. This make it possible to redesign or 'build' preventive steps into the system at the design stage.

3 *Set up time frames*. Time is related to cost in all services: faster often means more costly. The model helps to calculate acceptable standard times for the various stages in the service process. The time required is generally related to the complexity of the service.

4 *Analyse profitability*. Standard times help to avoid poor profitability and inefficiency. The standard times are also important for measuring quality and allocating resources in the best way.

Kingman-Brundage's development of blueprinting is 'service mapping'. Like blueprinting, service mapping is based on flow charting. The aim of both methods is to reveal the activities which together form the co-service process. Service mapping highlights four groups: customers, contact staff, support staff and management. The focus is on the customer path, which runs from left to right, and shows how the customer thinks and acts (see Fig. 8.5).

In the interaction between the company and the customer, there should be a correspondence between the logic of the customer and that of the company. There is internal interaction between front-line employees, support staff and management. The line of visibility divides the co-service process into a part that is visible to the customer and a part that is invisible. The line of implementation divides top management from operations.

Quality function deployment (QFD)

QFD was developed in Japan in the late 1960s by Shigun Mizuno and Yoji Akao and has been in use since the beginning of the 1970s. Mitsubishi was the first company to use QFD (King, 1987; Hauser and Clausing, 1988; Andersson, 1989; Chang, 1989; Conti, 1989; Ferguson, 1990). The strength of the method is that it systematically translates the customer's needs and expectations into specifications that are relevant to the company.

CUSTOMER'S PATH →

CUSTOMER
↑
↕
EXTERNAL INTERACTION
↕
FRONT LINE STAFF
↑
─── LINE OF VISIBILITY ───
↕
INTERNAL INTERACTION
↕
SUPPORT STAFF

─── LINE OF ───
IMPLEMENTATION

MANAGEMENT

PROVIDER'S ORGANIZATION

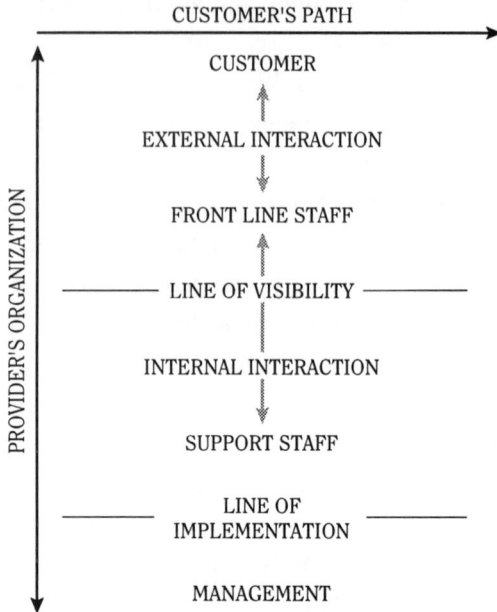

FIGURE 8.5   The Generic Structure of a Service Map

Source: Gummesson and Kingman-Brundage, 1992.

QFD is a systematic way to help identify customer desires and deploy them throughout all functions of the corporation, remaining faithful to the voice of the customer. During this deployment, QFD helps to identify the critical parameters that are then optimized by quality engineering to reduce functional variation and costs.

(Clausing and Simpson, 1990, p.44)

In many of the cases reported, the use of quality deployment has cut half the problems at the beginning (design) stage, and shortened development time from one-half to one-third ...

(King, 1987, p.277)

Although developed in manufacturing companies, we have found a modified approach to be useful for part of the design process for service companies.

QFD is a four-stage process

1 The first phase, as usual, is to identify the customer's needs and expectations – 'customer demands'. This involves identifying those customer preferences around which competition occurs.
2 The second phase, translated into service terms, is defining the requirements of the service and designing the co-service system – parts and the whole – so that the right quality is built in from the beginning.
3 The third phase is process planning. This is a matter of choosing the co-service process which 'best' produces what the customer requires, and defining it using service blueprinting.
4 Phase four, is planning the day-to-day production of the service. Working instructions and staff levels and training are defined.

An example of the use of the QFD method

The following is a simple demonstration of how to use QFD in designing a secretarial service. It uses a simplified version of 'the house of quality' (see Fig. 8.6).

Procedure
1 *Establish the aim of the project.* The members of the QFD team together determine the aim of the project. Is it a new service or an existing service that needs improving? What is to be the concrete result of the project?
2 *Define customers and others who make demands.* Here the team considers the customer demands to be satisfied.
3 *Compile customer expectations.* Customer expectations should not be filtered but come direct from the customer in his or her own words. Customer expectations are specified in the form of operational variables.
4 *Describe the elements of the service.* In the original version of QFD the next step is to describe the features of the product. Generally this does not cause any real problems where goods are concerned but it is much more difficult when it comes to services. We describe the service in the form of value-bearing elements, in this case: experience, business hours, printed matter, office equipment and number of secretaries. The service elements are then entered in a QFD matrix, shown in Fig. 8.6.

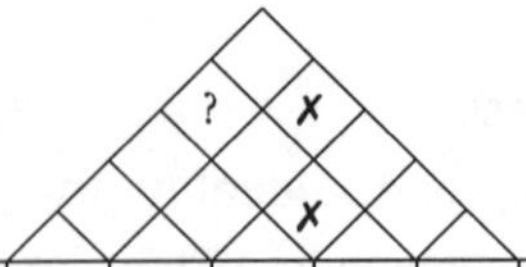

CO-SERVICE REQUIREMENTS / EXPECTATIONS	Experience	Opening hours	Publications	Office equipment	Number of secretaries	WEIGHTING	CUSTOMER EVALUATION our service competitor's service 0 2 4 6 8 10
Information easy to understand			9			3	
Reliability	9		1	1		9	
Willingness to oblige	5				1	6	
Accessibility		3			9	7	
Open 24 hours a day		9				3	
STUDY OF COMPETITORS	+ −						
WEIGHTING	111	48	36	9	69		
GOAL VALUES							

FIGURE 8.6   An Example of a QFD Matrix: 'The House of Quality'

5 *Mark the links between customer expectations and service elements.*
This involves examining how the various elements in the service affect
the service's capacity to satisfy the different customer expectations. The
strength of the link is indicated on a scale of 1–9 where 9=very strong
link and 1=some link.

6 *Mark the links between the service elements*. Links between the service elements may be supportive, antagonistic or non-existent. Analysing the links can suggest ways to design the service. In the matrix these links are indicated, under the 'roof', by: x=strong link and ?=possible link.

7 *Customer weighting and customer evaluation*. Customers decide the importance of the various demands in 'weightings', using a scale of 1–9. The next step is to consider competitor performance on the preferences against the service, using a scale of 1–10.

8 *Study of competitors*. Objectivity in assessing competitors is easier by establishing one or more measures for the service elements, or by having an outsider make an assessment. The results are entered in the same way as for customer evaluation.

9 *Weighting the service elements*. This step produces a measure of the customers' assessment of the service elements. The link between customer demands and service elements is multiplied by the customer weighting. The products are then totalled for each service element. For example, the calculation for the element 'experience' is: $9 \times 9 + 5 \times 6 = 111$. The figure for each feature is entered underneath the result for the competitor study. These weighted results have to be treated with caution because they partially depend on the structure of customer wishes and uncertain estimates.

10 *Goal evaluation*. This sets goals for which parts of the service should be given the highest priority for improvement. The goals are entered at the bottom of the matrix (Fig. 8.6).

11 *Strategic assessment*. Lastly, the company must make strategic assessments before finalizing goals. These include deciding which is the primary customer segment and which customers should be given priority.

What information do we gain using this approach and from 'the house of quality'? The matrix gives an overview of a large amount of information and a 'knowledge bank' about the following:

- The strong and weak points of the company and competitors.
- The position of the company on the market.

- The niche opportunities to be found on the market – the unsatisfied customer needs, demands and wishes.

QFD project groups

The project group working with QFD usually consists of five to eight people with the necessary competence to carry out the project, typically, product developers, designers, marketers, product planners and other specialists such as buyers and quality experts may be included. These may be involved throughout the project or included when needed. In addition, staff working with the service on a daily basis should be included, and, if possible, representatives of customers and suppliers as co-producers.

SERVICE INNOVATION THROUGH DESIGN: A MODEL FOR THE SERVICE DESIGN PROCESS

Designing services is one of the most important ways to innovate. Although a rigid approach can destroy innovation, and some approaches to quality are rigid, we do not believe that innovation is luck or incompatible with a systematic quality approach. We can plan for innovation, increase the chances of generating new ideas for new or existing services, and most important of all, ensure that these new ideas are given a chance to prove themselves in evaluation and market testing. This is all part of total quality service management which involves a systematic design process to make innovation less of a hit-and-miss affair. In this section we describe a model for systematically designing or redesigning a quality service consisting of four phases: idea collection, evaluation and concept development; customer and competitor analysis as a basis for concept evaluation and specification; design of the co-service system; and detailed design of the co-service process.

We note two other models of design with different stages: Donnelly *et al.* (1985, p.147) define six stages: strategic guidelines, exploration, screening, comprehensive analysis, development and testing, and introduction. The Scheuing (1989, p.371) normative model for new service evaluation we described above has 15 phases: formulation of new service objectives and strategy, idea generation, idea screening, concept development, concept testing, business analysis, project authorization, service design and testing, process and system design and testing, marketing programme design and testing, personnel training, product testing and pilot run, test marketing, full-scale launch, and post-launch review.

Phase 1: Idea collection, evaluation and concept development

Ideas for new services often come from customers – many new services were built by entrepreneurial customers who found that their supplier could or would not provide a service which they and others needed. Organizations frequently ignore such ideas because they do not have staff or a procedure to evaluate them, or even to seek them out. Other demanding and competent customers should be included in this evaluation process – Citibank and Telia (Swedish Telecom) are two companies that use customer input in a systematic way in their evaluation processes. Part of the idea evaluation is to assess it against the market by analysing customer needs and the value the service will provide, the competitive situation, and the size and growth potential of the market. This phase should also consider the technical possibilities for realizing the service at the right level of quality, as well as produce a first description and evaluation of the service concept, and the potential income and costs.

The purpose in this phase is to decide if it is feasible and profitable to proceed, and to identify key factors that will affect the quality of the service and its value for potential customers. People with knowledge and experience in this particular field, both employees of the service company and key customers, should participate in the evaluation process. The concept should be tested against other services and examined from a technical and economic point of view. With this information, management decides whether or not to proceed taking into consideration: how the new idea ties in with company goals, how well consumers' primary and secondary needs can be met, the relative advantage for the customer, and the competition in the market. In order to take both primary and secondary needs into account, the core service and the support services have to be specified. Further questions to be answered are: how well the new service fits in with the company's current range of services and to what extent the current co-service systems can be used.

Phase 2: Customer and competitor analysis for concept evaluation and specification

If management passes the new or revised service for further assessment, phase 2 of design is to undertake a more comprehensive analysis of many of the areas of phase 1. This involves assessing potential consumer needs, wishes and expectations concerning the proposed service, using a wider base of up-to-date information from and about potential customers. The more thorough analysis of phase 2 also considers competitors and other businesses with similar services. The results of this phase are: a detailed description and analysis of consumer needs and expectations; a detailed analysis of competing services; a detailed analysis of the core and support services in relation to consumers' needs and expectations; and a commercial (income and cost) evaluation of the service concept.

Phase 3: Co-service system design

If a proposed service is commercially viable and accepted for further design, then phase 3 is to design and specify the co-service system of resources. To realize the service concept at the right quality, managers need to specify the elements of and demands on the co-service system. These elements are the staff of the service company, the customers, the organizational structure and the physical environment. The demands on these elements can be specified using quality function deployment to translate customer needs into the resource requirements of the service. QFD can also be used in this way when the new service will use an existing co-service system, either part of this system (e.g. part of a building, or some staff), or all of this system, where an additional service is to be provided, or where the existing service is being redesigned into a new service. The results of this phase are: a specification of resources, based on the service concept; a thorough evaluation of the resources in the existing co-service system; and a detailed description of the design of the 'new' co-service system.

Phase 4: Co-service process design

Phase 4 is not really a phase in the sense of following phase 3, but should be undertaken in parallel with co-service system design, or overlap with this phase. This is because mapping the co-service process in detail helps to specify further the co-service system elements, for example by highlighting extra staffing at potential failpoints or high customer demand. Process design details the different activities in producing the service, and clarifies the role of the customer. It involves making detailed flow charts of how the service is to be produced, and considering alternative co-service processes sometimes using computer-based simulation techniques. This design phase results in a detailed process description of: activities; equipment; critical points and line of visibility (what the customer is allowed to see and not to see). It also gives more detailed costs and a value-based price as well as proposals for guiding customer expectations, marketing, and measurement and review.

CONCLUSION

Even more than manufacturing quality, service quality depends on prevention and design to avoid poor quality. In services, design of the product and of production are one and the same, and call for special methods. But like manufacturing companies, services are poor at recognizing profitable new ideas, developing them and bringing them to the market. They are even worse at realizing innovations than postwar British manufacturers are reputed to be, and mistakenly believe that they do not face international competition. The three purposes of this chapter were to emphasize the importance of design to service quality; to show how service can innovate and ensure that ideas for new service are realized in the market; and to describe approaches and techniques suited to service design.

The chapter considered strategies and techniques for developing services, service guarantees as a strategic issue and outlined our framework for designing services. This framework included the four phases of: idea collection, evaluation and concept development; customer and competitor analysis; design of the co-service system; and of the co-service process. This process has to be adapted to the conditions in individual organizations, but should form part of a comprehensive approach to quality.

Our argument was that service design is the way to get substantial and lasting results in higher quality and productivity in the service sector. It is a key part of total quality service management, both for innovation and for redesigning existing services to prevent quality problems. Successful quality improvement must be based on well-planned services, which are correctly designed to meet customer needs and expectations. The more managers understand how the service concept and co-service processes and systems for producing services are best constructed, the better chance they have of being successful in quality improvement and service innovation.

Leading quality improvement in services

The ability to think differently today from yesterday distinguishes the wise man from the obstinate.
(John Steinbeck)

The title of the book is *Quality of service: Making it really work*. We have stressed the human element of service, and the need to develop both a systematic approach and the spirit of service. We believe that the coming years will see a transformation in the role of the service manager, and call for new and different skills and attitudes. In the past we could say that many leaders were not managers, and many managers were not good leaders. In the future all managers must also be leaders. The new service manager, whether he or she works in a private or public service, is first and foremost a leader. By leadership we mean 'being in the vanguard' but also 'being together with others', clarifying visions and goals, generating commitment, finding and blazing new paths into the future in both thought and action. It is a matter of leading and supporting a mental, strategic and spiritual change in the organization, but also of initiating and enabling practical changes and ensuring that there are systems and measures.

The systems and technical changes are relatively easy – it is the cultural change which is more difficult yet just as important for ensuring that the systems do not become an end in themselves. Chapter 3 considered cultural change for improving quality, which involved introducing new ideas and directing existing ideas into new paths. Introducing the 'language of quality' with its special approaches, definitions and concepts helps to get cultural change of the right kind, so long as people know what they mean by the new terms. These are the tools for spreading the quality message, communicating quality thinking and implementing quality. Managers live in a world of non-stop activity, and are always expected to 'do' something – they often have opportunities to act in different ways to lead cultural change by example.

When management 'leads' and introduces new quality thinking into the organization, there is an impact which managers often do not recognize, but which we have observed. We do not mean formulating quality policies, but clarifying, both within and outside the organization, through commitment and personal demonstration what quality is, and showing that improvement of quality is a major priority. At the same time, managers show that quality improvement is not a separate activity but an integral part of everyday work. When management and everybody else in the organization 'are in step', far-reaching and lasting results can be achieved. Quality improvement should always 'be in the mainstream' of business development.

Leadership for service quality is different from many types of management leadership in the past: the way in which managers lead conveys the message more powerfully than their words. It involves creating a sense of participation, and giving staff the opportunity to implement ideas in their work. It involves removing obstacles to quality, some of which have given a sense of security in the past. These obstacles may be of the overarching kind, such as the structure of the organization, which frequently prevents the kind of vertical and lateral communication needed for quality. The obstacles may even be less complex, such as deficiencies in the work organization which are easy to rectify, or the lack of simple, practical aids.

Two obstacles of particular importance are those which managers create themselves. One is front-line staff not being able to take decisions. Service staff can and should take more decisions than they have been able to in the past. They often know customers and markets better than managers, and know what to do to avoid quality problems at the time, and in the future. Feeling threatened by the new approaches and demands, many managers and supervisors 'intrude downwards' into the easier operational tasks. Managers fail to delegate decision making because they do not work out ways to define the constraints and ensure accountability so as to free staff to respond in appropriate ways. They often do not have the training to be able to create the conditions for staff to do the work, and underestimate the ability and potential of staff to take responsibility if they are managed in the right way.

The second obstacle is that managers do not ensure that staff understand the overall service process and their part in it. Managers may explain and draw attention to the part an employee plays within a department, but tend not to explain the way the departments services form part of the whole, or the processes which cut through the department. We have found that staff frequently do not understand their work as a process, or the co-service processes and how their own work affects others. Following managers' example, employees often think no further than the limits of their department or sphere of work. It is managers who create the understanding that there are both internal and external customers whose expectations must be met, and that each person is a link in a long service chain consisting of a set of processes and activities.

TEN PROPOSITIONS ON TQM IN SERVICES

In these last pages we summarize some of the points of the book in a number of general propositions. The emphasis is on a systematic approach to quality, but not one which exorcizes the human element of service as a troublesome uncontrollable variable. It is an approach which aims to support and advance the human element – the spirit of service.

1 *The customers', employees' and owners' expectations are the basis for quality improvement.* Find out and keep yourself informed about the requirements, needs and expectations of the main interested parties. Define quality on the basis of these 'stakeholder' requirements, specifying customer, professional and management quality. Recognize conflicting requirements at an early stage and decide how these are to be resolved in design and service operation. Consider both customers and suppliers as part-time employees and co-producers. Analyse the current situation on a factual basis, and base the service concept on these requirements. Introduce the concept of internal customer and remove the barriers between departments and professional groups. Do not promise more than you can deliver.

2 *Decide a quality framework for the whole company, which sets a common approach to quality improvement in each area.* By quality framework we mean more than a quality system like ISO 9000, but a framework which links the market and business strategy to quality activities in all aspects of the organization. In some companies there are a variety of quality systems and improvement approaches which do not link properly. The company should develop a framework suited to its activities and market – we have suggested that the US Baldrige award is a good starting point as it is not bureaucratic, but ensures a systematic and comprehensive approach.

　　Part of this framework should be a customer-orientated quality policy valid for the whole organization. Base it on the company's business concept, its basic business processes and the unique nature of co-service. The quality policy will clarify and create understanding of fundamental, common values and approaches to work and customers.

3 *Quality goals are needed at all levels in the company.* Determine simple and clear goals for quality improvement. The goals should further the realization of the business concept, and be realistic, challenging, attainable and measurable. They must be known to everyone and broken down into sub-goals linked to daily activities. All must recognize that the goals are to be exceeded and reset, and that the overriding goal

is to keep removing causes of poor quality and prevent new ones from arising.

4 *Quality improvement requires internal marketing and a reward system.* Quality improvement has to be 'sold' to staff, especially if their past experience is of poor quality. Gaining support for quality improvement is often done unsystematically, and reward systems are often inappropriate. The quality framework, policy and goals must be made clear and communicated. Raise motivation by emphasizing, assessing and rewarding the results of quality improvements. Quality improvement must be seen to be more than one project among others and more than a destination: it must be seen to be a continual journey.

5 *Quality improvement requires organization.* Quality frameworks, quality systems and quality strategies all help to take an organized approach to quality. Managers have to get across the idea that quality improvement is not crisis problem-solving, but seeing and resolving the problems that cause crises. Discover inbuilt system faults, and be aware that you cannot find all the obstacles at once; as the work progresses, new obstacles will emerge. Chart the co-service processes and systems. Quality improvement is generally not a question of revolution, but of evolution. It is the continuous 'everyday improvement' (the Japanese term *kaizen*) that produces results in the long term. But radical structural changes in the processes may also be necessary. It is, thus, a combination of continuous improvement and process re-engineering.

6 *Measure yourself against the best.* Introduce benchmarking. Managers and staff need external standards and reference points, as well as their own goals and standards, where the yardstick is the best achievements available. Measure yourself against your competitors and against companies in other lines of business – learn from the best. Develop contacts with other service managers and academics who question well-tried methods and established ways of thought which may be out of date.

7 *Measure where you are, set goals and measure where you get to.* Without quality measures we cannot know the effects of changes, improvements, or of doing nothing. Managers should ask 'How do we

measure success in this, how do we measure our progress?' Start by measuring what is both easy and quick to measure, such as complaints, recognizing that this helps to establish measurement as a part of every-day work. Build on this by introducing quality methods to improve performance. Gradually develop monitoring methods that will accustom you to using qualitative measures for goal fulfilment which are difficult to interpret.

Our general advice to managers in a sentence is: define your processes, assign responsibility for parts of the process, establish measures and goals for parts and for the whole process, feed back measures to staff in an understandable way, give them responsibility for improving quality and the tools to do it, and reward them appropriately.

8 *Listening to the customers tells us where we are going wrong.* Exactly one reason why we tend not to listen, or deny what we hear by explaining why it is wrong. Set up a system for listening to complaints and 'could do betters' from both external and internal customers. The aim is to reduce the causes for complaints and to seek out dissatisfied customers. It is common policy to minimize complaints in a company, which means that it is easy to miss valuable information. Managers worried about increasing complaints should listen to demanding and critical custo-mers. Maximize complaints and deal with those complaining. Learn from your mistakes so that you do not go on repeating them (prevention). Practise handling critical incidents so that they can be turned into something positive (recovery).

9 *It is competent, motivated and committed people who create quality in an organization.* In service operations the staff concept, as a complement to the business concept, is particularly significant. Quality improvement presupposes that all employees are competent and motivated and work in a professional manner. In the final analysis, it is a matter of personal quality, of the attitude and commitment of the individual to quality improvement. In today's and tomorrow's company the competence, motivation and commitment of the employees comprise the main resource.

Create security for the employees through effective routines and back-up systems. Give them the right and opportunity to develop, both through education and new tasks. Re-establish professional pride. The reward system must be designed to encourage awareness of quality at all levels in the company. Gather new ideas by means of a suggestion scheme, where all the suggestions are studied and dealt with quickly, and where as many of them as possible are implemented.

10 *Quality and innovation in services depends on design.* Many quality problems are caused by poor service design or no design at all, and most of these problems keep reoccurring. Services should be carefully designed. Managers should seek out new ideas for service and have an established design process. This design process should systematically develop the service concept, the design of the service system and the service processes. Capturing and evaluating new service ideas and building-in the right quality from the start form the keystone for the development and future of the organization.

The aim of the book was to give managers and others an introduction to the new quality methods and concepts for services. We have selected ideas and examples which we felt to be of most relevance and use to service managers who are not expert in total quality management. The danger in a book of this type is to overwhelm the reader, and we hope our criticism of many practices in the service sector has not had the wrong effect. Because quality is so poor in many services, and quality methods little used, there are opportunities for managers to make significant improvements and to pioneer new approaches. We want to emphasize that quality development starts with and depends on people. It is personal responsibility and commitment to quality which is the basis for using the systems and techniques. It is this combination – the spirit and the systematic approach – which we have observed in the managers who have achieved quality improvements which others did not think possible.

Appendices: Measurement instruments

SERVICE QUALITY MEASUREMENT: COMPUTING SERVICE COMPANY

1 How are your application systems run by AVD?

    1 On line ☐

    2 Remote batch ☐

    3 Centrally initiated batch ☐

2 What application(s) is your system used for?
If several of the applications are used, order
according to extent from 1 to 3, where
1=greatest extent

    1 Materials control (ordering,
stocking, invoicing, planning
etc.) ☐

    2 Personnel administration
(wages, staff reports etc.) ☐

    3 Financial system (accounting,
cash management etc.) ☐

    4 Other. Indicate what

3 How long have you used AVDs services?

    1 10–12 months ☐

    2 1–3 years, etc. ☐

    3 More than 3 years ☐

4 What is your opinion of AVDs
current level of service?

	Very unsatis-factory	Unsatis-factory	Satis-factory	Very satis-factory

Comments ....

Delivery reliability

5 What is your opinion of delivery reliability
as regards batch jobs with respect to:

	Very unsatis-factory	Unsatis-factory	Satis-factory	Very satis-factory
a) delivery at the right time	☐	☐	☐	☐
b) delivery to the right addressee	☐	☐	☐	☐
c) quality, i.e. work correctly done?	☐	☐	☐	☐

Reply time

6 What is your opinion of 'on line' reply
time with respect to:

a) average reply time	☐	☐	☐	☐
b) reply time on a Monday morning	☐	☐	☐	☐
c) reply time on other occasions?	☐	☐	☐	☐

Accessibility

7 What is your opinion of the accessibility
of the system ('on line') with respect to:

a) length of downtime	☐	☐	☐	☐
b) number of downtime occurrences	☐	☐	☐	☐
c) quality of telephone lines	☐	☐	☐	☐
d) accessibility generally?	☐	☐	☐	☐

8 Does downtime have more serious
consequences at any particular point
in time? _____

Customer relations

9 What is your opinion of the telephone
operators at AVD with respect to:

a) how you are treated on the telephone	☐	☐	☐	☐
b) the length of time before anyone answers	☐	☐	☐	☐
c) the ability of the telephone operators to provide information	☐	☐	☐	☐
d) their ability to understand your problem/question and connect you with the right person?	☐	☐	☐	☐

10 What is your opinion of AVDs
   operation staff with respect to:
   a) the time you have to wait on
      the telephone before speaking
      to the right person ☐ ☐ ☐ ☐
   b) their ability to understand your
      problem/question ☐ ☐ ☐ ☐
   c) their ability to solve your
      application problems ☐ ☐ ☐ ☐
   d) their ability to solve your
      technical problems (e.g. operating
      the terminal) ☐ ☐ ☐ ☐
   e) the time it takes to solve your
      application problem ☐ ☐ ☐ ☐
   f) the time it takes to solve your
      technical problem? ☐ ☐ ☐ ☐

11 What is your opinion of the information
   you receive from AVDs operational
   staff with respect to:
   a) the way they convey information ☐ ☐ ☐ ☐
   b) the value/quality of the
      information? ☐ ☐ ☐ ☐

Other
12 Do you feel you have received enough
   training in the use of your application
   systems? Yes ☐
            No ☐

Further training?
13 What do you consider the three most
   important problems as regards level
   of service?

1_____

_____

2_____

_____

3_____

14 How do you feel these problems are
   best dealt with? (Refers to the
   problems taken up in 13)

1 _____

  _____

2 _____

  _____

3 _____

15 Have you any further comments or
   suggestions for improvement?

   _____

   _____

   _____

   _____

   _____

If necessary, please continue on a separate sheet.

HOTEL SERVICE

Welcome and thank you for choosing our Holiday Inn hotel.

Our Hospitality Promise assures that you will be satisfied with your stay and that we will meet the high standards you have come to expect from Holiday Inn hotels. **If, for any reason, you believe we have not met the standards we promise, or you should have a problem, please contact our front desk/Manager on Duty immediately**.

The quickest way to resolve any difficulty, no matter how small, is to let the Manager on Duty know as soon as possible so he can make it right. In most cases we can solve your problem before check-out. Please give us the opportunity to assist you.

If you still need assistance, after contacting our front desk, call our toll free Holiday Inn Guests Assistance Number: 1-800-621-0555. (Guest Assistance will need the names of our staff who attempted to resolve your problem.)

HOW WELL DID WE SERVE YOU?

Please let us know what you think about our service and accommodation so we can serve you better in the future. **Just complete this card and <u>leave it at the front desk.</u>** Please check the box which best describes your satisfaction with your stay at this Holiday Inn hotel:

How satisfied were you with:

	Very Satisfied	Somewhat Satisfied	Neither Satisfied Nor Dissatisfied	Somewhat Dissatisfied	Very Dissatisfied
Cleanliness of your room	☐	☐	☐	☐	☐
Working condition of the:					
● Television	☐	☐	☐	☐	☐
● Air conditioner/heater	☐	☐	☐	☐	☐
● Hot water	☐	☐	☐	☐	☐
● Brightness of bathroom lighting	☐	☐	☐	☐	☐
Service of Hotel Staff:					
● In responding to your needs	☐	☐	☐	☐	☐
● Friendliness of employees	☐	☐	☐	☐	☐
● Speed of check-in/check-out	☐	☐	☐	☐	☐

	Very Satisfied	Somewhat Satisfied	Neither Satisfied Nor Dissatisfied	Somewhat Dissatisfied	Very Dissatisfied
Hotel Safety/Security	☐	☐	☐	☐	☐
Value Received For Your Room	☐	☐	☐	☐	☐

Restaurant/Room Service (☐ Did not use)

	Very Satisfied	Somewhat Satisfied	Neither Satisfied Nor Dissatisfied	Somewhat Dissatisfied	Very Dissatisfied
● Quality of service	☐	☐	☐	☐	☐
● Value you received	☐	☐	☐	☐	☐

All things considered, please rate your overall satisfaction with your stay at this Holiday Inn hotel: ☐ ☐ ☐ ☐ ☐

If you were to return to this vicinity, how likely would you be to stay at this Holiday Inn hotel?

☐ Definitely
☐ Probably
☐ Might or Might Not
☐ Probably Not
☐ Definitely Not

Additional comments/suggestions

_____
_____
_____
_____
_____

Room#_____ Date of Stay_____

Optional
Name_____
Address _____
City_____ State_____ Zip_____
Telephone _____

Leave completed card at front desk

Reproduced by permission of Holiday Inn

253

SERVQUAL QUESTIONNAIRE

Directions Based on your experiences as a consumer of _____ services, please think about the kind of _____ company that would deliver excellent quality of service. Think about the kind of _____ company with which you would be pleased to do business. Please show the extent to which you think such a _____ company would possess the feature described by each statement. If you feel a feature is *not at all essential* for excellent _____ companies such as the one you have in mind, circle the number 1. If you feel a feature is *absolutely essential* for excellent _____ companies, circle 7. If your feelings are less strong, circle one of the numbers in the middle. There are no right or wrong answers—all we are interested in is a number that truly reflects your feelings regarding companies that would deliver excellent quality of service.

	Strongly Disagree						Strongly Agree
1. Excellent_____ companies will have modern-looking equipment.	1	2	3	4	5	6	7
2. The physical facilities at excellent _____ companies will be visually appealing.	1	2	3	4	5	6	7
3. Employees at excellent _____ companies will be neat-appearing.	1	2	3	4	5	6	7
4. Materials associated with the service (such as pamphlets or statements) will be visually appealing in an excellent _____ company.	1	2	3	4	5	6	7
5. When excellent _____ companies promise to do something by a certain time, they will do so.	1	2	3	4	5	6	7
6. When a customer has a problem, excellent _____ companies will show a sincere interest in solving it.	1	2	3	4	5	6	7
7. Excellent _____ companies will perform the service right the first time.	1	2	3	4	5	6	7

8. Excellent _____ companies will provide their services at the time they promise to do so.	1	2	3	4	5	6	7
9. Excellent _____ companies will insist on error-free records.	1	2	3	4	5	6	7
10. Employees in excellent _____ companies will tell customers exactly when services will be performed.	1	2	3	4	5	6	7
11. Employees in excellent _____ companies will give prompt service to customers.	1	2	3	4	5	6	7
12. Employees in excellent _____ companies will always be willing to help customers.	1	2	3	4	5	6	7
13. Employees in excellent _____ companies will never be too busy to respond to customers' requests.	1	2	3	4	5	6	7
14. The behaviour of employees in excellent _____ companies will instill confidence in customers.	1	2	3	4	5	6	7
15. Customers of excellent _____ companies will feel safe in their transactions.	1	2	3	4	5	6	7
16. Employees in excellent _____ companies will be consistently courteous with customers.	1	2	3	4	5	6	7
17. Employees in excellent _____ companies will have the knowledge to answer customers' questions.	1	2	3	4	5	6	7
18. Excellent _____ companies will give customers individual attention.	1	2	3	4	5	6	7

19. Excellent _____ companies will have operating hours convenient to all their customers.	1	2	3	4	5	6	7
20. Excellent _____ companies will have employees who give customers personal attention.	1	2	3	4	5	6	7
21. Excellent _____ companies will have the customers' best interests at heart.	1	2	3	4	5	6	7
22. The employees of excellent _____ companies will understand the specific needs of their customers.	1	2	3	4	5	6	7

Directions The following set of statements relate to your feelings about XYZ Company. For each statement, please show the extent to which you believe XYZ Company has the feature described by the statement. Once again, circling a 1 means that you strongly disagree that XYZ Company has that feature, and circling a 7 means that you strongly agree. You may circle any of the numbers in the middle that show how strong your feelings are. There are no right or wrong answers—all we are interested in is a number that best shows your perceptions about XYZ Company.

	Strongly Disagree					Strongly Agree	
1. XYZ Co. has modern-looking equipment.	1	2	3	4	5	6	7
2. XYZ Co.'s physical facilities are visually appealing.	1	2	3	4	5	6	7
3. XYZ Co.'s employees are neat-appearing.	1	2	3	4	5	6	7
4. Materials associated with the service (such as pamphlets or statements) are visually appealing at XYZ Co.	1	2	3	4	5	6	7
5. When XYZ Co. promises to do something by a certain time, it does so.	1	2	3	4	5	6	7
6. When you have a problem, XYZ Co. shows a sincere interest in solving it.	1	2	3	4	5	6	7

7.	XYZ Co. performs the service right the first time.	1	2	3	4	5	6	7
8.	XYZ Co. provides its services at the time it promises to do so.	1	2	3	4	5	6	7
9.	XYZ Co. insists on error-free records.	1	2	3	4	5	6	7
10.	Employees in XYZ Co. tell you exactly when services will be performed.	1	2	3	4	5	6	7
11.	Employees in XYZ Co. give you prompt service.	1	2	3	4	5	6	7
12.	Employees in XYZ Co. are always willing to help you.	1	2	3	4	5	6	7
13.	Employees in XYZ Co. are never too busy to respond to your requests.	1	2	3	4	5	6	7
14.	The behaviour of employees in XYZ Co. instills confidence in you.	1	2	3	4	5	6	7
15.	You feel safe in your transactions with XYZ Co.	1	2	3	4	5	6	7
16.	Employees in XYZ Co. are consistently courteous with you.	1	2	3	4	5	6	7
17.	Employees in XYZ Co. have the knowledge to answer your questions.	1	2	3	4	5	6	7
18.	XYZ Co. gives you individual attention.	1	2	3	4	5	6	7
19.	XYZ Co. has operating hours convenient to all its customers.	1	2	3	4	5	6	7
20.	XYZ Co. has employees who give you personal attention.	1	2	3	4	5	6	7
21.	XYZ Co. has your best interests at heart.	1	2	3	4	5	6	7
22.	Employees of XYZ Co. understand your specific needs.	1	2	3	4	5	6	7

XY&Z INTERNAL OBSERVATION SHEET

Date:_____ Account #:_____

CCE:_____ Observer:_____

Type of Call: _____ Length of Contact:_____

---

	1 2 3 4	A. COMMITMENT

NA No Yes   a. Identified/acknowledged customer's expressed needs.
    1. Restated or paraphrased the customer's inquiry.
    2. Assured customer that we could help to resolve the matter.

NA No Yes   b. Appropriate fact finding.
    1. Asked appropriate questions to clarify customer's needs.

NA No Yes   c. Took ownership.
    1. Representative took responsibility for the problem without shifting it back to the customer.
    2. Representative assumed responsibility for company practices and procedures.
    3. Representative handled problem without blaming other individuals, departments or the computer for customer's problems.
    4. Representative used 'we' or 'I' when speaking to the customer instead of 'they'.
    5. When transferring the customer reassured customer that they would be helped and educated customer as to reason being transferred.

NA No Yes   d. Resolved inquiry or made commitment.
    1. Appropriately addressed all of the customer's problems/concerns.
    2. Representative negotiated an agreeable solution/understanding with the customer before taking action.
    3. Representative ensured that inquiry was resolved to the customer's satisfaction/understanding by checking with the customer throughout the contact.
    4. When an inquiry was unable to be resolved, the representative made a definite commitment to follow up.

NA No Yes   e. Verified all concerns addressed.
    1. Recapped pertinent facts related to the customer's inquiry.
    2. Summarized multiple inquiries and resolutions at the close of the contact.
    3. Assured customer that problem would be resolved.
    4. After handling initial inquiry, asked customer if he/she had additional questions or concerns.

1 2 3 4	B. COURTESY

NA No Yes	a. Immediately answered call.
	1. Representative answered call without silent gap, typing, or side conversation being heard by customer.
NA No Yes	b. Identified self and XY&Z
	1. Identified self and XY&Z upon answering call.
NA No Yes	c. Acknowledged opening statement/gave immediate assurance/ established rapport.
	1. Asked customer, 'How may I help you?'.
	2. Conveyed immediate assurance to customer in a way that sounded enthusiastic.
	3. Empathized with the customer's problem by acknowledging the customer's emotions.
	4. Expressed regret or apologized in response to the customer's complaint or frustrations.
NA No Yes	d. Listened attentively, focused on customer.
	1. Allowed the customer to speak without interruption.
	2. Allowed customer to speak without talking over the customer.
	3. Allowed customer to finish explaining the reason for the inquiry without making assumptions or jumping to conclusions.
	4. Listened to customer carefully so that information did not have to be repeated by customer.
	5. Responded to customer to maintain an active conversation.
NA No Yes	e. Used proper hold procedures.
	1. Collected all relevant facts before leaving the line.
	2. Gave customer an explanation for leaving the line.
	3. Gained customer's permission to put them on hold.
	4. When returning to the line, acknowledged the customer by name and thanked the customer for waiting.
	5. Returned to the line within the defined time.
NA No Yes	f. Appropriately closed/branded.
	1. Closed the contact on a positive and personal note.
	2. When closing, representative thanked customer for choosing, calling or staying with XY&Z.
NA No Yes	g. Tone
	1. When speaking, the rep varied the tempo, stress and volume of his/her voice.
	2. Representative enunciated clearly and spoke at a rate and volume that could easily be understood by the customer.
	3. Representative's tone conveyed the same message as the words being used.
	4. Representative sounded sincere, friendly, enthusiastic and caring.

NA No Yes   h. Sensitivity/maintained rapport.
1. Demonstrated sensitivity and patience when dealing with diverse customers such as, those speaking a foreign language, the elderly or culturally different customers.
2. Used appropriate courtesies; please, thank you, etc.
3. Where appropriate, offered expressions of sympathy to the customer.
4. Used customer's last name.
5. Demonstrated judgement and sensitivity in addressing a female customer with Ms., Miss, Mrs. or Ma'am.
6. Empathize with the customer's problem by acknowledging the customer's emotion.
7. Expressed regret or apologized in response to the customer's complaints or frustrations.

---

1 2 3 4 C. KNOWLEDGEABLE (Customer Perception)

NA No Yes   a. Conveyed to customer that XY&Z maintains high standards of service and equipment.

NA No Yes   b. Demonstrated familiarity with appropriate XY&Z long distance services.

NA No Yes   c. When the recommended resolution was not agreeable, representative was able to offer appropriate alternatives.

NA No Yes   d. When customer's request could not be fulfilled, referred customer to the most appropriate XY&Z department.

NA No Yes   e. Delivered explanation to the customer in a clear, concise and understandable manner.

NA No Yes   f. Gave a personalized explanation to the customer.

---

1 2 3 4 D. CALL PROCESS CONFORMANCE (What the Representative SHOULD do)

NA No Yes   a. Provided accurate and complete information.
1. Followed call handling policies and procedures.
2. Utilized appropriate resources (P&P and/or Handbook).
3. Completed all associated work necessary to complete the agreement with the customer.
4. Took appropriate steps to ensure that the call would not result in a repeat call.

NA No Yes   b. Followed Billing adjustment guidelines.
1. Checked notations.
2. Checked listing/returns.
3. Reviewed call details.
4. Educated customer.
5. Noted account.

NA No Yes   c. Appropriate sustain attempt.
1. Made appropriate sustain attempt.

NA No Yes   d. Appropriate adjustment granted.
                  1. Used appropriate adjustment code.
NA No Yes   e. Accurate and Complete Terminal Activity.
                  1. Completed correct terminal activity including notations.
                  2. When appropriate, populated CI Field to flag account requiring
                     special attention.
                  3. When appropriate, corrected customer's address on all appro-
                     priate screens.
                  4. Used appropriate tracking codes (Media Code, Alt ID and
                     Notation Type codes).
                  5. Used appropriate feedback vehicles (CCF and MIMS).

---

          1 2 3 4 E. CONTACT EFFICIENCY/CONTROL (What the Representative DID)

NA No Yes   a. Directed the contact through a logical sequence in a timely
                  manner.
NA No Yes   b. Controlled a talkative customer by politely bringing them back to
                  the call inquiry.
NA No Yes   c. Spoke to the customer without unnecessarily repeating himself/
                  herself or overexplaining.
NA No Yes   d. Spoke to the customer without using company jargon, technical
                  terms or slang.
NA No Yes   e. Interacted with the terminal and/or reference materials while
                  conversing with the customer.
NA No Yes   f. Paused and clarified appropriately without rushing the customer.
NA No Yes   g. Asked customer to repeat only when necessary.
NA No Yes   h. Put customer on hold only when necessary and returned within
                  the defined time.
NA No Yes   i. Maintained the contact without initiating any idle/non-contact
                  related conversation.

---

          1 2 3 4 F. WINBACK PROBE/RESPONSE (What the Representative
                        SHOULD do)

NA No Yes   a. Asked Winback Probe
                  1. Determined whether customer uses XY&Z for all long distance
                     needs.
                  2. Used Winback probe only when appropriate (e.g., avoided using
                     with irate customer or customers in a hurry).
NA No Yes   b. Appropriate Winback Probe response.
                  1. Expressed appreciation for customer using XY&Z services.
                  2. Where customer does not use XY&Z made an appropriate
                     Winback attempt.
                  3. Educated customer when appropriate (rates, services, dialling
                     instructions, etc.).

261

				G. VALUE ADDED (What the Representative SHOULD do)
1	2	3	4	

NA No   Yes   a. Appropriate transition.
           1. Obtained customer's permission by using a customer benefit.

NA No   Yes   b. Used Service Support screen.
           1. Acknowledge value of customer's existing services.
           2. Addressed customer needs/opportunity to save.

NA No   Yes   c. Fact-finding and discovering clues.
           1. Determined needs by reviewing call details.
           2. Obtained information by asking questions based on clues provided by the customer.

NA No   Yes   d. Appropriate OCP save effort.

NA No   Yes   e. Personalized recommendation.
           1. Demonstrated how a particular XY&Z service could meet the customer's needs.
           2. Educated the customer on the best use of XY&Z services.
           3. Provided clear information on the benefits of the service to the customer.

NA No   Yes   f. Addressed questions and concerns.
           1. Clarified areas of concern and possible confusion.
           2. Provided additional information, where needed.
           3. Demonstrated empathy while dealing with the customer's objection.

NA No   Yes   g. Asked for the sale.
           1. Asked customer for 'sale' at an appropriate point in the contact.
           2. Offered to process the order.

				H. RETENTION/SAVE EFFORT (What the Representative SHOULD do)
1	2	3	4	

NA No   Yes   a. Value Statement.
           1. Communicated that XY&Z values the customer.

NA No   Yes   b. Determined reason customer is requesting cancellation/identified vulnerability.
           1. Determined reason customer requesting Dial-1 or Optional Calling Plan cancellation.

NA No   Yes   c. Used Service Support screen.

NA No   Yes   d. Used appropriate competitive response aids.

NA No   Yes   e. Appropriate personalized save effort/offered appropriate alternatives.
           1. Asked open-ended questions to discover customer needs and feelings about XY&Z.
           2. Offered an appropriate alternative based on customer needs and concerns.
           3. Explained benefits of XY&Z service to customer.
           4. Clarified customer's misunderstandings about XY&Z service or calling plans.

NA No   Yes   f. Left door open/invited customer back to using our services.
                    1. Expressed appreciation for past use of XY&Z when save efforts
                       are not successful.
                    2. Express hope that customer will use XY&Z in the future.

Yes.......No.......Was this a repeat contact?

If 'yes', what was the cause?
*   CHANNEL
    ... Missed commitment
    ... Inaccurate/incomplete information
    ... Inaccurate/incomplete order
    ... Other _____
*   LEC
*   OTHER XY&Z ENTITY
    ... Telemarketing
    ... Operator Services
    ... RAMP
    ... CPP
    ... Other _____
*   CUSTOMER-INITIATED
*   UNABLE TO DETERMINE
*   OTHER

References and further reading

Achabal, D., Heineke, J. and McIntyre, S. (1984). 'Issues and perspectives on retail productivity'. *Journal of Retailing*, Vol. 60, No. 3

Achabal, D., Heineke, J. and McIntyre, S. (1985). 'Productivity measurement and the output of retailing'. *Journal of Retailing*, Vol. 61, No. 3

Adam, E., Hershauer, J. and Ruch, W. (1981). *Productivity and quality: Measurement as a basis for improvement*. New Jersey: Prentice-Hall

Adams, F. and Faulhaber, G. (1989). 'Measuring services output: The Wharton Index of Services Production'. Discussion Paper, Fishman–Davidson Center for the Study of the Service Sector, University of Pennsylvania

Albrecht, C. and Bradford, L.J. (1990). *The service advantage – How to identify and fulfill customer needs*. Homewood, Illinois: Irwin

Albrecht, C. and Zemke, R. (1985). *Service America*. Homewood, Illinois: Dow Jones-Irwin

Albrecht, K. and Zemke, R. (1985). *Service America: Doing business in the new economy*. New York: Warner

Alderfer, C.P. (1969). 'An empirical test of a new theory of human needs'. *Organizational Behavior and Human Performance*, No. 4, pp. 142-5

Allen, F., Faulhaber, G. and MacKinley, C. (1989). 'Unbalanced growth redux. Sectoral productivity and capital markets'. Discussion Paper, Fishman–Davidson Center for the Study of the Service Sector, University of Pennsylvania

Andersson, G. (1985). 'Kritiska händelser i banken' (Critical events in banks). Paper presented at the Second Nordic Meeting on Services Marketing, Lund, 24 April

Andersson, R. (1989). 'QFD–Kundcentrerad planering för hög kvalitet' (QFD – Customer-centred planning for high quality). *Verkstäderna*, No. 6

Armisted, C., Johnston, R. and Slack, N. (1988). 'The strategic determinants of service productivity'. In: *The management of service operations*. Proceedings of the Annual Conference of the Operations Management Association, January 1988, pp. 1–16

Arnerup, B. (1989). 'Tjänstesektorns struktur och utveckling internationellt' (The structure and development of the international service sector). Working Paper, Service Research Center, University of Karlstad, Karlstad

ASQC (1989). QUALITY: *Executive priority or afterthought? Executives' perceptions on quality in a competitive world*. Milwaukee: ASQC

Atkinson, P. (1990). 'Creating cultural change'. *TQM Magazine*, February, pp. 13–15

Atkinson, R. (1992). 'Motivating people for success'. *TQM Magazine*, Vol. 4, No. 4, August

Atle Berg, S., Försund, F. and Jansen, E. (1989). 'Bank output measurement and the construction of best practice frontiers'. Paper presented at the 16th Meeting of the European Finance Association in Stockholm

Babakus, E. and Mangold, W.G. (1992). 'Adapting the SERVQUAL scale to hospital services: and empirical investigation'. *Health Services Research*, Vol. 26, No. 6, February, pp. 767–86

Bailey, D. and Hubert, T. (1980). *Productivity measurement: An international review of concepts, techniques.* Programmes and Current Issues, British Council of Productivity Associations

Barra, R. (1989). *Putting quality circles to work. A practical strategy for boosting productivity and profits.* New York: McGraw-Hill

Baum, S. (1989). *Making your blueprinting pay off.* Paper presented at the American Marketing Conference, San Francisco, 23 October

Baumol, W. (1986). 'Productivity growth, convergence and welfare: What the long-run data show'. *The American Economic Review*, Vol. 75, No. 5

Baumol, W. and Wolff, E. (1986). 'Input and output composition changes: Measuring the effect on the productivity slowdown'. Discussion Paper, Fishman–Davidson Center for the Study of the Service Sector, University of Pennsylvania

Baumol, W., Blackman, S. and Wolff, E. (1989a). 'Unbalanced growth revised: Asymptotic stagnancy and new evidence'. *American Economic Review*, Vol. 74, No. 4

Baumol, W., Blackman, S. and Wolff, E. (1989b). *Productivity and American leadership: The long view.* Cambridge, MA: MIT

Bearman, C., Guynup, G. and Milevski, S. (1985). 'Information and productivity'. *Journal of the American Society for Information Science*, Vol. 36, No. 6

Bellenger, D.N. and Greenberg, B.A. (1978). *Marketing research – A management information approach.* Homewood: Richard D. Irwin Inc.

Bergman, B. and Klefsjö, B. (1991). *Kvalitet – från behov till användning*

(*Quality – from needs to applications*). Lund: Studentlitteratur

Bergstedt, M. (1983). 'Affäsidéer och personaladministration' (Business ideas and personnel management). In: Mabon, H. (ed.) *Personaladministration* (*Personnel management*). Stockholm: Norstedts

Berry, L. (1989). *The service quality agenda for the 1990s*. Distinguished Papers, Business Research Institute, St John's University, New York

Berry, L., Zeithaml, V. and Parasuraman, A. (1985). 'Quality counts in services too'. *Business Horizons*, May–June

Berry, L., Parasuraman, A. and Zeithaml, V. (1988). 'The service-quality puzzle'. *Business Horizons*, September–October

Bitner, M.J. (1988). 'A model of service encounter and marketing mix effects'. Paper, presented at the QUIS symposium, Service Research Center, University of Karlstad, Karlstad

Bitner, M.J. (1991). 'The evolution of the services marketing mix and its relationship to service quality'. In: Brown *et al.*, Service Quality, Massachusetts: Lexington Books

Bitner, M.J., Nyquist, J.D. and Booms, H.B. (1985). 'The critical incident as a technique for analyzing the service encounter'. In: Bloch, T.M., Upah, G.D. and Zeithaml, V.A. (eds) *Service marketing in a changing environment*. Chicago: American Marketing Association

Bitner, M.J., Booms, H.B. and Tetreault, M.S. (1990). 'The service encounter: Diagnosing favorable and unfavorable incidents'. *Journal of Marketing*, Vol. 54, No. 1

Bjurek, H., Försund, F. and Hjalmarsson, L. (1988). *Parametric and nonparametric estimation of efficiency in service production: a comparison*. Göteborg University

Blois, K. (1984). 'Productivity and effectiveness in service firms'. *The Service Industries Journal*, Vol. 4, No. 3

Blumberg, F. and Gershowitz, G. (1982). 'Improving field service productivity'. *Journal of Systems Management*, March

Boakes, K. (1988). *Britain's productivity miracle: More to come*. London: Greenwell Montague

Boström, M. (1987). 'Dialektiken i sanningens ögonblick' (The dialectic of the moment of truth). Working Paper, Service Research Center, University of Karlstad, Karlstad

Brown, S., Gummesson, E., Edvardsson, B. and Gustavsson, B-O. (1991). *Service quality – multidisciplinary and multinational perspectives*. Lexington MA: Lexington Books

BSI (1987). *BS 5750 Quality systems part 1: Specification for design/ development, production installation and servicing*. London: British Standards Institute

BSI (1992). *BS 5750 for Services*. London: British Standards Institute

Camp, R.C. (1989). *Benchmarking: The search for industry best practices that lead to superior performance*. Milwaukee, Wisconsin: ASQC Quality Press

Carlzon, J. (1989). *Moments of Truth*. New York: Perennial Library, Harper & Row

Chang, C. (1989). 'Quality function deployment (QFD) processes in an integrated quality information system'. *Computers and Industrial Engineering*, Vol. 17, No. 1–4

Chase, R.B. and Aquilano, N.J. (1977). *Production and operations management. A life cycle approach*. Homewood, Illinois: Dow Jones-Irwin

Clausing, D. and Simpson, B.H. (1990). 'Quality by design'. *Quality Progress*, Vol. 23, No. 1

Conti, T. (1989). 'Process management and quality function deployment'.

Quality Progress, Vol. 22, No. 12

Cowell, D. (1984). *The marketing of services*. London: Heinemann

Crane, F.G. and Clarke, T.K. (1988). 'The identification of evaluated criteria and cues in selecting services'. *Journal of Services Marketing*, Vol. 2, No. 2

Crawford, C.M. (1983). *New products management*. Homewood, Illinois: Irwin

Crosby, P.B. (1980). *Quality is free*. New York: New American Library

Crosby, P.B. (1988). *The eternally successful organization – the art of corporate wellness*. New York: Plume

Dale, A. and Wooler, S. (1988). *SOS – Strategy and organisation for service, a content and process model for decision-making*. Uxbridge, Middlesex: BIOSS, Brunel University

Dale, A. and Wooler, S. (1990). 'Strategy and organization for service: A process and content model'. In: Brown, S., Gummesson, E., Edvardsson, B. and Gustavsson, B-O. (eds) *Service quality – multidisciplinary and multinational perspectives*. Lexington, MA: Lexington Books

Dale, B. and Lascelles, D. (1992). *The road to quality*. Available from IFS, Kempston, Bedford

Dalin, Å. (1987). *Kompetensutveckling i arbetslivet (The development of competence in working life)*. Lund: Studentlitteratur

Davidow, W.H. and Uttal, B. (1989). *Total customer service*. London: Harper & Row

Davis, F. (1990). 'Enabling is as important as empowering: A case for extended service blueprinting'. Working Paper

Davis, S. (1987). *Future perfect*. Reading: Addison-Wesley

De Bandt, J. (1988). *La mesure de la productivité dans les activités de service*. Nanterre: Nanterre, Université de Paris

De Brentani, U. (1989). 'Success and failure in new industrial services'. *Journal of Product Innovation Management*, Vol. 6, No. 4

Deming, E. (1986). *Out of the crisis*. Cambridge, Massachusetts: MIT

Denton, D.K. (1989). *Quality service*. London: Gulf Publishing

Donelly, J.H., Berry, L.L. and Thompson, T.W. (1985). *Marketing financial services*. Homewood, Illinois: Dow Jones-Irwin.

Edström, A., Norbäck, L.E. and Rendahl, J.E. (1989). *Förnyelsens Ledarskap (Leadership for renewal)*. Stockholm: Norstedts Förlag

Edvardsson, B. (1986). *Tjänster som konkurrensmedel (Services as a means of competitions)*. Research Report 86(1), Service Research Center, University of Karlstad, Karlstad

Edvardsson, B. (1988a). 'Analys av verksamheten inom Lokaltrafik AB med fokus på kvalitetsutveckling' (Analysis of operations in local traffic: Focusing on quality improvement). Unpublished Working Paper, Service Research Center, University of Karlstad, Karlstad

Edvardsson, B. (1988b). 'Kritiska händelser i fösäljningsprocessen – En studie av tjänstekopplade kritiska händelser inom verkstadsindustrin' (Critical incidents in the sale process – a study of service-related critical incidents in the manufacturing industry). In: Edvardsson, B. and Gummesson, E. (eds) *Management i tjänstesamhället (Management in the Service Society)*. Malmö: Liber

Edvardsson, B. (1988c). 'Service quality in customer relationships: a study of critical incidents in mechanical engineering companies'. *The Service Industries Journal*, Vol. 8, No. 4, pp. 427–45.

Edvardsson, B. (1989). Varu- och tjänsteproduktionens ökade integrering (The growing integration of the production of goods and services). In:

Benndorf, H. and Henriksson, H. (eds) *Framtida perspektiv på marknadsföring (Future perspectives on marketing)*. Stockholm: MTC

Edvardsson, B. (1991). *Service breakdowns – a study of critical incidents in an airline*. Research Report No. 91 (10), Service Research Center, University of Karlstad, Karlstad

Edvardsson, B. (1992). *Principles of service design*. Unpublished Working Paper, Service Research Center, University of Karlstad, Karlstad

Edvardsson, B. and Gummesson, E. (eds) (1988). *Management i tjänstesamhället (Management in the service society)*. Malmö: Liber

Edvardsson, B. and Gustavsson, B-O. (1988a). 'Uppföljning av programmet för företagsutveckling' (Review of the programme for corporate development). Unpublished Working Paper, Service Research Center, University of Karlstad, Karlstad

Edvardsson, B. and Gustavsson, B-O. (1988b). *Quality in services and quality in service organizations*. Working Paper No. 88(5). Service Research Center, University of Karlstad, Karlstad

Edvardsson, B. and Gustavsson, B-O. (1990). *Problem detection in service management systems – A consistency approach in quality improvement*. Working Paper No. 90(13). Service Research Center, University of Karlstad, Karlstad

Edvardsson, B. and Gustavsson, B-O. (1991). Quality in services and quality in service organizations – A model for quality assessment. In: Brown, S., Gummesson, E., Edvardsson, B. and Gustavsson, B-O. (eds) *Service quality – multidisciplinary and multinational perspectives*. Lexington, MA: Lexington Books

Edvardsson, B. and Magnusson, L. (1988). *Tjänstesverige (Service Sweden)*. Lund: Studentlitteratur

Edvardsson, B. and Thomasson, B. (eds) (1989). *Kvalitetsutveckling i privata och offentlig tjästeföretag (Quality improvement in private and public service companies).* Stockholm: Natur och Kultur

EFQM (1992). *The European Quality Award 1992.* Brussels, Belgium: European Foundation for Quality Management

Eiglier, P. and Langeard, E. (1987). *Servuction.* Paris: McGraw-Hill

Eneroth, B. (1984). *Hur mäter man 'vackert'? Grundbok i kvalitativ metod (How can we measure 'beautiful'? A basic course in qualitative methods).* Stockholm: Akademiliterratur

Eriksson, L.T. (1990). *Marknadsorientering – en introduction (Market orientation. An introduction).* Malmö: Liber

Feigenbaum, A.V. (1963). *Total quality control.* New York: McGraw-Hill

Ferguson, I. (1990). 'Process design', *Total Quality Management.* April

Finkelman, D. and Goland, T. (1990). 'The case of the complaining cuştomer'. *Harvard Business Review,* May–June, pp. 9–25

Fitzenz, J. (1984). *Human resources management?* New York: McGraw-Hill

Flanagan, J.C. (1954). 'The critical incident technique', *Psychological Bulletin,* Vol. 5, July, pp. 327–58.

Fletcher, J. and Snee, H. (1982). 'The services industries and input–output analysis'. *The Service Industries Journal,* Vol. 2, No. 1

Fletcher, J. and Snee, H. (1985). 'The need for output measurements in the service industries: a comment'. *The Service Industries Journal,* Vol. 5, No. 1

Forsman, A. (1989). 'Den offentliga sektorn är inte problemet' (The public sector is not the problem). *Svenska Dagbladet,* 20 September

Fortune International (1989). The Race to Quality Improvement. Vol. 120, No. 20, 25, September

Garvin, D.A. (1987). 'Competing on the eight dimensions of quality'.

Harvard Business Review, 65 (November–December), 101–9

Garvin, D.A. (1988). *Managing quality*. New York: Free Press

George, W.R. and Gibson, B.E. (1991). 'A tool for managing quality in service'. In: Brown *et al.* (eds) *Service quality – multidisciplinary and multinational perspectives*. Lexington, Massachusetts: Lexington Books

Giarini, O. (1986). 'Coming of age of the service economy'. *Science and Public Policy*, August

Glaser, B. and Strauss, A. (1967). *The discovery of grounded theory: Strategies for qualitative research*. New York: Aldine

Glisson, C. and Yancey, M.P. (1980). 'Productivity and efficiency in human service organizations as related to structure, size and age'. *Academy of Management Journal*, Vol. 23, No. 1

Godfrey, B.A. (1986). 'The history and evolution of quality at AT&T'. *AT&T. Technical Journal*, Vol. 65, No. 2, March–April

Grönroos, C. (1983). *Marknadsföring i tjänsteföreta (Marketing in service companies)*. Malmö: Liber

Grönroos, C. (1990). *Service management and marketing*. Lexington, Massachusetts: Lexington Books

Grönroos, C. and Monthelie, C. (1988). *Service management i den offentliga sektorn (Service management in the public sector)*. Malmö: Liber

Gummesson, E. (1985). *Forskare och konsult – om aktionsforskning och fallstudier i företagsekonomi (Researcher and consultant – on action research and case studies in business administration)*. Lund: Studentlitteratur

Gummesson, E. (1987). *Quality – the Ericsson approach*. Stockholm: Ericsson

Gummesson, E. (1988). 'Att utveckla servicekvalitet eller "Varför finns det inga servicekonstruktörer?" ' ('Improving service quality or "Why are there no service designers?" '). In: Edvardsson, B. and Gummesson, E. (eds) *Management i tjänstesamhället (Management in the service society)*. Malmö: Liber

Gummesson, E. (1989a). Service quality in the 1990s: a note from Northern Europe. In: *Distinguished Papers*, Business Research Institute, St John's University, New York

Gummesson, E. (1989b). 'Nine lessons on service quality'. *TQM Magazine*, February

Gummesson, E. (1990a) 'Service design'. *TQM Magazine*, April

Gummesson, E. (1990b). *Service Quality – A holistic view*. Research Report No. 90(8), Service Research Center, University of Karlstad, Karlstad

Gummesson, E. (1991a) 'Kvalitetsstyrning i tjänste- och serviceverksamheter. Tolkning av fenomenet tjänstekvalitet och syntes av internationell forskning' (Quality management in services. An interpretation of the phenomenon of service quality and a synthesis of international research). Research Report No. 91(4), Service Research Center, University of Karlstad, Karlstad

Gummesson, E. (1991b). *Qualitative methods in management research*. Newbury Park, California, SAGE Publications Inc.

Gummesson, E. (1991c). Servicekvalitet – en ledningsfråga för privat och offentlig sektor (Service quality – a management issue for both private and public sectors). In Arvidsson, G. and Lind, R. (eds) *Ledning av privata och offentliga verksamheter (Management of private and public businesses)*. Stockholm: SNS

Gummesson, E. (1991d). 'Service quality – a holistic view'. In Brown, S.W., Gummesson, E., Edvardsson, B. and Gustavsson, B-O. (eds) *Service*

Quality - Multidisciplinary and multinational perspectives. Lexington, Massachusetts: Lexington Books

Gummesson, E. (1992a). 'Quality dimensions: What to measure in service organizations'. In: Swartz, T.A., Bowen, D.A. and Brown, S.W. (eds) *Advances in service marketing and management.* Greenwich, Connecticut: JAI Press Ltd

Gummesson, E. (1992b). 'Service productivity: A blasphemous approach'. *Studies in Action and Enterprise,* pp. 1992:2. Stockholm University, Stockholm.

Gummesson, E. (1993). *Quality management in service organizations.* New York: ISQA

Gummesson, E. and Grönroos, C. (1987). *Quality of products and services - A tentative synthesis between two models.* Research Report No. 87(3). Service Research Center, University of Karlstad, Karlstad

Gummesson, E. and Grönroos, C. (1989). 'Kvalitet på varor och tjänster - ett fösök till helhetssyn' (Quality of goods and services - an attempt at a holistic view). In: Edvardsson, B. and Thomasson, B. (eds) *Kvalitetsutveckling i privata och offentliga tjänsteföretag (Quality improvement in private and public service companies).* Stockholm: Natur och Kultur

Gummesson, E., Arnerup, B. and Edvardsson, B. (1990). *Kvalitet - en hävstång för produktivitet och lönsamhet i tjänsteverksamheter (Quality - a lever for productivity and profitability in service businesses).* Report to SAF Congress 1990.

Gummesson, E. and Kingman-Brundage, J. (1992). 'Service design and quality: Applying blueprinting and service mapping to railroad services'. In: Kunst, P. and Lemmink, J. (eds) *Quality management in services.* Assen/Maastricht, The Netherlands: Van Gorcum

Hart, C. (1988). The power of unconditional service guarantees. *Harvard*

Business Review, Vol. 66, July–August, pp. 54–62

Hart, C. (1990a). 'Service guarantees: How good can you be?' Working Paper. Harvard School of Business, Boston

Hart, C. (1990b). 'The power of unconditional service guarantees'. In: Zemke, R. and Bell, C.R. (eds) *Service Wisdom*. Minneapolis: Lakewood Books

Hauser, J.R. and Clausing, D. (1988). 'The house of quality'. *Harvard Business Review*, No. 3, May–June

Heskett, J.L. (1986). *Managing in the service economy*. Harvard Business School Press

Hippel, E.V. (1979). 'A customer-active paradigm for industrial product idea generating'. In: Baker, M.J (ed.) *Industrial innovation, technology, policy, diffusion*. London: Macmillan

Hjern, B. (1990). *Problemet med produktivitetsutveckling (The problem of increasing productivity)*. Research Report No. 90(2), Service Research Center, University of Karlstad, Karlstad

Holm, K. and Thorburn, D. (1989). 'Kostnadskalkylering i tre banker' (Cost estimation in three banks). Thesis, Stockholm School of Business, Stockholm

Hudiburg, J.J. (1991). *Winning with quality: The FPL story*. Quality Resources, A Division of the Kraus Organization Ltd, New York

Imai, M. (1986). *Kaizen*. New York: McGraw-Hill

Ishikawa, K. (1985). *What is total quality control? The Japanese way*. Englewood Cliffs, New Jersey: Prentice-Hall

Jaques, E. (1989). *Requisite organisation*. Arlington, Virginia: Casson Hall

Jones, P. (1988). 'Quality, capacity and productivity in service industries'. In: Johnston, R. (ed.) *The management of service operations*. Proceedings of the Operations Management Association UK Annual International Conference. London: Springer-Verlag

Juran, J.M. (1982). *Upper management and quality*. New York: Juran Institute

Juran, J.M. (1992). *Juran on quality by design – the new steps for planning quality into goods and services*. New York: Free Press

Juran, J.M., Gryna Jr., F.M. and Bingham Jr., R.S. (eds) (1979). *Quality control handbook*. New York: McGraw-Hill

Kahn, A. (1989). 'Målstyrd kvalitetsutveckling – tankar och tips kring det praktiska kvalitetsarbetet' (Goal-steered improvement – thoughts and suggestions for practical quality improvement). In: Edvardsson, B. and Thomasson, B. (eds) *Kvalitetsutveckling i privata och offentlig tjänsteföretag (Quality development in private and public service companies)*. Stockholm: Natur och Kultur

Kanter, R. (1991). 'Even closer to the customer'. *Harvard Business Review*, January–February

Karlöf, B. (ed.) (1985). *Det nya kvalitetstänkandet (The new quality thinking)*. Lund: Liber

Karlsson, U., Engström, T., Hörte, S-.Å, Nonås, K., Norbäck, L-E. and Thomasson, B. (1985). *Bilreparationer (Car repairs)*. Göteborg: IMIT

King, R. (1987). 'Listening to the voice of the customer: Using the quality function deployment system'. *National Productivity Review*, Vol. 6, No. 3

Kingman-Brundage, J. (1988). 'The ABCs of service blueprinting'. In: Bitner, M.J. (ed.) *Designing a winning service strategy*. Chicago: American Marketing Association

Kingman-Brundage, J. (1989). 'Blueprinting from the bottom line'. Paper presented at The 8th Annual Services Marketing Association, San Francisco, 23 October

Krauss, C. (1987). 'Customer satisfaction: A bottom-line performance indicator'. Arthur D. Little Inc, presentation at the American Marketing Association's Sixth Annual Services Marketing Conference, San Diego, CA, Sept.

Kunst, P. and Lemmink, J. (eds) (1992). *Quality management in services.* Assen/Maastricht, The Netherlands: Van Gorcum

Langeard, E., Bateson, J. and Eglier, P. (1981). *Marketing of services: New insights from consumers and managers.* Marketing Science Institute, Report No. 81(104), Cambridge

Långtidsutredningen (1990). *Privat tjänstesektor (The private service sector).* Appendix 17 to LU 90, Ministry of Finance, Stockholm

Lawrence, P.R. (1969). 'How to deal with resistance to change'. *Harvard Business Review* 47, No. 1, January–February

Lennerlöf, L. (1986). *Kompetens eller hjälplöshet. Om lärande i arbetet (Competence or helplessness. On learning at work).* An Overview of Research. Survey No. 1986(52), Arbetarskyddsstyrelsen, Forskningsavdelningen, Stockholm

Lee, C. (1987). 'Productivity: What exactly are we talking about?' *Training,* May

Lehrer, R. (1983). *White Collar Productivity.* New York: McGraw-Hill

Lehtinen, J. (1985). 'Improving service quality by analysing the service production process'. In: Grönroos, C. and Gummesson, E. (eds) *Service marketing – Nordic School perspective,* University of Stockholm, Stockholm

Lehtinen, U. and Lehtinen, J. (1983). 'Service quality: A Study of quality dimensions'. Working Paper, University of Tampere, Finland

Levitt, T. (1984). *Lysande marknadsföring (Brilliant marketing).* Stockholm: SvD förlag

Lewin, K. (1947). 'Frontiers in group dynamics: Concept, method and reality in social science'. *Human Relations*, Vol. 1, No. 1

Lilja, O. (1989). 'The SAS approaches to quality'. *TQM Magazine*, May

Lilja, O. and Schröder, H. (1990). 'Quality management at Saab'. *TQM Magazine*, April

Lindqvist, L. (1988). *Kundernas kvalitetsupplevelse i konsumtionsfasen (Customers' perception of quality in the consumption phase).* Research Report No. 17, Swedish School of Business and Economics, Helsinki

Luchs, R. (1986). 'Successful businesses compete on quality – not costs'. *Long Range Planning*, Vol. 19, No. 1

Lundmark, A. and Söderström, M. (1988). *Personalutbildning och ekonomi (Staff training and economy).* Lund: Studentlitteratur

Maccoby, M. (1989). *Arbeta varför det? (Why work?).* Stockholm: Svenska Dagbladets Förlag

Marton, F. (1978). *Describing conceptions of the world around us.* Report from the Institute of Education, University of Gothenburg, No. 66

Mattsson, J. (1991). *Better business by the ABC of values.* Lund: Studentlitteratur

Mattsson, J. and Edvardsson, B. (1991). 'Strategic management thinking in service firms: Modeling the qualitative dimension in casual maps'. Paper presented at the EIAS workshop on quality in services in Brussels, 16–18 May

Mintzberg, H. (1989). *Mintzberg on management: Inside our strange world of organizations.* New York: The Free Press

Möller, C., Finkelman, D. and Goland, T. (1990). 'The case of the complaining customer'. *Harvard Business Review*, May–June, p. 24

Moores, B. (ed.) (1986). *Are they being served?* Oxford: Phillip Allen

Morgan, C. (1986). *Images of organization.* Beverly Hills: Sage

Musgrove, C.S. and Fox, M.J. (1991). *Quality costs: Their impact on company strategy and profitability.* TQM Practitioner Series. Letchworth, Hertfordshire: Technical Communications (Publishing) Ltd

Nicolin, C. and Lyttkens, L. (1989). *Ledarskap och moral (Leadership and morality).* Stockholm: SAF

NIST (1990). *The Malcolm Baldridge National Quality Award 1990 Application Guidelines,* National Institute of Standards and Technology, Gaithersburg, MD 20899, USA

Normann, R. (1980). *Skapande företagsledning (Creative Management).* Stockholm: Bonniers

Normann, R. (1984). *Service management.* Chichester, Sussex: John Wiley & Sons

Normann, R. (1988). 'Service Management och därefter – en vision' ('Service management and after – a vision'). In: Edvardsson, B. and Gummesson, E. (eds) *Management i tjänstesamhället (Management in the service society).* Malmö: Liber

Normann, R. (1991). *Service management. Strategy and leadership in service business.* Chichester, Sussex: John Wiley & Sons

Nyström, H. (1979). *Creativity and innovation.* New York: John Wiley & Sons

Olsen, M.J.S. (1992). *'Kvalitet i banktjänster. Privatkunders upplevda problem med bnaktjänster – en studie med hjälp av kritisk-händelsemetoden' (Quality in banking services. Problems in banking services experienced by private customers – a study with the aid of the critical incident technique).* Department of Business Studies, Stockholm University and Service Research Center, University of Karlstad, Karlstad

Øvretveit, J. (1989). *Total quality service management: The new approach to managing service quality*, Research Report, BIOSS, Brunel University, Uxbridge, Middlesex

Øvretveit, J. (1990a). 'What is quality in health services'. *Health Service Management*, June, pp. 132–3

Øvretveit, J. (1990b). *Quality health services*, Research Report, BIOSS, Brunel University, Uxbridge, Middlesex

Øvretveit, J. (1991a). *Primary care quality through teamwork*, Research Report, BIOSS, Brunel University, Uxbridge, Middlesex

Øvretveit, J. (1991b). 'Quality costs – or does it?' *Health Service Management*, August

Øvretveit, J. (1992a). *Health service quality*. Oxford: Blackwell Scientific Press

Øvretveit, J. (1992b). 'Towards market-focused measures of customer/purchaser perceptions'. *Quality Forum*, Institute of Quality Assurance, London, Vol. 19, No. 3, pp. 21–4

Øvretveit, J. (1992c). 'Maps-Qual quality audit software'. *Quality News*, Institute of Quality Assurance, London, March, Vol. 18, No. 3, pp. 116–17

Øvretveit, J. (1993a). *Measuring service quality*. Aylesbury, Buckinghamshire: Technical Communications Publications Ltd

Øvretveit, J. (1993b). *Coordinating community care: Multidisciplinary teams and care management in health and social services*. Milton Keynes: Open University Press

Øvretveit, J. (1993c). 'Quality awards and auditing for purchasers of services: Towards partnership contracting'. *International Journal of Service Industry Management*, Vol. 4, No. 2, pp. 74–84.

Øvretveit, J. (1993d). 'Auditing for service quality'. *Quality Forum*, Institute of Quality Assurance, London, Vol. 19, No. 1, pp. 4-9

Parasuraman, A., Zeithaml, V. and Berry, L. (1985). 'A conceptual model of service quality and its implications for future research'. *Journal of Marketing*, Vol. 49, pp. 41-50

Parasuraman, A., Zeithaml, V. and Berry, L. (1988). 'SERVQUAL: A multiple-item scale for measuring consumer perceptions of service quality'. *Journal of Retailing*, Vol. 64, No. 1

Parasuraman, A., Berry, L. and Zeithaml V.A. (1991). 'Understanding customer expectations of service'. *Sloan Management Review*, No. 39

Peters, T. (1988). *Skapande kaos (Creative chaos)*. Stockholm: Svenska Dagbladets Förlag

Peters, T. and Austin, N. (1986). *Besatt av mästerskapet* (In search of excellence). Stockholm: Svenska Dagbladets Förlag

Pirsig, R.M. (1975). *Zen and the art of motorcycle maintenance*. New York: Bantam Books

Porter, M.E. (1985). *Competitive Advantage*. New York: The Free Press

Quinn, J. and Gagnon, C. (1986). 'Will services follow manufacturing into decline?' *Harvard Business Review*, November-December, pp. 85-103

Quinn, J., Baruch, Jordan and Paquette, P. (1987). 'Technology in services'. *Scientific American*, Vol. 257, No. 6, pp. 50-8

Quinn, J., Baruch, Jordan and Paquette, P. (1988). 'Exploiting the manufacturing-service interface'. *Sloan Management Review*, summer, pp. 45-56

Quinn, J.B., Doorley, T.L. and Paquette, P.C. (1990). 'Products: Services-based strategy'. *Harvard Business Review*, March-April, pp. 58-67

Rathmell, J.M. (1974). *Marketing in the service sector*. Cambridge, Massachusetts: Winthrop

Reichheld, F.F. and Sasser, W.E. (1990). 'Zero defections: Quality comes to services'. *Harvard Business Review*, September–October, pp. 105–11

Rogers, B. (1987). *Så lyckades IBM (How IBM succeeded)*. Stockholm: Forum

Rosander, A.C. (1985). *Application of quality control in the service sector*. New York: Marcel Dekker/ASQC Quality Progress

Sandberg, J. (1989). 'Competence analysis as a strategic tool'. Working paper presented at the European Foundation for Management Development Conference on Knowledge as a Corporate Asset: An International Perspective, 24–25 April, Barcelona, Spain

SAS (1987). *Kvalitetsboken – kunderna och SAS (Quality book – the customers and SAS)*. Stockholm: SAS

SAS (1990). *Från luftakrobatik till världscirkus (From aerobatics to world circus)*. Stockholm: SAS

Schein, E.H. (1987). *Organizational culture and leadership*. San Francisco: Jossey-Bass Inc.

Scheuing, E.E. (1989). *New product management*. Columbus, Ohio: Merrill Publishing Company

Scheuing, E. E. and Johnson, E. (1989). 'A proposed model for new service development'. *Journal of Service Marketing*, Vol. 3, Spring.

Schonberger, R.J. (1990). *Building a chain of customers*. New York: Free Press

Shaw, J. and Capoor, R. (1979). 'Quality and productivity: Mutually exclusive or independent in service organizations?' *Management Review*, March.

Shewhart, W.A. (1931). *Economic control of quality of manufactured product*. New York: Van Nostrand

Shostack, L. (1977). 'Breaking free from product marketing'. *Journal of Marketing*, April, pp. 73–80

Shostack, L. (1981). 'How to design a service'. In: Donnelly, J. and George, W. (eds) *Marketing of Services*, pp. 221–9. Chicago: American Marketing Association

Shostack, L. (1984). 'Designing services that deliver'. *Harvard Business Review*, January–February, pp. 133–9

Shostack, L. (1985). 'Planning the service encounter'. In: Czepiel J., Solomon M. and Suprenant C. (eds) *The Service Encounter*, pp. 1–23. Lexington, Massachusetts: Lexington Books

Shostack, L. (1987). 'Service positioning through structural change'. *Journal of Marketing*, January, pp. 34–43

SIPU (1991). *Allmänhetens syn på den offentliga sektorn, SIPUs servicebarometer 1990/91 (The public's view of the public sector, SIPUs service barometer)*. Report, March

Smirchich, L. (1983). 'Concepts of culture and organizational analysis'. *Administrative Science Quarterly*, No. 28, pp. 33–358

Södergren, B. (1988). *När pyramiderna rivits (When the pyramids have been pulled down)*. Stockholm: Timbro

Solomon, M.R., Suprenant, C.F., Czepiel, J.A. and Gutman, E.G. (1985). 'A role theory perspective on dyadic interactions: The service encounter'. *Journal of Marketing*, Vol. 49, pp. 99–111

Spencer, P. (1987). *Britain's productivity renaissance*. London: Credit Suisse First Boston

Stamp, G. (1989). 'The individual, the organisation and the path to mutual appreciation'. *Personnel Management*, July

Statistisk Årsbok (Statistical Yearbook) (1991) Stockholm: Statistics Sweden

Stauss, B. and Hentschel, B. (1991). 'Attribute-based versus incident-based measurement of service quality: Results of an empirical study in the German car service industry'. In: Van der Wiele, T. and Timmers, J.G. (eds) *Proceedings of the Workshop on Quality Management in Services, Brussels, 16–17 May*

Surprenant, C.F. and Solomon, M.R. (1987). 'Predictability and personalization in the service encounter'. *Journal of Marketing*, Vol. 51, pp. 73–80

Sveiby, K.E. and Risling, A. (1986). *Kunskapsföretaget (Knowledge firms)*. Malmö: Liber

Swedish Post Office (1990a). *Satsa på kunden (Focus on the customer)*. Stockholm: Swedish Post Office

Swedish Post Office (1990b). *Kunddialog (Dialogue with customers)*, March. Stockholm: Swedish Post Office

Thams, R. (1985). 'Hur fastställs vilka kvalitetsaspekter man bör satsa på?' (How do we determine what aspects of quality we should improve?) In: Karlöf, B. (ed.), *Det nya kvalitetstänkandet (The new quality thinking)*. Lund: Liber

Thomasson, B. (1989). *Bilverkstadskunders kvalitetsuppfattningar (Customers' perception of quality in the services offered by garages)*. Research Report No. 89(2), Service Research Center, University of Karlstad, Karlstad

Thomasson, B. (1990) *Kvalitetsutveckling inom Linjeflyg AB (Quality improvement in Linjeflyg AB)*. Research Report No. 90(9), Service Research Center, University of Karlstad, Karlstad

Tjänsteförbundet (1989). *Nyhetsbrev (Newsletter)*, No. 1

Tjänsteförbundet (1990). *Verksamhetsberättelse för 1989 (Annual Report for 1989)*

Torgovnik, E. and Preisler, E. (1987). 'Effectiveness assessment in public service systems'. *Human Relations*, Vol. 40, No. 2

Townsend, P. and Gebhardt, J. (1986). *Commit to quality*. New York: John Wiley & Sons

Townsend, P. and Gebhardt, J. (1988). 'The policy is still quality'. *Best's Review*, June.

Vasilash, B.S. (1989). 'Hearing the voice of the customer'. *Production*, Vol. 101, No. 2

Zairi, M. (1992). *Competitive benchmarking: An executive guide*. Letchworth, Hertfordshire: Technical Communications (Publishing) Ltd

Zeithaml, V.A. (1988). 'Consumer perceptions of price, quality, and value: A means–end model and synthesis of evidence'. *Journal of Marketing*, Vol. 52, July

Zeithaml, V.A., Parasuraman, A. and Berry, L.L. (1990). *Delivering quality service – balancing customer perceptions and expectations*. New York: The Free Press

Zemke, R. and Schaaf, D. (1991). *The service edge*. New York: North American Library.

Zetterberg, H.L. (1983). *Det osynliga kontraktet. En studie i 80-talets arbetsliv (The invisible contract. A study of working life in the 1980s)*. Vällingby: SIFO 83170

Index